THE BACK ROAD TO THURBER

Published by Thurber Historical Association, Box 192, Gordon, TX 76453

People's names and certain applications mentioned in this book have been changed to protect the privacy of the people involved. However, we have attempted to convey the essence of the experience and the underlying principles as accurately as possible.

1st printing Joy Presswork Collection 1993

2nd printing Thurber Historical Association 2000

3rd printing Thurber Historical Association 2009

ISBN-10: 0-9638476-2-7

ISBN-13: 978-0-9638476-2-1

Cover: From top center---clockwise

American Citizenship papers

Polish Band in 1920 home celebration

Rocky Creek Bridge, site of important 1903 UMW meeting

Thurber token for one stick of dynamite

Bocce balls for the Italian game

TO MY DAUGHTER JENIFER

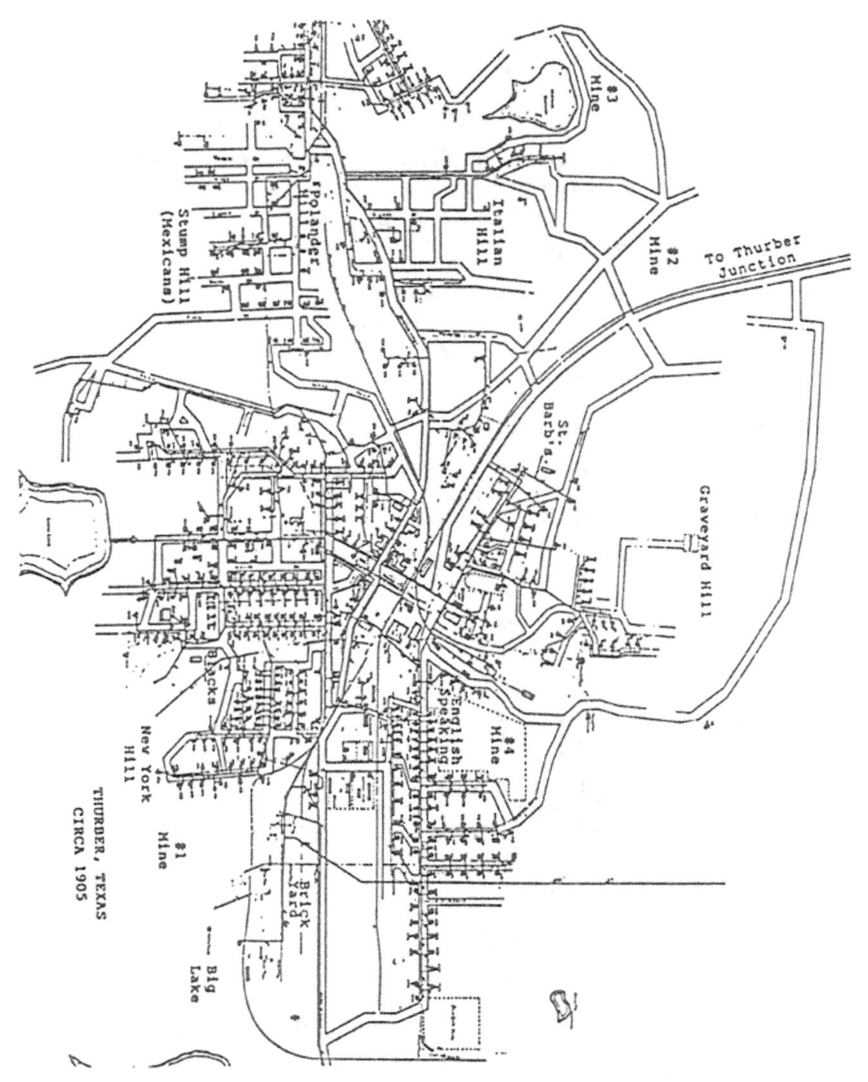

Thurber, TX 1905

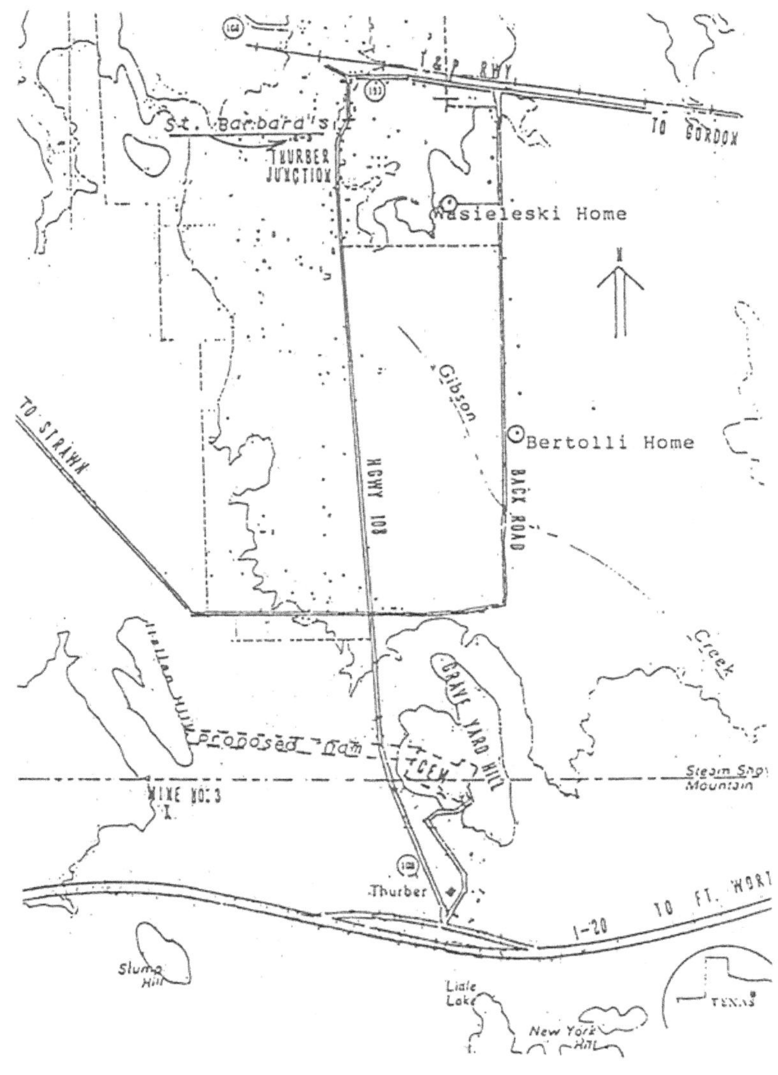

Today's Thurber & Thurber Junction (Mingus)

ACKNOWLEDGMENTS

Kate Nowak reviewed the original manuscript and gave helpful suggestions.

Dr. Francaviglia, UT Arlington, a writer and authority on old mining camps, offered some fruitful ideas and encouragement.

Laura Butler, a local artist who has an interest in preserving Thurber's past, sketched some of the pictures herein.

All of the old-time Thurberites who through the years, from conversations, anecdotes, or questioning, imparted a panorama of Thurber; particularly my mother, Lottie Bielinski, who lived all her 90 years in Thurber and Thurber Junction; my uncle, Joe Daskevich, who went to work in the mines at the age of 12; John Zinanni, Uncle Joe's mining buddy, and probably the finest bocce ball player around here; "Gigi" Biondini, who dug coal at Grant Town, years after the Thurber mines were closed; my uncle, Marche Zimicki, whose accordion was always the centerpiece of any Polish get-together and whose lively polkas I can still hear; Lawrence Santi, secretary of the Italian Miners' Local, who steadfastly and correctly maintained that John L. Lewis never set foot in Thurber, although many swore he had; Frankie Martin, who moved in with the "oil people" in 1917; Ted Bott, Thurber's popular ice man; and especially my good friend, Geno Solignani, who though now 80 years of age, has almost perfect recall of the people and events, as if it were yesterday.

FOREWORD

Thurber, Texas. Around the turn of the century, the name was familiar to American industry. After all, it was Thurber coal that made possible the expansion of rail lines through the southwestern United States. It was the Thurber coal miners' strike of 1903 which marked the beginning of the labor movement in the southwest. Thurber brick paved miles and miles of Texas highways and streets as Americans discovered the pleasures of automobile travel. Thurber played a key role in the 1917 discovery of the Ranger, Texas Oil Field; "The Oil Field That Won WW I". But most importantly, it was the city of Thurber which became the beckoning star on the horizon to hundreds of repressed European immigrants who sought a beginning in a new land.

As a child growing up in Thurber Junction, a suburb of Thurber, I paid little heed to the stories of Thurber and the company which owned it. The stories were too familiar, and in the familiarity was bred the contempt that youngsters have for that which is of their parents. I had no time for stories of coal and bricks and the complicated politics of labor. Only later, when I realized the "old-timers" were fading away, and that soon the stories would cease to be told at all, did I begin to take notice. Then I knew I must listen and record before the stories and their meanings disappeared forever.

In the years since, my research has led me through many inaccurate reports and written accounts of Thurber and its history. And in each of these accounts I have found the treatment of the immigrant, so important to the success of Thurber and its founding company, to be cursory and impersonal. However, without this durable, dependable Eastern European labor force, Thurber might not have been. With a grandfather who came to Thurber from Sierpc, Poland in 1890, my personal exposure to Thurber has been from the immigrants' perspective, so it is through their viewpoint that the idea of this novel was conceived.

A few of the characters within the following pages are composites of the many colorful personalities who lived and worked and loved and died in Thurber and its suburb, the Junction. In several instances, circumstances have been rearranged or created for continuity. However, the setting, the time frames, the key events, and the principal characters are real and now reside peacefully in the memories of the few who remain.

Religion was absolutely essential for the Eastern Europeans, for through the Mass they felt a communion with home and loved ones thousands of miles away. To emphasize this, I have used a religious subplot which may seem controversial.

Thurber is gone now. The once vibrant city has been reduced to a few derelict buildings and blackened earth mounds which rise from the ground like blisters, marking the locations of once active mines. Also gone are the rails that formed the junction to Thurber, and with them the name Thurber Junction, or simply the Junction, as I knew it. Today, what remains of the Junction is known as Mingus, a tiny hamlet seemingly unaware of its colorful history.

Unlike Gino Bertolli, I have been able to return to the home of my youth. I still roam the hills and the coal-cropped mine dumps and the ruins. I still walk the Back Road to Thurber, feeling my grandfather's presence with each step, and I hear a whispered rush of immigrant voices; voices so long dead. I hear once again the laughter, and I am reminded once again of the tears. And I realize how very important it is that the Thurber immigrants' story be told.

Leo S. Bielinski, October 1992

ONE

They buried Gino Bertolli the other day. Although Gino lived the last fifty years of his life in California, the final rites were held in the ghost town of Thurber, Texas. Not unnaturally, this caused some people to wonder. Why, after fifty years would one want his funeral rites to be held in a ghost town where there were only a few people in the whole county who might even recall the family name? And to be interred in the abandoned, untended Thurber cemetery? Such an act seemed ludicrous. But there were reasons, and there were those who readily understood those reasons. What was difficult to understand, however, is how one small funeral, out in the back of nowhere, for one old man whom anyone hardly knew, could set off brush fires of controversy which involved not only the Bertolli family and steadfast friends, but the Fort Worth Diocese of the Roman Catholic Church, Peacock Energy and Exploration Corporation, one of the largest fossil fuel producers in the nation, and a handful of local and state politicians.

As for Gino Bertolli, his burial in Thurber Cemetery was merely to acknowledge a bonding and a heartfelt debt to Thurber, his place of origin. The Bertollis got their start in America when Gino's father hired on as a miner in the Thurber coal mines in 1889. And Gino was not one to forget such ties. However, even he might not have remembered how important the city of Thurber had been to his family had he not attended the thirty-fifth annual Thurber Reunion in 1970. It was then, as he spoke with many of his old friends and ex-Thurberites, when Gino first realized the extent of his family's indebtedness to that now defunct company town. It was also the first time in thirty-five years he and his wife Lena had been back to their old hometown, or what was left of it. Seeing so many old friends made his eyes misty. Many memories were stirred that day. And in each conversation nostalgia bubbled forth like a perking coffee pot. Afterward, Gino never left Thurber out of any future plans.

The 1970 reunion, like the ones to follow, was held in the spacious old dry goods store, one of three remaining brick structures left after Thurber closed down operations and was abandoned. As Lena, his grandchildren, and his son Leo watched, Gino indicated the layout of old Thurber with the sweep of a hand. "See here? The train tracks ran right through the middle of town. Over here on the left side was the grocery store, and over there, on the right, was the Opera House. And the music! The music of heaven could be no sweeter than the sounds that came from that place! And see up there, with all the trees, the yellow house? That was Gordon's house; it looks the same as it did. Then let's see...Oh, yes; the bandstand. It was in the plaza between the dry goods store and the drug store..."Gino's thoughts drifted back to the days when Maestro Dan Raffael and the old Hunter Band played those spirited marches by John Phillip Sousa. Gino could feel his heartbeat quicken as the memory of the music pounded in his thoughts. Rah, ta, ta, tum. Rah, ta, tum, tum. For a moment, time spun backward to the days of spectacular Labor Day celebrations which profusely acknowledged the unionization of Thurber after the long, bitter fight between the company and the miners had ceased. What wonderful celebrations those were! Gino could see it all once more in his mind's eye. The parades, the horse-drawn floats, the games, the beauty pageants, and the long-winded speeches by politicians. And then finally, after Gino had almost given up, the baseball game. Later there would be drinking and dancing far into the night, but the big game was what Gino had come for, and what he would always remember best. He and his brother Pete, along with their father, had watched the baseball game with spirited enthusiasm while his mother and two sisters, not inclined towards sporting events, attended the festivities downtown. Gino could still remember how the Thurber Colts had torn up the Stephenville Sluggers that day, winning the game twelve to one. That was the game when Gino's idol, Clifford Gibson, belted two home runs. Had that Labor Day game been the kindling of his desire to play baseball? But it would be several years before Gino, a young baseball phenomenon in his own right, would wear the Colt uniform. How he loved the roar of the crowd back then! Gino shook free of his momentary reverie and walked a little farther down the street. "Over there," he said, pointing for the benefit of his grandsons, "behind the livery stable. That's where I beat up that bully, Bill Black. I was about your age, then; maybe eight. Bill, he was ten, and big! He was always taunting the immigrants' kids. He called us names like **wop** and **dago,** or maybe **polack** or **fish eater**. One time I asked my Papa John what a **wop** was, and Papa said, 'You are an American of Italian descent. If somebody calls you a **wop**, you teach them a good lesson. I don't like you fighting, but don't you let that stand in your way when somebody calls you a bad name. You may even have to take a bloody nose, or a black eye, or maybe torn clothes. But in America, everybody's the same. You remember that. It is what makes this country great. And if you must fight so others will understand that, then you fight.' So I followed Papa's instructions. I went after Bill Black. Some of his friends were going to let me have it, but then some of those **wops** and **polacks** and **fish eaters** stepped in and for a while we had quite a ruckus. After that, when Bill's friends saw how outnumbered they were by sons of immigrants, they backed down. From then on it was nice and peaceful from the kid's point of view.

Gino and Lena and the family walked on a little farther. Soon they were standing on the spot where the old Opera House had once stood. The plain wooden exterior of Thurber's Opera House, Gino recalled, belied the first-class interior of the building with its thirty by fifty foot stage, private boxes for dignitaries, a "dress circle", a "family circle", and parquet seating. Several touring companies made yearly stops in Thurber to give outstanding performances. The Italians were opera-starved and a sell-out crowd could nearly always be expected. Since a railroad track ran directly in front of the Opera House, the performing troupes could park their private railroad cars very near the building. Everyone in town knew whenever a new troupe arrived, and the excitement would build throughout the day as the townspeople awaited the troupe's first performance. Gino could remember his family dressed in their Sunday best and excited as they attended certain performances. Like all Italians, the Bertollis loved music, and the classical operas were their favorites.

After Thurber died out, the Opera House was torn down. Now the plaza where it once stood was empty. Gino looked at the desolation of the place and a melancholy spirit descended upon him. Nothing but a ghost town now, and to make it worse, he could even recall stories of a ghost to go with it. In 1935, just before he and Lena had moved to California, Gino heard "Nigger" Albert Whitehead and his wife Liza tell of a spooky operatic ghost they'd seen late one night, wandering through the deserted Thurber plaza singing a mournful song. "Yes, suh," 'Nigger' Albert had told him, "dressed in like a white bedsheet, she wuz, and singin', tho' it be a mighty mournful wail, more like screamin', she was a singin' out. No suh, you don't be ketch me passin' through town afta' dark, no mo!"

Gino smiled as he remembered that conversation of so long ago, and wondered if anyone else since had seen the singing ghost making her nightly rounds, filling the evening air with her song.

"Papa, you all right?" Lena nudged Gino to break the spell his thoughts had cast.

"Hmm? Oh, yeah; just thinking of things that happened a long time back." Then, as he shook free of his reverie, Gino noticed for the first time the man standing beside Lena. He threw his wife a questioning glance.

"You remember Tony Scarlotti, Gino? They lived by Rossi on Italian Hill." Lena tilted her head toward the man at her side.

"My goodness, yes! Tony! So good to see you after all these years!" And once again, as he had so many times during that day, Gino allowed his mind to drift back to the past as he and Tony reminisced about growing up in and around Thurber.

In its heyday, the Thurber of Gino Bertolli and Tony Scarlotti was a booming coal mining center, but when oil was discovered nearby at Ranger, Texas, coal was suddenly "out" and the population of Thurber declined from 6,000 people to that of a ghost town in a remarkably short span of time. A poem recited during that era succinctly stated the situation:

> "Thurber was,
> But Thurber ain't no more,
> The trains they went from coal to oil,
> Locking Thurber's door."

The majority of people in Thurber were immigrants; some three thousand Italians, a thousand Poles, another one thousand Mexicans, and a dozen or so other nationalities mixed in with two thousand native-born Americans. The town was a true melting pot.

Gino's family, the Bertollis, had not lived in Thurber but in Thurber Junction, a suburb of Thurber. When Gino left the area in the mid-1930's, the Junction's population was around fifteen hundred. Upon returning for the reunion, Gino was shocked to see how the town had dwindled down to a handful of people. Not more than two or three hundred were left in the whole area. Because the Junction was so economically dependent upon Thurber, it, too, had no way to go but down after Thurber was abandoned. The only difference was that while everything in Thurber was company owned, and could be "company dispensed with", property in the Junction was privately owned. Both Gino and Tony recalled that when Thurber had closed down, many unmarried miners went back to the Old Country. Some went to the coal mines in Illinois and Pennsylvania, others to California. One, Gino remembered, had even gone to work for Al Capone. Then there were those like Gino's family who owned homes in the Junction. Not a few of them turned to bootlegging as a way of hanging on through the hard times, all the while hoping for resurgence in the coal industry.

The Bertollis had been among that group, but finally, realizing the end was in sight, they moved to California. None of the family, however, had been able to make that final severance with Thurber Junction; for they never sold the old family home.

After the reunion was over for the day, Gino went to the old homestead on the Back Road to Thurber; to his place of birth. But the visit proved too heart-rending, and Gino soon broke into sobs. The old ramshackle place had been his home for twenty seven years of his life. As he gazed at the sad looking structure overgrown with weeds and cacti and mesquite, he saw once again the home of his childhood, and in an instant he knew in his heart where he wanted to be.

"Mama," he said to Lena, his voice soft, tentative with questions. "How would it be if we retired back to here, to this place?" he gently probed as he tested for her reaction, fervently hoping she would be agreeable.

"But Gino, look at it! The house would take so much fixing."

"That's the idea," Gino answered quickly, his thoughts already arming him for verbal battle, if necessary, while the contemplation of new beginnings made him feel all at once as though he were young again. "In four years when I retire I'm going to need something to keep me busy, so I won't be under your feet all the time. How about restoring this old house? Can you think of a more wonderful task for an old man than rebuilding the home of his youth? I'll make it exactly like it was. You'll see. Even down to the old furniture. But of course, I'll make it more modern for you. Indoor plumbing. No one would dream of using an outhouse today. While I'm working on it, we can live in the motor home. Finally get our money's worth out of that contraption. And I can plant a garden. When I was a kid, my dad used to grow some pretty good grapes here. Might try my hand at it. Wouldn't hurt." He looked at his wife and waited for her to say something. Silence was her answer. "Well," he said finally, feeling weak and tied in knots.

"What do you think, Lena? Could we?"

Lena smiled up at her husband, knowing that if living on the Back Road to Thurber would make Gino happy, then she, too, would be happy. It would be nice, she conceded, to come back home. Gino was right when he said earlier in the day that they'd stayed away too long. It would be good to move back. The more Lena thought about it, the more she liked the idea.

"Whatever, Gino," she said with a soft shrug of her shoulders. "If it's what you want."

Gino put his arm around her and hugged her close to him. It was settled. In four years, when he retired, they would sell out in California and come back here to stay for the rest of their lives.

But it was never to be. Not long before his retirement, Gino Bertolli suffered his first heart attack and he never fully recovered.

Another 11 years would go by and though he longed to be back in Thurber, both he and Lena knew he could not risk the trip. And so, he was never allowed to live out his dream of restoring the old home place. Now finally, 15 years after that 1970 Thurber Reunion where so many plans for the future were made, Gino Bertolli came home. It seemed to Lena that bringing her beloved husband back to his place of birth, and now his place of final rest, was the very least she could do.

TWO

The physical and spiritual arrangements, for what should have been a simple funeral, created several difficult problems. Shortly before he died, Gino told Lena he wanted a traditional Latin Mass in the St. Barbara's Church in Thurber Junction with burial in the old Thurber Cemetery. Of course Gino had no way of knowing that the church in Thurber Junction had not been used since 1962. And how could Gino, living in California all these years, know that the Diocese in which St. Barbara's was located was overseen by Bishop Gregory Solezel, a man who had cut his bishopric teeth on Vatican II? A clergyman who would never agree to anything as unecumenical as a Tridentine Latin Mass with black vestments. And lastly, how was Gino to know that securing a final resting place in Thurber Cemetery, better known locally as Graveyard Hill, would be difficult at this particular time because a large energy corporation had plans for the cemetery?

There were only fourteen Italian families remaining in the Junction with ties to Thurber. Following Gino Bertolli's death, Lena called the family of Joe Venutti. At first Venutti was perplexed by Lena's call. How he could set up a Latin Mass, he wondered. But too stunned by the news of his old friend's death to consider the many roadblocks he would encounter, Joe promised Lena he would take care of everything. "Lena," he told her, "you know how close the Bertollis and the Venuttis have always been. I'll make all the arrangements. Right now I am just so sorry about Gino's passing. I kept thinking you and Gino would be moving out here soon, just like he talked about. It's hard to think of him gone. But don't worry; I'll take care of everything. I'll see about the church as soon as we hang up. And we'll pick you up at the airport. You can stay at our house on the lake as long as you like."

Joe's eyes misted over as he thought about his father and

Gino's father and the hundreds of other immigrants who had been such an important part of Thurber. He marveled at the love former residents felt for that once lively, but long gone, coal mining center. Would Gino's generation be the last to care? Joe cleared his throat and spoke into the phone. "Do you have a priest in mind who would say the Latin Mass, Lena?"

"No, not really. We've been going to Father Musser here," Lena answered, her voice sounding weary and strained. "He has the Mass each Sunday in his home. But Father has emphysema and like us, he's in his seventies. I'm afraid he could never make the trip, Joe. But he's making some phone calls, trying to find a priest out your way."

"And you're certain it has to be a Latin Mass, Lena?"

"Gino never went to the New Mass in all his life," she answered. The weariness in her voice was tinged now with bitterness. "He said he'd go to hell before he attended one. If it was so important to him in life, Joe, then I won't let him down in death. Can I have Father Musser call you?"

"Sure Lena, have him call." For the first time Joe thought about how hard all this must be on her, and his voice became gentler, each word now swathed in understanding. "You know, Lena, we haven't had a Mass at St. Barbara's for, God, it must be close to twenty-five years now. Most of us here go over to Strawn for the so-called New Mass. But, Lena, I can certainly understand Gino's love for the Old Latin Mass and St. Barbara's. I feel the same way. There is something special about that old Church, isn't there?"

"There sure is, Joe," Lena answered. "Gino and I were married there, and Gino was baptized and served Mass there. You can see why it is so important for his funeral to be there."

"Of course, Lena. Of course. Now don't you worry; I'll see what I can do. Gino will have his last request, I promise."

After he hung up, Joe immediately began having second thoughts. How could he go about arranging a Latin Mass in St.

Barbara's? To Bishop Solezel, Vatican II was gospel. How did one parishioner in one tiny church out in the sticks of the Diocese go about bucking the system? Joe didn't have any idea, but he knew he was going to find out.

His first call was to Father Frank Hopper, his own parish priest, who served two other churches in the area. Father Frank was a young, Ecumenical Catholic priest, assigned to a rural locale in the hope that he could, in time, acquire the polish and diplomacy necessary to be given one of the larger metropolitan parishes. As a result, Father Frank looked at his three churches and the accompanying parishioners with an eye jaundiced by outright boredom. The Church mandated he bide his time. There was no mandate that he bide it enthusiastically.

Though he couldn't quite pinpoint why, Joe had never cared for Father Frank. The man just didn't seem like a priest. He wore open-necked sports shirts, and he called everyone, young and old alike, by their first names. No show of respect for those older, and probably much wiser, than he. No, Joe Venutti decided, he would never like Father Frank. But he would have to ask him about the Mass. A man does not have to be liked to be needed or useful.

As expected, Father's reaction was one of total disbelief. The priest paused for a long interval as though he were trying to determine if the older man were completely demented. "I can't believe, in this day and time," he finally said to Joe, "that anyone is old-fashioned enough to request an outdated Latin Mass. Well, you can ask the Bishop, Joe, but I doubt you'll get it. I know the Bishop's feelings on this. He's not going to change his mind for you or anyone else. I'm sorry, Joe, but don't expect me to ask the Bishop for such an unusual request like a Latin Mass in an unused church."

Joe felt anger rising like bile in his throat. "I'm sure there's a great deal about the old ways you'll never understand. For instance, I thought the Tridentine Latin Mass was 'in perpetuity', and would never be outdated. But now you say that's not the case. So, you've expressed your opinion, Father Frank. So now I've expressed mine, and I'll leave you to your work, which must be demanding since you have so little time for the concerns of your parishioners." Joe paused and took a deep breath before continuing. "Gino Bertolli was a good friend, Father, and a devoted **Roman Catholic**. His last request was for a Latin Mass, and by damn, he'll have one. It would be nice to have it officially sanctioned, but the lack of sanctioning won't keep it from happening. And as to the place, hopefully it will be at St. Barbara's, but it could be done in the funeral home, or even the Legion hall. That won't be the problem. But you can bet we'll have the Latin Mass. So don't worry, Father, I will call Bishop Solezel, and I wouldn't dream of asking you to make the call for me. Now, if you will excuse me, I too have a great deal of work to do. Good day." Joe was shaking with anger as he hung up the phone. *Pompous little fool,* he thought as he replaced the receiver, *we'll see about outdated!*

Joe's second call was to the Diocese office in Fort Worth. After spending a few minutes dealing with a receptionist who seemed over-zealous in her task of screening calls, he was finally put through to Monsignor George Flippin.

"Yes, I see," Monsignor Flippin replied after Joe stated his request. There was a degree of officiousness in the Monsignor's voice that rankled Joe, but the agitated parishioner could do nothing but will him self to remain calm. "I understand your reason for being upset, and I regret your inability to deal with Father Frank Hopper, in whom I've always had a great deal of faith. But I suppose that is neither here nor there." He paused for a moment, and then added, "You say you want a Latin Mass. I suppose that is not entirely unheard of these days. It is, however, a bit out of the ordinary, and this is a matter which only the Bishop can decide."

"I realize that, Monsignor. That's the reason I called. I asked to speak to the Bishop, but they put me through to you instead. But frankly, Monsignor, I'm having trouble seeing what the problem is. Gino Bertolli is dead. He wanted a Latin Mass. With the Pope's Indult, I fail to see why the Bishop would not permit the Mass. This is, after all, a man's last request. Looks like that should carry a little weight with the Bishop."

"What about the church?" the Monsignor inquired, steering the conversation away from the Mass. "I understand the church has not been used for some twenty years. Do you think the church would be suitable even if the Bishop were willing to permit the Mass?"

"I've been taking care of the church myself ever since it's been closed. I put a roof on it six years ago. The building is in fine shape. The church building is not the problem." Joe could feel his patience dwindling.

The Monsignor harumphed, then in a pedantic tone, responded, "I know his Excellency's position on the matter, Mr. Venutti. I also know the position of the Church. And you must realize that even with such unusual circumstances, I don't think the Church or the Bishop will deviate from accepted practice. But since you are sincere, I will speak with the Bishop and get back in touch with you. Leave your number with my secretary, and I'll call you as soon as I have an answer."

Time was short. Joe knew Monsignor Flippin was giving him the run-around. Gino couldn't wait forever to be buried, and the Monsignor probably figured if he delayed long enough, the problem would most likely resolve itself. Joe was furious as he listened to the Monsignor's rhetoric. "Okay, Monsignor, the ball's in your court," he responded bluntly. "But you might keep a few facts in mind as you approach the Bishop on this matter. Number one, St. Barbara's Church is almost one hundred years old. It hasn't been used for over twenty years, so apparently the Diocese has no use for it, but the Texas Historical Society might be interested. I could be in your office within two hours with earnest money to buy the church for the Historical Society. And

Monsignor, while you're thinking over that possibility, why don't you also do a little checking before you speak with the Bishop? Check the Diocese Wills and ask about the Venutti Will. That's V as in Victor, E-N-U-T-T-I. I'll be waiting to hear from you or the Bishop within the next thirty minutes. Thank you, Monsignor, and do have a nice day."

Joe slammed down the receiver. "By damn!" he shouted into the empty room. "Stubborn jackasses opposed to the Latin Mass! If it was good enough for my parents and Gino's parents and countless generations before them, then why does the Church suddenly find the Latin Mass no longer valid? The new Mass is supposed to be in the vernacular. Why then, does Father Frank say the Mass in Spanish for the 'wetbacks' in the parish? I don't understand Spanish, so a lot of good the Spanish Mass does me! The Pope's Indult says a Latin Mass can be at the discretion of the Bishop; looks like he could grant this one request. It's not like we're having a big production in some cathedral in Fort Worth or Dallas." Joe stared down at the silent phone for a moment as the resolution within him rose and solidified. "Damn!" he swore through gritted teeth. "Gino Bertolli's going to have his Latin Mass, Bishop or no Bishop!"

Monsignor Flippin wasted no time in looking up the Venutti Will. According to the paper before him, Joseph Venutti and his wife Carmen had no children. Upon their death, "...all physical assets will be sold or auctioned under the auspices of the First National Bank of Strawn, Texas, and all moneys received there from, as well as all other financial assets, stocks and bonds, after disposal of all claims against the Venutti estate, will revert to the Fort Worth Diocese of the Roman Catholic Church..." Monsignor studied the Will for several minutes. How much money, he wondered, was involved? It seemed to him that a man like Venutti, living in such a small town, so far from anywhere, and in such a depressed area as Thurber Junction, couldn't have acquired much wealth. Might just be a case of self-inflated ego. Venutti was probably the wealthiest man in a town of paupers, but in truth, a man of quite meager means. To be on the safe side; however, Monsignor Flippin thought he'd better have a talk with Father Frank Hooper. Just in case.

Within seconds of his conversation with Father Frank, Monsignor Flippin was scampering down the hall to the Bishop's office. Joseph Venutti, resident of Thurber Junction, was a multimillionaire! This muddled up the problem! How was a man, like Venutti, able to make so much money, the Monsignor had asked. Had he or his wife inherited money? No, Father Frank assured him, every cent had been hard earned. Joe Venutti started out as a welder, working forty years for a gas company while taking extra welding jobs after work and on weekends. His wife ran a beauty shop in the Junction and they put money away for a "rainy day". There were no children to care for or spend on, and they were able to buy land and cattle. As their situation improved, they put more money into land. Then there were royalties from the gas wells drilled on their land. Joe and Carmen Venutti acquired stock in the Strawn bank, and it wasn't too many years before Joe was sitting on the board of directors of that bank. According to Father Frank, Joe Venutti and his wife were the All-American success story. Monsignor Flippin felt a knot growing in the pit of his stomach. With Diocesan finances steadily declining since Vatican II, Venutti's Will would be an element to be weighed very carefully by the Bishop when he considered the request for a Latin Mass. Monsignor earnestly hoped he had not angered Joe Venutti too much. This was certainly a case where great diplomacy would be needed. As he knocked on the Bishop's door, Monsignor was only too glad this one responsibility would fall upon the Bishop's shoulders and not his own.

Joe Venutti's immediate task was to let everyone know of Gino's death and the upcoming funeral. In a town as small as the Junction, word of mouth was the fastest way of getting news out. His first call was to Vic Belizza, a long-time friend, and one man, he knew who would have a sympathetic ear.

"Gosh, yeah, I remember Gino well," Vic said. "I remember all the Bertollis. They lived up the back road by the Engstroms. Gino was one good ball player."

Vic listened as Joe recounted the difficulties he was having in arranging the Funeral Mass for Gino. "I agree one hundred and ten percent with what you say about today's Church and the Bishop, Joe," Vic declared. "You know, Vatican II never threw out the old Latin Mass like the Ecumenics would lead you to believe. The New Mass was stated as a wish, but every liberal weirdo grabbed it as the gospel truth. Part of the social revolution of the sixties, I guess. Bishop Solezel allows a Mass for the homosexuals, and that's absolutely forbidden by the Bible and the Church! Why don't you point that out to him? Tell him you don't think it's right for him to provide a Mass for queers but no Mass for a long-time faithful Roman Catholic like Gino." Vic paused as he recalled the Bishop's previous comments on the Latin Mass. "I guess though, it won't matter much what you say to him. Remember when he said the Latin Mass was nothing more than nostalgic history? Yep, Joe, you've got your hands full."

"We'll see. Before I get through with the Bishop, maybe he'll have his hands full, too."

"Well, Joe, Latin Mass or no, St. Barbara's could still use a good cleaning. Let me see if I can get Rico and Bill and maybe Mrs. Petrelli to help, and we'll get her nice and clean."

"Gosh, Vic, that would sure be a big help. I really appreciate it. You might ask Mrs. Petrelli about the altar linens; she took care of that for years and years. With the funeral on Saturday, we're going to have to hurry to get everything done, even if Bishop Solezel decides to be agreeable."

"OK, Joe. We'll take care of this end. Just hang in there with the Bishop. It's about time somebody took him on. I'll get on the horn to Rico and Bill. You do what you have to do and good luck." Vic hung up and whistled low. For years he'd been hoping someone would straighten out the Bishop, and if anyone could, it would be a guy like Joe Venutti with plenty of money and some clout. Wouldn't that be something, he thought, if the Latin Mass were revived right here in Thurber Junction — all because of Gino Bertolli's funeral.

Saint Barbara's Church

THREE

Al Lyons had been funeral director of Strawn Merchandise Company since 1948. He was a tall, reticent man, with pale gray eyes, pale gray hair, and pale gray skin. Folks in the area said Al Lyons had been around dead people so long he looked like one of them. With so many years of experience, Al had seen more than his share of peculiarities where funerals were concerned. Because of this, the difficulties with the Latin Mass that Joe Venutti had recounted made little impression on him. As an occasional church going Methodist, the problems within the realms of the local Catholic Church didn't mean much to Al, anyway. His knowledge of Catholicism was limited to those rites which were performed at funeral services. Although he could vaguely recall from way back the Old Latin Mass which Joe talked about, his recollection was too scanty to be of much good. Well, he thought as he picked up the handwritten list on the desk before him, the Catholics could take care of the Mass; his only concern at this point in time was the preparation.

The list was a schedule his wife, Heddy, had written for the Bertolli funeral. "Pick up at DFW Airport—Thurs. P.M." Heddy's handwriting was precise, controlled; straightforward and to the point. The handwriting, like Heddy herself, gave him comfort. "Visitation: Fri. Rosary: Fri. 7:00 P.M. Funeral Mass: Sat. 10 A.M. St. Barb. Thurber Junction?" Would the Mass be at St. Barbara's, Al wondered. Joe Venutti had some doubts.

Right now though, Al had to get over to the Thurber Cemetery and stake out Gino's grave plot. On the drive to Thurber he thought about how funerals and the hoopla that went with them had changed since he began working at the funeral home all those years before. He could well remember that until about 1950, a good many people held wakes in their own homes with all-night vigils over the corpse until time for burial. And after the funeral, everyone would bring gobs of food to the home of the bereaved. And the drinking and dancing that followed! Like a celebration! Nowadays the body remained at the funeral home until time for the service, which made it much easier on the family and the funeral director.

When he arrived at the cemetery, Al was baffled by a large chain and padlock on the gate. To his knowledge, there had never been a lock on the gate before. He'd have to drive two miles to the Lazy T headquarters to find out about the lock. If Gino was to be buried Saturday, it was a trip he'd have to make.

Al found Slim Burch, the ranch foreman, welding on an iron pipe railing of a corral near the barn. A big man with a big potbelly which belied his nickname, Slim had a quick smile and a hearty handshake for the funeral director. "I hope you're not out here trying to drum up business Al," he said. "If you don't mind I'd just as soon stick around a little longer. But I might have an enemy or two I could let you have if you're real hard up for work right now..."

Both men laughed, and after a few minutes of conversation which covered everything from weather to politics, Al directed the talk toward the locked cemetery gate.

"Beats me," Slim told him. "Maybe Peacock energy put it there. Peacock's got mineral rights to all our thirty thousand acres, but they own outright the eight hundred acres surrounding the cemetery. All they care about is the minerals so they let us run cattle up there when we want to. But we haven't had any cows in there in a long time. So we haven't used the gate, and I can't tell you about the lock. But I guess with Gino Bertolli dying, you'll need to get in there pretty quick." Slim looked at Al and said, "Tell you what. Let me give Buck a call. If anybody'd know, he would."

Slim dialed Buck Buchannon, owner of the Lazy T. After getting Buck on the phone, Slim handed the phone to Al. But the padlocked gate was as puzzling to Buck as it was to his ranch foreman. Although Buck had Peacock's number and was more than willing to call, he knew that since it was already after five o'clock it would do no good. "They shut their offices up tighter than a drum at five sharp," he told Al. "Hell, I'll just cut the damned chain. I've had about as much of those bastards as I can take. They keep my roads and grass tore all to hell with their trucks, and they're damned slow about making repairs. I'll just tell them I had a sick cow I had to get to. Dammit to hell anyway! They can't be locking up cemeteries. You'd think the damn fools would know better!"

"Naw, Buck, don't cut the chain," Al said. "I've got time in the morning before I drive to the airport. Give me their number and I'll call them first thing tomorrow morning."

"OK. But if you don't get the right answers, call me back. One thing I've learned after all these years with those fools is how to talk their lingo. I can't believe those idiots would lock a cemetery. I might have some kinfolk buried up there I want to visit. What the hell am I supposed to do, climb the fence? Did you ever hear of such bull crap in all your life?"

Al slipped the piece of paper with Peacock's Dallas number into his shirt pocket after hanging up the phone. Buck's thoughts remained on the locked gate. Something wasn't right. Peacock was up to no good, but what kind of no good, he couldn't tell. Peacock Energy and Exploration Corp.-PEEC. They were one of the country's energy giants and boastfully proud of it. The TV was full of their commercials. But what the general public didn't realize was that the company had gotten rich by bilking hundreds of small landowners out of their mineral rights and leases. PEEC had an army of attorneys who were specialists in deceit and circumvention. And if there was a lock on the gate at Graveyard Hill, Buck knew PEEC was up to no good.

Two Peacock Energy executives in Dallas were in a tizzy. Ties loosened, coats tossed aside, the men pored over maps and reports.

It was long past martini time, and with the exception of the night crew, the building was empty.

"Look, like I've been trying to tell you guys," one told the other, taking a deep drag off his cigarette before setting it back in the ash tray, "our man in Austin didn't get our bill before the legislature. So unless we can get the governor to call a special session, we've got a hell of a long wait before we get the Thurber gasification going. That's why I had the surveying done, and why I want the cemetery fence moved right now; we need to get the show on the road."

"Yeah, but what I'm trying to explain to you," said the other, jabbing at a chart for emphasis, "is that our ass will be mud if some bug-eyed bastard from around Thurber gets to snooping around the cemetery and figures out what we're doing. Too dicey! Big George won't like it, but we'd better see about slipping this project a year."

"What? And Peacock loses twelve million bucks production? Hell, I like Dallas. I don't want to be shipped out to Helena, Montana. Nobody's buried at Thurber any more. We can quietly move the fence over and nobody will know the difference. I say it's worth the risk, and that's what I'm shooting for."

FOUR

The difficulty in securing a final resting place for Gino Bertolli was far from a precedent in the Thurber area. William Whipple Johnson, the man who began the Thurber coal mines, lay in his coffin almost nine years before entombment. More amazing is the fact that Johnson's son and daughter, who preceded him in death, remained unburied for even a longer time. The children's coffins were kept in a brick structure behind the Johnson house in Strawn, Texas. Later, when the Johnsons moved to a new home north of Gordon, Texas, the two small coffins were carried on the back of their wagon. When Will Johnson died in 1914, his coffin was placed alongside his children's in the small frame, shingle-sided edifice at the rear of the family home. It wasn't until 1922, following the death of Will's wife, Anna, that the children, along with their father and mother, were permanently entombed in a stone mausoleum on the Johnson ranch.

In life, Will Johnson was a crafty promoter with his fingers in many enterprises. His skill seemed to lie in putting together a scheme and then selling it. He had little interest in the day-to-day operation of the businesses he started, for this provided little challenge. Once any venture became an ironclad reality, Will would sell out and come up with another promotion.

Will Johnson was a good-looking, average size man with a reputation as a "lady's man." Lady friends described him as entertaining, kindhearted, generous and agreeable. But Will Johnson was a procrastinator who often broke dates and received complaints about his belated personal and business appointments.

Born in Ionia, Michigan, Will established himself as a businessman shortly after finishing school. Along with his father, Ethan, and his brother, Harvey, Will was a partner in a general merchandise business in Ionia. This business, coupled with his ability to wheel and deal in buying and selling property, and leasing lumber lands, kept Will busy and provided valuable experience he could fall back on later in life.

For many years the Johnsons' business interests in Ionia prospered. Will considered himself a fortunate man, but felt there was one thing lacking in his life: a wife. In school he was infatuated with a young girl, Anna Fatzinger. Anna's family moved to Waterloo, New York while she and Will were still in school, but her physical absence only served to cause Will's thoughts of her to grow stronger.

Keeping in touch through family members, Will was heartbroken when he learned Anna had married a man named W. C. Campbell. From what friends told Will, Campbell was several years older than Anna and the newly-married couple had little in common. W. C. Campbell bought a sheep ranch near San Antonio, Texas, and expected Anna to take up housekeeping on the ranch. But in Will's wildest imaginings, he could not picture Anna being happy as a sheep rancher's wife, especially out in the sticks somewhere, because Anna cared too much for big cities and crowds. Will, therefore, decided to bide his time because he felt it wouldn't be long before Anna and W.C. Campbell parted ways, and when they did, he intended to be around to lead Anna in a new direction.

At the age of thirty-five, however, Will abandoned his infatuation with Anna Fatzinger Campbell, and took another as his wife. But the marriage was short-lived, and Will's longings soon returned to Anna.

In the Panic of 1873, the Johnsons' business enterprises in Ionia began to fail. Although they held on for a few more years, Will and his brother Harvey were astute enough to realize the hopelessness of their financial condition. Burdened by debts in excess of $20,000, the Johnsons considered bankruptcy but knew it would not remedy their situation since collateral would soon be needed if they were ever to get back on their feet. After weeks of anguish, Will consulted with his closest friend, Harry Taylor.

"Will," Harry told him, "the best thing you could do would be to start signing your name 'G.T.T.'"

"What the hell's that suppose to stand for?"

"Haven't you heard the expression, 'Gone to Texas'? Hell, I can name a dozen friends from New York and Ohio who have run off to Texas to escape their debts. Texas has some crazy law that says after several years' residence in Texas; you're no longer responsible for your indebtedness. And once in Texas, you'd be surprised at the opportunities you'd find, so a shrewd young buck like yourself could make a new fortune, fast."

Harry knew what he was talking about, for he was a wheeler-dealer who had inherited considerable property and had moneyed connections. He traveled widely throughout the United States and Mexico, and when a cousin of his, Ira Taylor, became a land agent in Weatherford, Texas, Harry saw his chance to get on the inside track in that young and growing state. After scouting the Weatherford area, Harry soon wangled himself a position as Secretary of the Beef Producers and Butchers Association that was headquartered in the Parker County town.

Harry soon arranged for Will to buy his cousin Ira's seven hundred acre farm and timber land in East Texas. Leaving their collapsed business behind them, Will and Harvey migrated to Texas in the fall of 1878. The Johnson brothers had secretly cached away some $18,000 in merchandise, and shortly after he arrived in Texas, Will made a trip to New York to arrange for shipment of the goods to his new home in Texas.

William Whipple Johnson

Will stored the merchandise from New York in a barn on his East Texas farm, but he had no intention of being tied to the farm. There was too much quick money to be made from unclaimed land, land sold for taxes and speculative land. For the first several months after their arrival in Texas, Will and Harvey worked closely with a Corsicana land agent to study entrepreneurial locations. Then, when visiting Harry Taylor in Weatherford, Will learned of the rumor that Jay Gould would soon take over the Texas and Pacific Railroad that had been stranded at Fort Worth.

"If there's any truth to this rumor, Will," Harry told him, "the best thing you could do would be to determine the railroad's route and buy land at a favorable location and set up a business. And one thing more, Will. If this railroad pushes west, farmers and ranchers are going to have to start fencing their land, and the real money makers are going to be fence posts and barbed wire. You mark my words."

Recognizing sound advice when they heard it, Will and Harvey quickly bought two tracts of land located seventy-five miles west of Fort Worth in the community of Strawn, in Palo Pinto County. The land lay adjacent to the proposed Texas and Pacific Railroad right of way.

As a newly established landowner in Texas, Will wrote to Anna's sister, Mattie, to boast of his business prowess in the raw new state. Anna, and her young daughter Fannie, now lived in Chicago with the Fatzingers, and Will's letters to Mattie naturally found their way into Anna's hands. Though still married, Anna could not resist such a wonderful excuse for a flirtatious and perhaps suggestive correspondence with an old beau. In October of 1878, in what was probably her first letter to Will, Anna wrote:

> My Dear Friend,
>
> In your letter to Mattie received today you mentioned a subject that has been uppermost in my mind for the past year-namely Texas...I can go to San Antonio but Mr. C. will not be there and I should go alone unless I can persuade Mamma and Mattie to go.
>
> Do you not pass through Chicago either coming or going? I should like an opportunity of talking Texas with you.
>
> You have no idea how tiresome it is to keep house without a man; it is like playing Hamlet with Hamlet left out (I don't know but I do wrong to acknowledge this to one of your vain sex and you too, as I remember had your full share.) We have some idea of going abroad next year. I am quite anxious to go while Mr. C. is away and I have no household cares at present. One might as well enjoy oneself as to mope when one's husband is away.

I am anxious to talk with someone who has seen my "El Dorado." I think I see your smile and say, "Anna is as enthusiastic as ever." I confess I am perhaps as unchanged in some ways as in the school days when you last saw me, although my path has not always been strewn with roses.

I should be pleased to hear from you when you are in Texas. Any information, from or concerning that part of the country, is interesting to me.

Yours sincerely,
Anna F. Campbell

While Will was flattered and amused by Anna's letters, his thoughts for the most part remained on his new business enterprises. By early 1880, Will and Harvey, spurred on by the growing talk of the coming railroad, established the Strawn Feed, Lumber and Grain Company on land adjacent to the proposed Texas and Pacific Railway.

By April of that same year, the T & P began laying rails westward from Fort Worth to El Paso. The Johnson brothers' business flourished. And when the railroad offered to buy 50,000 cedar ties from the Johnsons, Will looked toward the Palo Pinto Hills surrounding Strawn and the abundance of cedar that covered them. Cedar "hackers" eagerly sold or traded posts and ties to the Johnsons, who in turn wasted no time in selling them to the railroad and ranchers for a tidy profit. As track moved farther westward, the demand for barbed wire was so great it was not even necessary to unload the wire from the boxcars and carry it to the Johnson store. Farmers and ranchers, with money in hand, would pay for the wire and then load it directly to their wagons from the rail cars. Texas became the land of milk and honey for Will and Harvey Johnson.

While Will was more than pleased with his business successes in this frontier post, he was discouraged by the acute shortage of suitable female companionship. His thoughts turned more to Anna, and through her letters to him, he sensed her marriage to W. C. Campbell was about to come to an end.

> "I had expected to accompany Mattie but a hitch in the machinery of my household required, as I flatter myself, a master (or either mistress' hands) present. That is the misfortune of being married, you see."

Other letters to him boosted Will's ego as the words portrayed a woman earnestly seeking his help in money matters:

> "Yours of the 18th was duly received. I see you are as much a flatterer as ever. I have vanity enough to think you like to receive my letters.
>
> You need not apologize for minding of business for I am always interested in that and really feel you are paying me quite a compliment in telling me of some of your plans and investments. I shall be very glad to take your advice about investments.
>
> I have been watching the stock reports closely and am happy to say I did not invest. Really, I expect my remarks on stocks will appear refreshingly verdant to you so I won't say any more on the subject."
>
> AFC

By February 1880, Anna Fatzinger Campbell had obtained a divorce from W. C. Campbell. She was awarded custody of their eight year old daughter, Fannie, although full visitation rights were granted the father who remained on his sheep ranch outside San Antonio. Fannie had spent her entire life in the Fatzinger household, and since she was adored and fussed over by her grandmother and her Aunt Mattie, as well, it was obvious from the onset of the divorce whose custody Fannie would really be in. For the first time in many years, Anna Fatzinger was free to pursue a relationship with Will Johnson.

In the spring of 1880 Will paid a visit to Anna in Cincinnati where she had moved following the divorce from Campbell. Harry Taylor also made the trip to Cincinnati during that time, and from the moment he saw Will and Anna together he realized how much in love the couple were.

The day following his return to Texas, Will received a letter from Anna.

My Own Darling,

It is not yet 48 hours since you rolled away from your love, but still I would be just as delighted to see you now this minute as many would hail their love as had been gone a year. So you must abandon all thoughts of ever leaving Anna a year, no matter what your call.

I dream of the happiness we will experience when you return to me, Darling, and we can visit undisturbed. 'Tis all I ask of life to be permitted to love you uninterruptedly till death calls yours, Darling William.

William, Dear, look to your health in every way. Don't be up late at night. Arrange your rest and be regular. Regularity is the foundation of health.

I love you madly, sweetly, dearer than life, (and I know I am loved at last! God bless you dearest) "Who could not lightly love, He would to keep such love." I never thought to know what I have known through rapture, Dear, of being loved by you. Mr. Taylor was very kind, offering his arm, and saying not a word until I had choked back all my sobbing sufficiently to speak. Then he spoke very nicely that you would soon be with me again. Our loving is no mystery to him now, I guess.

So bye, bye, sweet one.

God guard you safely.

Anna

Five days later Anna wrote again.

Dearest, Dearest William: How much I love you, no tongue can tell. Your letter is all-everything to me. It is so lovely. Sounds differently from any ever received from you before. I know, Dear, it is the honest sentiments of your heart. I feel certain that nothing, no one can deprive me of your affections. Yes, I would now venture my life upon your love without a moment's hesitancy...and I find myself talking and calling you endearing names, but my last words to you before extinguishing the light is "God bless my Darling, grant him prosperity and health."

Anna

By the end of June, Anna had mentioned the term "husband and wife" at least once in her letters. As it turned out, she would soon become Mrs. William Whipple Johnson. First, however, she would need to serve as a very necessary "business associate" to William and Harvey.

Will's bragging about his business prowess was not limited to his letters to Anna and her sister Mattie. In his letter to his family in Ionia, Michigan, Will had also done a sufficient amount of boasting, which in turn, was passed on as "how well the boys in Texas are doing." In leaving Michigan and the debts they incurred there, the Johnsons left behind angered creditors who would be forced to settle for fifteen cents on the dollar, thanks to the craftiness of the Johnson brothers' attorney, Albert Williams.

It was not long after word of the Johnsons' success in Texas spread throughout Ionia that the Johnsons received an urgent letter from Williams that advised them to place their Texas holdings with another party before courts in Michigan could seize their assets for debts left in Ionia. Since the "Gone to Texas" law would not grant them immunity until 1889, Will, and Harvey signed over their business and property to Anna F. Campbell.

Will and Anna were married in September, 1880, almost twenty years since their school infatuation. At last, all of Will Johnson's dreams were finally coming true.

By the summer of 1881, "Campbell and Company" opened a general merchandise store in conjunction with the Johnsons' feed and lumber company. With their businesses thriving in a growing community, Will, Anna and Harvey could look forward to a rosy future. With complementary personalities, the Johnsons' marriage seemed close to perfect. For the first time in their lives, Anna and Will realized total contentment. Their life in Texas was safe and comfortable, but in following attorney Williams' advice, the life they portrayed in letters to Ionia painted a much different picture: They were forced to live a rugged life on the Texas frontier harassed by Indians, outlaws and various wild creatures while they struggled to eke out an existence as horse ranchers.

Not long after opening the general merchandise store, Will spent a day scouting the area southeast of Strawn in search of cedar posts. As he approached a log cabin, Will called out, as was the custom, "Hallo, the house!"

A settler appeared from the rear of the cabin. "Git down, mister, and rest yourself, Jowell's the name."

"Thank you. Will Johnson's mine; from Strawn way. I'm out looking for cedar. I own a post yard. Right now I sure could use a drink of water, if it's not too much trouble."

"Got some water," Jowell told him. "Well water. It's cool, but it ain't the best tastin'. Danged black rock makes a bitter taste."

As the two men walked to the well and the bucket of water, Will noticed a small pile of "black rocks" that he instantly recognized as coal. A dozen thoughts bombarded his mind at once. Texas and Pacific RR was hurting for coal. That was common knowledge, although Will doubted a settler like Jowell would know anything about that. Six miles to the northeast, near Gordon in Coalville, coal was already being mined. Was this the same vein, Will wondered. Did Jowell have any idea of the value of coal? Since he referred to it as "black rock," Will doubted it. If the

Johnsons could buy Jowell's land, and if the vein were extensive, they could make a fortune! Will could think of nothing else when he stopped at the well. In his elation at the prospects of coal, Johnson's hand was shaking as he put the dipper to his lips. He was unmindful of the "gyp" taste of the water as he drank, only of the "black rock" beside the house. Trying to mask his excitement, he pointed with the dipper and with a croaky voice asked, "Is that the black rock that gives the water a bitter taste?"

Will's thoughts took him far, far away from the drone of Jowell's voice. If there was any way the coal could be exploited, he thought... In his mind's eye, Will could see a huge mound of coal standing alongside the railroad tracks, and train cars, one after the other, being loaded. And the tremendous profits! A magnificent home for Anna! Hobnobbing with the likes of Jay Gould himself! And no more lies to the folks back in Michigan. Why, with that kind of money he could buy out every one of his creditors, a hundred times over!

"Strawn, huh?" Jowell was saying when Will finally allowed his mind to drift back to the present. "Ain't never been there, but I git over to Gordon 'bout every three weeks or so."

"Right now, I'm looking for cedar," Will replied, forcing the conversation back to the original reason for his mission. "The railroad coming through has caused a lot of ranchers to fence in their range land."

"Reckon so. But the railroad bein' so far away, and all," Jowell said, chuckling as he talked, "it ain't gonna bother me none."

"Might make things a sight cheaper for you, and the cattlemen will be able to ship their stock instead of having to make those long drives."

"Guess I can see where the railroad 'ud be purty good for ranchers and city folk, but I cain't see it'ud do me much good. Me and the Missus, we git along alright. Ketch the weather right, and we can git a fair oat crop and a purty good garden. An' I sell a few fur in winter. It's them hot dry summers that makes it bad. I don't mind so much, but the wife 'ud like to be in Tennessee when it goes to gittin' hot."

Did that mean there was a chance the Jowells might sell out, Will wondered. He ached with excitement of his discovery, and more than anything he wanted to hurry back to Strawn to discuss the idea of a coal enterprise with Anna and Harvey. But right now he needed to earn Jowell's trust. Willing his manner to stay calm and patient, Will carried on with the conversation. "The train will make travel easier, too. For instance, if you and your wife wanted to go back to Tennessee for a visit..."

The two men talked for almost an hour. Will learned Jowell owned 2300 acres of land, had lived on it the past four years, and had never seen an Indian about. As once more Will steered the conversation to cedar posts, his hopes for obtaining the coal deposits soared.

"Looks like you've mostly got mesquite around here, Mr. Jowell," Will told him. "A little cedar on the hill. Maybe we could make a deal with you to cut cedar on your land, or maybe you'd cut some for us."

"Once I git my hay in, I might cut some fer yuh."

"Fine, Mr. Jowell. I need to be getting back to Strawn before it gets dark, but I'll be by to see you again. See if we can't make a deal on those posts. And if you ever get to Strawn, drop by and see us. Campbell Merchandise, and next door is the post yard. I own them both. And the trail between here and Strawn is passable in a wagon, so bring the Missus with you."

It was well after dark when Will rode into his barnyard. Anna popped out the back door of the house with a lantern in hand. "Oh, Will!" she cried upon seeing him. "Where have you been? I've been so worried! Scared to death you'd been attacked by Indians, or thrown from your horse!"

Will took his wife into his arms and held her tight. “It’s all right, Anna. I’m home and safe. You worry too much about me. I know how to take care of myself. But good news! I’ve found a way to make more money than we ever imagined!” The excitement in his voice reached a higher pitch as he summarized his discovery.

“I went southeast looking for cedar post and came upon this cabin; owned by a fellow named Jowell. And Anna, you won’t believe this, but the man’s cabin is sitting right in the middle of a field of coal. I saw the coal he got from digging his well. And the best part, this man doesn’t even know what he’s got!”

“I don’t see what you’re getting at, Will,” Anna said as they entered the kitchen.

“Anna, don’t you see? If we can buy the land from Jowell, we’ll mine the coal and sell it to the railroad. We’ll get rich! Really rich! You’ll have the finest house in all of Texas!”

Anna laughed at her husband’s exuberance. “I don’t need the finest house in Texas, William Johnson. I have you and you’re all I need. But if getting rich from coal is what you want, let’s look into it. Go get Harvey, and we can discuss this over supper.”

Harvey, although younger than Will, was far more business minded and not nearly as impulsive as his brother. “Calm down, Will,” he cautioned after Will enthusiastically presented his views on the coal. “First, we know absolutely nothing about mining coal. Secondly, we’re doing right well with what we now have. Coal mining is a big investment and a risky one. I’m not sure we can afford such a risk.”

“Hell’s bells, man!” Will shouted across the table. “You know you’ve got to spend money to make money. And we can learn what we need to know about mining coal. We can probably get the land for a song. Jowell has no idea what he’s sitting on!” Will rose from his chair and paced the kitchen floor. Then sitting back down, he stared across the table at his brother. “Look, Harvey, when you see what I’ve seen, you won’t be so pessimistic. The way I see it, we stand to get rich! And I have nothing against being filthy rich!"

For two hours the Johnsons discussed the possibilities. Harvey's caution was understandable, although Will had a hard time fathoming it. And Anna, while finding her husband's exuberance contagious, had several questions of her own. Of course, investing in a coal mine was a gamble, and she didn't want to lose everything they already owned. She was content with her present status. So, while Anna and Harvey took a "wait-and-see" attitude, Will was ready to get right into it. But it would be another five years before the Johnsons began extracting coal from the ground, for there was much preliminary work and many questions.

How, for instance, did one go from merchandiser to coal operator with limited capital and no knowledge of coal mining? And while they might be able to buy the land from Jowell, what was the extent of the coal deposits? What were the railroad's present and future needs? Were the land titles clear? How could they study the coal situation without stirring up the curiosity of the unsuspecting owners? It was obvious the Johnsons would need advice from someone with far more knowledge of coal than they had; someone who would be discreet and not locally known.

Anna came up with a solution. "My brother John will help us," she told Will and Harvey. "I'll write to him. He studied mining in college and he's wanted an excuse to come west."

In the late summer of 1881, John Jacob Fatzinger, a recent engineering graduate of the Pennsylvania Military College, stepped off the train in Strawn, Texas. He had come to help the Johnsons in their quest for coal.

FIVE

The railroad's need for coal became insatiable as the rail mileage increased and more rail services were added to the Texas and Pacific line. In the beginning, coal was mined at Bridgeport, north of Fort Worth. Coal had also come from Rock Creek, near Mineral Wells, and then from Santo, a small town located directly on the railroad line. After that, a meager amount of coal was found in Panama, a few miles to the west of Santo, but not enough to meet demands of the new railroad. Then in 1881, just prior to Johnson finding coal on the Jowell place, mines were opened just north of Gordon, in an area that would be called Coalville. Although the Coalville mines had satisfactory potential, union demands would allow the mines to remain open only five years. In 1886, while the T & P clamored for more coal, the Coalville mines were shut down, but by then, Will Johnson was ready.

In 1881, in those exciting days following John Fatzinger's arrival, Will and his brother-in-law spent endless hours prowling the land around Jowell's acreage. John made notes and drawings until a rough map evolved. In several locations John found outcroppings of coal, primarily along stream beds. There were three old Indian campsites where coal had been burned, and at one of the sites the two men saw their first metal arrowheads, fashioned from the metal rim of a wagon wheel. A few settlers in the area used coal for heating water, washing clothes and hog butchering, but the "black rocks" were too dirty for use in the cook stove. They found three other settlers, who like Jowell, encountered the black substance while digging water wells. There was no doubt about the availability of coal.

The thought of all that coal and the riches it symbolized became the driving force in Will's dreams. The businesses in Strawn were left to Anna and Harvey, while day in and day out, Will and John continued with their survey. Physically worn by the long hours of riding and walking, the sleepless nights, and a mind that would not rid itself of coal for even a few moments, Will became more and more haggard and weary, despite Anna's concern and protests.

Names of settlers and various acreages were noted on John's map, along with a brief description of the property "...a rock, big cottonwood tree, center of creek bed, flat topped mountain to east, an oak post." In all, John Fatzinger's map roughly defined a 20,000 acre field of coal, but there were many criss-crossings of boundary lines and overlapping acreages. It would take time to sort out and trace all the rightful owners or their heirs. Will was impatient, but he knew from his years of dealing in land transactions that it must be done. Falling back on those years of experience, Will also realized he had a certain knack, for he could quickly spot a clouded title, a quick claim possibility, a void, or an adverse possession opening. With this kind of experience, no high priced attorney would be needed. For that, Will was grateful.

With the maps complete, Will and John rode thirty miles to Stephenville, the county seat of Erath County. While the courthouse provided some answers regarding boundary lines, they found that in several cases, there were no descriptive deeds on record. Thankfully, the Jowell property, the anchor to the entire scheme, had been duly recorded as a portion of the Pedro Hererra Survey. Will knew it would be necessary to begin with the Jowell acreage and work outward. In the months ahead, Will would have to speak with each landowner personally, and study their deeds carefully if he were ever to succeed in this venture. This, he knew, would require a great deal of tact and time.

The next step for Will and John was a visit to the Coalville mines, eight miles east of Strawn. Here, they hoped to learn something of the day-to-day operation of a coal mine. When they arrived in Coalville, Will used his typical pretentious manner to introduce his brother-in-law as a "mining engineer from

Pennsylvania studying mining techniques in the Southwest." It was the key they needed to gain working knowledge of coal mining.

A drift mine had been opened on the west side of Clayton Mountain at Coalville, two miles north of Gordon. The mined coal was hauled by wagons to Gordon, piled alongside the tracks and then lifted into coal chutes for dumping into the locomotive tenders.

The town of Coalville was a typical rough mining camp. With a population of several hundred, the town was wild and brawling with an assortment of saloons. Drunken fights were the norm, and fatal knifings and shootings were commonplace. Will had heard tales of miners who simply disappeared, never to be heard from or seen again. Both Will and John quickly realized that while the Coalville mines might be profitable at present, the undisciplined work force, the excessive drinking by workers and the domination by the local union would soon make the Coalville mines a money loser. Will made a mental note to benefit from his observation.

Charley Finnigan, Coalville mining superintendent, made a grand show of it for the "mining engineer from Pennsylvania." As he led the two men down the shaft of a slanted tunnel, Will experienced a sudden and totally unexpected attack. They had gone no more than fifty feet, well short of where the coal was being dug, when Will became overwhelmed by feelings of suffocation. When John turned back to see how Will was progressing along the shaft, he noticed his brother-in-law was panting and sweaty and seemed disoriented. His forehead was covered by sheen of sweat, and he was stumbling as he walked. "Will, are you okay?" John asked.

"Yeah, fine," Will said weakly. "Probably something I ate. You two go on without me." Before his words were out, Will was heading for the mine entrance. Instinctively he knew if he could only get to the shaft opening and the wide spaces beyond it, he would be all right. As he reached the opening, Will realized his problem. A problem, considering his current ambition, which was laughably embarrassing, for William Whipple Johnson, Texas entrepreneur about to become a mine owner, suffered from claustrophobia. Although in the future, Will would try several times to conquer this phobia, it would plague him throughout his life.

On the train back to Strawn that day, John, slightly embarrassed and not wanting to draw undue attention to his brother-in-law's attack, hurriedly looked over his notes and gave his first impressions. "First off, the Coalville operation is paying its miners too much," John said. "The owners need to pay by the ton, rather than by the day because the miners just laze around in their work. Back east they'd be paid about a dollar a ton, and even at that, most miners make two-fifty, maybe three dollars a day." He paused and thought for a minute. "Then, too, back in Pennsylvania they use a lot of foreign labor. I didn't notice any foreigners here. Maybe a few Mexicans, but that's all. It's a pity because immigrants work hard and for practically nothing. And they don't understand that damned union business, either. They're just glad to get the work. The Knights of Labor are too strong a force here, Will. High pay to the miners will eat your lunch. I figure if the owners at Coalville have to go any higher in wages, it'll shut them down. And there's already talk that the Knights of Labor are fixing to demand a fifty cent a day increase for their workers. Coalville might as well shut down the mines right now as pay it because they'll never see another cent profit."

John Fatzinger had a few more specific ideas for his brother-in-law. "You should immediately buy Jowell's land, and then as much of the surrounding lands as you can get at a reasonable price. If the owners get wind of what you're doing, they might not sell, or they may ask too much. Ideally, if you could get it, the entire 20,000 acres will give you all the coal land you'll ever need. If you can buy at even a dollar an acre, that's still a mighty big investment. And you're going to need twenty thousand for equipment and you'll have to haul the coal to the rail lines." John studied the maps in his lap. "Oh, and Will, give up the idea of hauling coal all the way to Strawn for the railroad. It's too far, and it'll eat up your profits. If I were you, I'd bring it here," he pointed to a location on his map. "It's about two miles north. Just haul it to the tracks there. If the railroad wants coal badly enough they'll be glad to make a pick up stop there."

John had been an invaluable help to Will in his quest for coal, but once the lands had been studied and plotted and the mining at Coalville studied firsthand, both men knew John's work was finished. It was time for him to head back to Pennsylvania. The night before his departure the Johnsons gave a huge barbecue in John's honor. When the last guest was gone and Will and Harvey were cleaning up, John found a few minutes to spend privately with Anna, to whom he'd barely had time to speak; it seemed, since his arrival.

Knowing her brother intended to stop in Chicago and visit their mother and sister, Anna began their conversation by asking, "Just how long are you intending to stay with Mama and Mattie?"

"Not more than three days, I suppose. I must be getting back to my own work soon."

"I envy you the visit," Anna said. "I'd love to see them again, but even more so, I long to see my daughter Fannie. I do wish Mamma and Mattie were more disposed toward Will, they seemed to like him as a family friend, but since our marriage, they seem not to particularly want him as a member of the family."

"They'll come around, Anna," John said comforting. "Give them time. Why, if they got to know Will as I have in these past few weeks, they'd have much better feelings toward him. I guess we've ridden several hundred miles together, and the one thing I've noticed is that everything Will does, he does with you in mind; even this coal thing. All Will can think about is how the money it makes will provide you with a better home and more comforts."

"I know," Anna agreed with a smile. "And you know what I like about him best, John? He acts like my opinion really matters to him. He's always asking me about business matters, and what I think he should do. You have no idea how flattering that is to me, and it makes me feel as though I'm part of everything he does."

"You are, Anna. You most certainly are."

Anna allowed her thoughts to drift for a moment as she stared out of the darkened window into the night. Finally she turned back to her brother and in a resigned voice asked, "Can you take a package for my little Fannie? It's a frilly dress. Isn't that silly? Buying a frilly dress for a little girl you never get to see?" Tears stung her eyes, she twisted her hands together, and she bit tentatively on her bottom lip before speaking again. And then it was in a voice so anguished it tore at her brother's heart. "Oh, John, I miss Fannie so much! I want her with me so badly some times I think I can't stand it if she doesn't come out here. But Mamma and Mattie keep saying it's too uncivilized, but you know that's not so. Lord, how I miss that child!" Anna struggled to regain her composure and headed toward the kitchen. "Anyway, would you mind taking the package for me?"

"Sure, Anna, I'll be glad to." He wanted to say something sympathetic, some little word that would allow his sister to realize he understood how she felt. But no such word would come to mind, and he realized Anna could deal far more easily with his jesting than his sympathy. "And I'll be certain to tell Mamma and Mattie about the scorpions and red ants and rattlesnakes and copperheads. You know, I'd bet Mamma doesn't even know that poisonous snakes have triangular heads. Won't she be thrilled when I tell her?"

"Oh, John! Stop it!" Anna laughed, instantly banishing her sadness. She brushed past Will and Harvey as they entered the room while she was retreating. "Do something with my incorrigible brother, William, if you can," she teased. With a sweep of her skirts she was out of the room only to return a moment later bearing a tray replete with her finest coffee service.

Anna winked at Will, and Will stepped quickly to the bureau. Reaching into the top drawer, he took out a small package and handed it to his brother-in-law. "A tribute," he said softly. "A small measure of our thanks."

John opened the package and flipped open the lid of a gold pocket watch. On the inside of the lid were inscribed the words: "To John. In Appreciation. W. W.- Anna - Harvey. Texas, 1881."

"When the coal mines are a success," Will added, "It will be because of you. We're indebted to you, John; mighty indebted."

"Oh, no, Will, it's me who's indebted to you," John grinned. "Why if it hadn't been your idea about this coal business, I should never have had the opportunity to become acquainted with every shinnery patch and cedar brake within a ten mile radius of here. Thank you so much." He looked down at his new watch, then added, "And thanks for the watch, too. Don't mind telling you I needed one."

"Well, on this festive occasion, then," Anna stated, pouring the coffee, "I'll add another happy note. It seems we'll be having an addition to the Johnson family next spring." For several seconds she kept her eyes down, not looking at her husband until she handed him his cup. Then Will noticed the bright sparkle in her eyes and the rosy glow that lighted her cheeks.

With misting eyes, Will set down the coffee cup and took his darling Anna in his arms. What a complete fool he had been, he thought as he held her. Not once had he noticed anything out of the ordinary! And then once again, for perhaps the millionth time, he realized just how extraordinary his wonderful little wife was. For the past few months he'd been gone twelve hours a day, traipsing about the countryside, neglecting Anna, and never once had she complained!

"Anna, my dearest," Will said, completely blanking out the two men still present in the room. In his mind, he and Anna were the only two people in the world. They and the tiny infant they would soon have as a symbol of their love. "I've been so busy with coal, I've neglected you terribly, and how do you repay me for my negligence? By making me the happiest man on earth, that's how! Oh, darling, how can I make this up to you? I know! Bill Allen is having a shindig this Saturday to get ready for fall roundup, and we can ride out with the Stuarts." He smiled at his wife, feeling his chest would surely burst with the swelling pride he felt inside it. "There'll be a fall moon, a full one; just right for lovers. The ride to the dance and spinning around the dance floor won't be too much for mother and baby, will it?" he asked as an afterthought.

"Don't worry about me or the baby, Will. The ride will do us both good. And the dancing shan't hurt either. But William Johnson, I'll not have you utter one more word of negligence, especially in the presence of Harvey and John, who might think I really feel that way," she chided. "I should have said something sooner, but you were already too excited about coal, and I didn't want to burden you."

"Burden him!" Harvey cried, "Looks to me as if the weight of the world's been lifted from his shoulders. If his smile grows any broader, it'll break!" Stepping forward, Harvey took his brother's hand and pumped it vigorously. "Congratulations, big brother. So you're going to be a papa, but I'll be an uncle!"

Anna laughed at the feigned look of shock on Harvey's face. "Come to the dance with us, Harvey," she begged. "It's time you started looking for a wife. If we let you, you'd stay married to the business. Why, Harvey Johnson, I've noticed pretty ladies flirting with you in the store all the time, and you never give them any attention! We really must remedy that situation and the sooner the better. Harvey, please say you'll come."

"Okay, Anna, if it will make you happy, I'll go to the dance. I only wish John could stay with us a little longer, so he might come with us, too. Maybe he could find a Texas belle to take back east."

"Leave me out of it," John warned with a smile. "I've had all of your wild Texas I can stand. Just think how thrilled Mamma and Mattie will be when I tell them the news!"

Before his departure, John Fatzinger left a clear outline for Will to follow in his quest for coal. he biggest hurdle, Will knew all too well, would be money. As John had figured, it would require at least $20,000 for land and an equal amount for equipment and mules. Impatient as he was, Will was forced to bide his time, for there was absolutely nothing he could do without the needed funds. And where the money would come from was another matter. John suggested approaching outside investors, but Will wouldn't hear of it, for William Whipple Johnson intended answering to no one. The coal mining venture had been the Johnsons' from the beginning, and he wanted no outside interference.

In the days that followed, Will was busy tracking heirs and checking deeds and legal documents. He wrote dozens of letters requesting geological surveys, maps and information on mining procedures. He kept a chart on the railroad's daily coal requirements, and from this, projected their future needs.

And each night, as he returned home to Anna, Will was again reminded of his great fortune. Anna never looked lovelier, and her glowing radiance provided the incentive in everything Will did. Throughout the day his thoughts were with her and the child she carried within her. As time passed and Anna bulged out, Will insisted she give up all but the least demanding tasks.

"Oh, Will," she chided. "You're like a mother hen watching over her one chick. I'm fine. And when I feel this tiny little life inside me kick, I know the future will be more joyous than ever. My happiness would be totally complete if only Fannie were here with us. She could be a little mother to the baby. Will, do you suppose there's the slightest hope Mamma and Mattie will relent? They still think of this place as being totally uncivilized."

"Uncivilized, my foot! That's bunk. We have three churches

and a school in this town, and I've seen several girls who are about Fannie's age. After the baby is born and you're well enough to travel, you take a trip up north and bring Fannie home with you and your mother and Mattie will have to understand."

Anna was beside herself with joy, and when Will left, Anna thought of fixing up a room for Fannie. Bright, flowery curtains; the kind that billowed in the breeze.

That evening when Will returned home, however, it was not to further discussion of Fannie's coming. It was a surprise visitor, Harry Taylor, who was entertaining Anna with talk of his travels when Will walked in the door.

"My goodness, Harry! Of all people! What brings you to Strawn?"

"On my way to Houston, Will. Just dropped by to see how you folks are making out on the frontier." Harry handed his business card to Will. "H. M. Taylor," the card read, "Cattle Dealer. Houston, Texas."

"Looks like your business is expanding, Harry." Will said as he placed the card on the table between them.

"Lots of money to be made in cattle, Will. I'm still secretary of the Beef Producers Association in Weatherford. It allows me some good connections in the industry I might not have otherwise. As the cattle industry grows, I find myself increasingly indebted to the railroad. No problem getting them to market any more."

Over supper that evening, Harry raised his glass to toast his host and hostess. "Dog-gone, Will! You folks have done remarkably well in just three short years. Probably the best move you've ever made. Just look at you, Will. A lovely wife," he paused and bowed, smiling at Anna across the table. "A baby coming, your business prospering and you own several hundred acres of land. Do you have any idea how many men would long to be in your shoes right now?"

Will smiled and winked at Anna as Harry continued.

"And what's this deal you keep hinting at? You said something about it being the biggest deal in your life. What are you into, Will Johnson? Since I'm the one who got you to Texas in the first place, I think you at least owe me an answer."

Will threw back his head and laughed. "You're right, Harry, I do owe you. And I hope you brought a fat roll of bills with you, because I have a feeling that tomorrow morning after we take a little trip east of here, you're going to be wanting in on my deal."

"Damnation, Will!" Harry swore the next morning after they had ridden out the Jowell place and Harry had seen the coal outcroppings himself. "Wish I had some capital to go in with you on this. Right now, though, I'm tapped with sugar cane in Cuba."

The two men were in the back office of the store. On the desk between them lay John Fatzinger's maps and a stack of surveys Will had requested. Harry studied the maps for several moments. "You say you need forty thousand? You sure that's enough to get this thing going? Don't short change yourself."

"It'll be enough, Harry. I'm certain of it, but what I'm not certain of is where it's coming from."

"It'd be pretty sweet if you could handle it yourself, but I'm afraid you may need outside money. For now you just buy up all the land you've got money for and remain patient. Hell, Will, knowing you, forty thousand is just a little hill to climb! I'll check on investors when I get back to New York and St. Louis. I know you'll get rich off this deal, Will. And old friend, I wish you the best."

The next morning Harry Taylor departed for Houston. "I'll see you in a few months, Will; until then, good luck."

"Thanks, Harry." Will did not realize that two years would pass before he'd see his closest friend again.

SIX

In June of 1882, baby daughter Marion was born. Will was beside himself with pride as he boasted to all who would listen. "She has her mother's beauty and her father's intelligence," he jested within hearing of several customers in the merchandise store.

"I'd rather she had your looks and her mother's good sense," Harvey replied good-naturedly, then slapped his brother on the back as laughter echoed throughout the store.

But even being the brunt of Harvey's jokes could not dim the joy in Will's heart, for little Marion became the central jewel in the crown of his life. Will and Anna fawned over the baby, and Will's only fear was that they might be guilty of loving the child too much. But this could never be, he reasoned. No one could love too much.

Time passed quickly and in what seemed far too short a span, Marion reached her first birthday. Anna looked forward to taking the toddler north where she hoped to be reunited with her first daughter, Fannie. Although Will had promised Anna the trip, he did not dare think of how he would pass the days without Anna and Marion.

Will made idle conversation as he helplessly watched Anna pack. "I hope traveling with Marion will not be too hard on you, and I hope you won't have any problems."

"If you have any doubts, then come with me, Will," Anna answered as she carefully placed the beautiful dress of black silk she had purchased for Will's mother into her traveling trunk. "It would do you good to see your family, and it might give mine an opportunity to realize what a wonderful husband and father you are." Anna smiled warmly up at him, and Will felt a knot of longing in his stomach.

"God, woman, don't you know I'd be on that train with you in a moment if I could? And the creditors back in Ionia would have my hide just as quickly, and that would be the end of our coal mining." He took his wife's hand in his and looked deeply into her eyes. "But, I'd still risk it, Anna, if I thought my being there would help persuade your family to let Fannie come to Texas. I'm afraid however; I'd only make matters worse. Judging from Mattie's letters, your mother doesn't care much for me as it is."

"That's only because she doesn't know you, darling, but don't fret about it. If you can't make the trip, you can't. It's that simple."

Will smiled and said, "You have no idea how difficult it is to deal with a woman of logic and beauty."

"I hope your trip will be happy and successful, darling," Will said to Anna as she and Marion boarded the train.

"I'm confident it will be, my dearest. I shan't spend any longer than necessary away from you. I shall retrieve Fannie from Chicago, make a fleeting stop in Ionia, just long enough for your mother and sisters to rave over our beautiful little Marion, and then I shall be on the next train home," Anna said with a quick smile and a kiss before turning away.

Will stood watching and waving his arm until the window where Anna was seated faded from his sight.

Ten days went by with agonizing slowness before Will heard from Anna. And then his heart and soul went out to Anna as he learned of her troubles with her family.

> A shop girl told me that she saw Fannie with Mattie about two weeks ago. Mattie said Fannie's father had paid expenses, so they let Fannie go with him since he had control over her.

Mattie, it seemed, had conspired with the Campbell relatives to hide Fannie away during Anna's visit. From the few shreds of information Anna was able to gather, she was fairly certain Fannie had been taken to Guelph, Ontario, Canada, where Campbell's relatives lived. And Anna had traveled to Guelph hoping for an opportunity to spend a few minutes with Fannie. But the Campbell family refused to let Fannie see Anna and accused Anna of deserting her daughter and now wanting her back for spite.

At times, frustrated beyond endurance, Anna had no recourse but to allow her fury and pain to flow into her letters home to Will. She could not believe the actions her own family had taken against her, and the anger festered as she tried time and again to reason with her sister Mattie and her more reticent mother.

Her reasoning, however, was met with condescension and belittlement. As a result, her letters home to Will became even more pain-filled. But while Will was more than ready to board the first train to Chicago and help Anna in dealing with the matter, she continued to caution against it.

Will remained in Strawn and tried to keep his mind on business while the majority of his thoughts were on Anna and the struggle she was forced to endure alone. As the weeks passed without news of a satisfactory outcome, Will's thoughts took a more deviant turn. "By damn!" he told Harvey. "If those bastards in Canada can kidnap Fannie, I see no reason why we just can't kidnap her back!"

"How do you propose to do that?" Harvey asked.

"I'll contact Pinkerton's Detective Agency and let one of their boys handle it. It'll be no time at all before Fannie is back with her mother where she belongs."

But kidnapping did not fall under the auspices of the famous detective agency, especially when national borderlines entered. The refusal sent Will into an even more dejected state, but he was forced once again to bide his time waiting for Anna.

Anna, in the meantime, considered several options of her own. She, too, thought about a turnabout kidnapping, but the weight of legalities was too heavy on her mind. She had also given consideration to purchasing a house in the same neighborhood as her mother's and then just "waiting it out" until Fannie's return. While studying the real estate market, Anna took time to consult with an attorney, although his advice was far from what she hoped to hear.

"Can you prove your ex-husband and your sister kidnapped your daughter?" the attorney asked. "Do you have any proof at all, other than your own feelings?"

"No," Anna said weakly.

"And supposing Mr. Campbell wants to file a counter suit for custody on the grounds of desertion? Can you prove that in moving to Texas you did not willfully desert your daughter?"

"Yes! I would never desert Fannie! Mother and Mattie persuaded me to leave her with them because they thought Texas was too uncivilized."

"But in three years you've never been back to see your daughter. That won't look good to the judge. Also, the court will want to know what sort of life you're living in Texas, if that's where you plan to take Fannie. Can you convince the court your life is wholesome and in an environment favorable to the growth of a young child?"

"Certainly!" Anna said, her voice gaining strength as she realized a glimmer of hope. "We own successful businesses and can give Fannie anything she needs or wants."

"And your husband? From what you've told me, his move to Texas was for the purpose of starting anew. Why did he want to start anew? What of his past in Michigan? What I'm getting at is that the court will want to know your husband's reputation, and you can be assured opposing attorneys will seek character references from both Michigan and Texas."

Anna's hopes were dashed with the attorney's last statement.

There would be no way she could win if Will Johnson's debts in Michigan were brought up. No judge would consent to Anna's request without a thorough check into her present life and circumstances. But Will was her life! And to make matters worse, even as she poured out her pain to Will in her letter she knew she could never allow him to know he was in any way responsible for her failure to reclaim her daughter.

As she and little Marion departed Chicago, Anna realized just how futile her hopes of having Fannie with her had been from the very beginning. For the last few years, eleven year old Fannie had never known any family but Mattie and Anna's mother. And though Anna had faithfully written her daughter since moving to Texas, there was not one instance where a letter had been acknowledged. In all probability, Anna's letters never reached Fannie. God only knew to what extent the child's mind had been poisoned against her mother. Had Anna been successful in getting Fannie back, the child might have always remained totally embittered. In the long run, it might be better her fight for Fannie had been lost. Such hostile emotions as the child no doubt held would have been destructive to the Johnson household. And it was this latter thought that allowed Anna to continue her journey on to Will's family in Ionia, Michigan with even the slightest semblance of happiness.

While her own family had turned against her, Anna soon discovered the Johnson family welcomed her with the warmest affection. Little Marion was the cause of much exuberance and joy, and Anna was in many ways able to put thoughts of the problems she endured in Chicago behind her.

Will was overjoyed when Anna's letter from Ionia arrived, and he could tell her depression had been lifted.

My Dear Will,

Yours of the 16th reached me this morning. I am so glad to hear from you.

Our little daughter Marion was baptized yesterday. I, of course, took charge of Marion who looked like an angel. She was dressed in her best dress and a lovely white cashmere cloak trimmed with ottoman ribbon and Rousseau pearl buttons. Blue shoes (glove kid) and stockings to match. She was the first baby baptized in the new church so her name will be first on record. I subscribed $25.00 toward a new baptismal font. Your sister Alice was delighted.

I ordered a carriage to take us and bring us home. Mother Johnson wore the new black silk dress I gave her and how proud she was. Everyone told Alice Marion was the loveliest child they had ever seen. So your infant's first appearance was an immense success. She behaved well and never looked better.

Marion sends a kiss for you. Mother Johnson was so anxious to hear from you.

Yours, Anna

As time for Anna's return approached, Will found he was less able to focus on his work. Every bit of spare cash available had been cached away for the coal mining venture, and Will was jubilant as he realized how close they were to seeing their dream come true. However, Anna's homecoming took precedence over everything, and in those last few days before her arrival home, Will could think of little else.

"They're here!" Will cried out as he heard the train's whistle, and he took off running to arrive breathlessly at the depot just as Anna, with little Marion asleep in her arms, stepped off the train.

Grabbing her and their child into his arms, Will kissed her soundly on the lips and held her tightly as though in fear of ever letting her go. "My God, Anna, I never knew I could miss someone so much!"

"Me too, Will. And Marion wanted her daddy."

"Come on, Mommy. Let's go home where we belong."

Later, Anna recounted the misery she experienced in trying to see Fannie. "I can't believe Mattie would be so deceitful," she told her husband. "To keep me away from my own child! Can you imagine any one wanting to do something that hurtful?"

"No, Anna, I can't. I only know we must put this behind us. Just pick up the pieces and go on, darling. That's all we can do. We may have lost Fannie, but we still have Marion."

But Marion would not be with them long.

SEVEN

It began as a croupy cough in the middle of the night. Two days later, at the age of three, little Marion Johnson was dead. The light had gone out of Will and Anna's life.

Will found it impossible to reconcile himself to his daughter's death, but for Anna, who had already given up one child, Marion's death was devastating. When time came to discuss funeral arrangements, Anna refused to talk of the child's burial.

As her eyes brimmed with tears and filled with panic, she screamed at Will. "I won't let them put her in the ground! I won't! They can't put my baby in a dark, cold hole! Oh, please, God, Will, do something! Don't let them take her away! Please!"

Perhaps it was the pain in Anna's voice, or the vivid memory of his seeming "entrapment" in the constricting, dark hole of the Coalville mine with John Fatzinger. Whatever the reason, Will agreed with his wife not to bury their only child.

For weeks following her death, Anna gently and lovingly brushed the corpse's hair and dressed her in the clothes she had worn in life. Though the situation was macabre and morbid, Will said nothing. But silently he agonized over the loss of his daughter and of Anna's inability to deal with reality.

"Anna, we can't keep her here any longer," he told his wife softly a month after the child had died. Immediately Anna's eyes filled with terror. Will placed his hand gently over her mouth to stifle her cry. "Don't worry, darling. I know how we can keep her with us. We'll build a small playhouse in the back yard. We'll let her stay there from now on, and we can visit her every day."

Anna hesitantly nodded, "But not burial," she said in a firm voice. "I won't have her in the ground."

"No burial," Will promised. Within a week, Marion's body was housed in a small wooden structure behind the Johnson house. If this caused a stir among the neighbors, Will was totally unaware of it. His only concern was for his wife, and he prayed he would not soon lose her, too.

Since Marion's death, Anna's spirit had died, too. She ate only when Will firmly insisted, and there was severe weight loss. Each day she wandered about in a trance-like state. The only time she showed any emotion was when she made her daily visits to the small coffin within the brick playhouse, and then the emotion was one of sadness and tears. Watching her tore at the core of Will's soul, but more than anything, he wanted his wife, the Anna he had once known and loved, returned to him.

Several doctors examined Anna, and each diagnosed her problem as "acute dementia." Most of them recommended she be sent to an institution, but Will would not permit it.

"Anna's strong," he told Harvey. "She'll pull through, I know she will. But, my God, man, she's been denied not one but both of her daughters. That would be a blow to any woman. It's going to take time for pain like that to heal."

"Of course they know it'll take time, Will. They're only thinking of what's best for her. Maybe an asylum might be better because God only knows how much more you can take before your health goes, too."

"But I don't care! I spent two months without her once and I won't be without her again, and as long as she needs me, I'll be there."

"Well, you know I'll always be here, too."

"Thanks, Harvey. I've left everything to you. This is hard on everyone."

Anna's recovery was slow. Will stayed near, venturing out only for pressing business matters. Had it not been for Harvey and the capabilities of a young engineer, R. S. Weitzell, who Will had hired, the Johnson's mining enterprise might never have gotten off the ground. But while Will looked after Anna, Harvey and Weitzell took care of the mining interests.

Jowell's 2300 acres were bought for $2500. W. F. Cummins, a state geologist, was paid to ensure a clear title to Jowell's land. Cummins would also place in Johnson's hands a state survey on coal that was favorable to Johnson's plans, and Will pretended this survey was his own undertaking.

In November 1886, almost a year after Marion's death, the Johnsons were ready to open the first mine. At long last, Will felt Anna was strong enough for him to leave her, and he was ready to take charge again.

Another factor also gave Will motivation. The miners at Coalville had struck against a cut in pay from $3.00 a day, but finally went back to work six months later at $2.64 a day. However, even with the lower pay, the mines were not profitable, and the owners shut down the mines. This was exactly what John Jacob Fatzinger had predicted three years previously. The labor union leased and reopened the mines, but there was no profit, and the mines permanently closed in 1886. Now the railroad was without a principal source of coal. But the closing of the Coalville mines was both fortuitous and unfortunate for the Johnsons.

The ex-Coalville miners swarmed to the new coal location, and the Johnsons had a ready, but mediocre, labor force on hand. The bad part was that the Knights of Labor organization also shifted to the new mine and the inexperienced coal operators unwisely recognized union representation of the miners, and this would become a major hindrance to the Johnson dream.

As the first coal came up, Will Johnson's spirits soared. Anna was much better, and the mine he had dreamed of for so long had finally become a reality. Perhaps, he thought, as he walked in the door shortly before Christmas, the bad times were over. Anna greeted him, looking more like her old self than she had in a year. She had gained some weight, and the color was back in her cheeks. He kissed Anna then asked, "If the weather's good tomorrow, could you pack a picnic basket? Harvey and I want to show you our mine and the little town of Johnsonville that the mine has caused."

"Oh, Will," she exulted, "I'd love to! I can't think of a nicer way to spend the day."

Once again Will felt fortune smiling down on him as he arose the next morning. It was mild and sunny, one of those blissful winter days peculiar to Texas. Anna and Harvey were waiting when Will pulled the buggy in front, and soon the trio was making their way across the rutted trail to Johnsonville. Daily trips to the store in Strawn for supplies had marked out a well-traveled but rough road. Anna was cheerful, chattering away, calling out in glee each time a deer, rabbit or squirrel came into view. Will's eyes watered up as he studied his wife and recalled the heartbreaks they had been forced to endure. But she was well now, he assured himself, and from now on only good would come to them, he prayed.

As the buggy crested the last rise, Will halted the horses so the Johnsons could view their domain. It was a quiet moment, as not one word was spoken, but each knew what the others felt. The spell was broken when Anna leaned over to give each man a quick peck on the cheek. "I love you both," she said.

As the buggy approached Mine Number One a few minutes later, they were again touched when the workers paused in their labors, and respectfully bowed toward Anna Johnson. It was a small but touching tribute. Anna, looking dignified and noble, nodded in turn to each group of men.

They stopped on a small hill to the south, later named New York Hill, which overlooked the mine and the disorderly arrangement of shacks that made up Johnsonville. They spread a quilt on the winter grass beneath the limbs of a leafless mesquite, and Anna laid out the food she had prepared. Within moments of their arrival, R.S. Weitzell made his way up the hill.

As the gracious hostess Anna was trained to be, she offered the young mining engineer a plate that was gratefully accepted. She suspected the food within the confines of the mining camp was probably deplorable, and appreciated Mr. Weitzell's tackling his lunch with great relish. Soon Anna began plying him with questions.

"You mean that smoke over there?" Mr. Weitzell asked, "That's two miles away where the railroad is. We take coal there to be loaded onto railcars." Weitzell glanced in Will's direction and then stated, "Mr. Johnson, it would really help us if we could persuade the railroad to lay a track out to here. Then we wouldn't have so far to haul the coal. We could take it right out of the mines and load it right on the cars. We'd save time and labor."

"It's already been taken care of, R. S., Will responded. "I talked with T & P yesterday, and they had no reservations whatsoever. In fact, they promised to start laying the track within the next two weeks."

It was a memorable day. As the Johnsons returned to Strawn, Anna thanked Will and Harvey for a marvelous day. "You have given me my best day in a long time, and now, I want to share my secret with you. We will have a baby about next June. If it's a boy, we'll name him William Harvey Johnson." Will was speechless. He took out a handkerchief, wiped his eyes, then blew his nose and strongly held Anna. His life had been restored; for all that God had taken from him, He was now generously giving back.

EIGHT

In March 1887 Harvey carefully analyzed the mine accounts and realized there was not a profit. The pay scale would have to be cut back to $1.50 a ton. Although Fatzinger's earlier advice was heeded and the Johnsons paid by the ton, rather than by the day, the $1.75 scale was too high. The Johnsons had not had any guidelines on wages, and at $1.75, most miners would make $3.50 or $4.00 a day, compared to the $3.00 at Coalville. The miners balked at the $1.50 scale and went on strike. The Johnsons were in a tight spot. They had to continue supplying the railroad with coal if they were to keep the railroad's business. And they needed a cash flow, even at a loss, until a solution could be found. After a two-month strike, the labor union and miners won, and rather than retain the $1.75 scale, the Johnsons were forced to up the pay to $1.95 a ton! This was disaster! They could not afford this pay scale and would soon be wiped out, much worse than Ionia, Michigan. An urgent wire went out to the normally hard to find Harry M. Taylor. Luckily, Taylor was at his home in St. Louis. Three days later, he appeared in Strawn.

On the evening of his arrival, talk at Anna's supper table soon turned to business. "I still say there's a great potential for profit in this coal deal of yours, Will," Harry said after being apprised of the situation. "The assay reports say you have a pretty fair grade of coal. And the railroad apparently has good faith in your product because they put a track out to your mine. But it looks like this rail spur might be one of the ways you've been painted into a financial corner."

"Of course it is," Will hurriedly agreed. "When T& P agreed to the spur, I signed a contract which stated we'd never charge the railroad any higher than $2.75 a ton. Now, with the miners getting $1.95, and the cost of equipment, mules, feed, and other expenses, we're going farther under every time a ton of coal comes out of the ground."

"I know, Will," Harry said. "It's little wonder you're losing money. And this $2.75 maximum certainly does limit your future income; that is, if you continue to look at this as a one mine venture. But Will, stop a minute and consider. The railroads will continue to expand all over Texas and the southwest. And with that expansion an ever increasing need for coal will result. From the surveys you've done, there's a vast field of coal out there, and you've bought up most of this land, 20,000 acres in all, isn't it?" Will nodded.

"That was a smart move," Harry continued. "Now, engineer Weitzell says you're getting 3500 tons to the acre. That's 70 million tons of coal! If you cleared only fifty cents a ton, man, we're still talking about a profit of 35 million dollars!"

"It sounds wonderful," Anna said. "But, how are we supposed to clear fifty cents a ton when our profits are limited and our expenses so high?"

"Good question," Harry replied. He was surprised to discover Anna's interest in the business. So many wives would have gladly dismissed themselves while the men folk discussed the matters at hand. But not Anna, who seemed as much a partner in business as either Will or Harvey, and she seemed to have just as much say. Will Johnson had chosen wisely when he made Anna Fatzinger his wife, Harry decided, for she was his greatest asset. "The way I see it, Anna, the main problem right now is vulnerability. You must incorporate immediately. Then, if the mining fails, you'll lose only the mine and not the store and lumber business, and you'll also keep your home and ranch that way."

"That sounds sensible to me, Harry," Anna replied. Turning to Will and Harvey, she asked, "Is that all right with you?"

"Remember, boys," Harry intervened before either could answer. "That store and lumberyard is your anchor right now.

Lose that and you'll have nothing to fall back on. When you incorporate, you'll need three people. I suggest one be an outsider. Think of someone you can work with and get a lawyer to draw up the papers. And you need to do this quickly."

"Incorporation sounds good to me," Harvey said. "You, Will?"

"I have no problem with it," Will quietly responded. "What about making Bill Allen the third person?" he asked. All agreed the well-liked rancher would be a good choice.

"Then that part's settled," Will said. "What's next, Harry?"

"Okay," Harry answered, as he rearranged his lanky frame in the chair for more comfort. "The biggest obstacle you have right now is the high pay. Had you been able to keep it cut back at $1.50 a ton, you would be showing a good profit by now. So, you know from experience you're not going to cut pay without a strike, and you have miners making in excess of $4.00 a day, while you're going broke. In the Illinois mines across the river from St. Louis, they use foreign-born miners. Those boys earn $2.00 a day, and they're pleased to get it. If you expanded your operation here, and brought in immigrant miners, you could have enough to outnumber your union workers. Hire the foreigners at lower pay and tell them they'll have a job as long as they stay away from that damned union! Nah, that wouldn't work; the Union would hound the devil out of those foreigners."

"What about steam machinery?" Harvey asked. "Wouldn't that help us mine the coal faster?"

"Of course, Harvey," Harry agreed. "Steam power would be wonderful, but it's terribly expensive, and right now, where are you going to get the money?"

"So far everything we've discussed comes back to two problems," Anna spoke up. "The high wages and no available money, and the way I see it we'll have to bring in outside investors. We must have working capital."

Will nodded his head in affirmation. "From the very beginning, I've been against outside investors because I wanted us to maintain control, but like Anna, I see no other way out. The question is: who? I've already approached the railroad, and they say their business is railroading, not banking. I've talked to Fort Worth banks, but they say it's all they can do just keeping up with Fort Worth businesses. And there's not a bank within a fifty-mile radius of Strawn with enough holdings to do us any good. I've thought of private investors, but all we have here are ranchers, and they like to hold back for drought or disease years. All the big money is still up north."

"I'll see what I can do when I get back to St. Louis," Harry promised. "I know a few moneyed men always on the lookout for a good investment, but in the meantime, you could mortgage your coal lands. Set up a bond issue, say, one hundred bonds at a thousand each at six percent for twenty years. That'll put you in shape for immediate needs until we can come up with something better."

"But it still won't solve our problem," Anna said, shaking her head in disagreement. "The problem will still be high pay, and we can't cut without a strike. We'll have to have a solution where the pay is concerned before we can ever get anywhere. I don't care how much money you raise for machinery, or new shafts, or whatever. Until we settle this problem of pay, we're in for trouble."

"She's right, and we all know it," Harvey said.

"Okay," Will declared. "The railroad is crying for more and more coal. They'll take all we produce and then some, but even if we hire twice as many miners, open up new shafts, and take out ten times as much coal, like Anna said, the high wages will still be there. Getting rid of the union or cutting wages are our only choices, and we can't do either. So, I say shut her down, get rid of all the workers, wait a few months, hire new workers and start over. The railroad will scream like a panther, but let them. In a few months we can start back up without a union and its high-priced miners. Then the railroad will be happy and so will we."

Will rose from his chair and began to pace the room while they mulled this over. Then, pausing to stand directly behind Anna's chair, with his hand resting on her shoulder, he said, "Wait a minute. I've got a better idea. Why don't we just sell out? After all, everything we've talked about is fraught with risk. Let's just end it, here and now. If T & P Railroad wants coal so badly, then they can buy us out, and let Jay Gould straighten out this mess with the union and high wages. We all agree the potential is there to make millions. So we can sell out, take our money and start over elsewhere. There's coal north of here, near Lyra. We can start up again there."

The group was silent for a few moments and then Harvey spoke up. "What would we ask for our holdings, Will?"

"Two million for the Johnson mine and the land. That ought to be fair enough. If the mine is set up right, they stand to make half a million a year. They'll have their initial investment back in three or four years."

Anna rose to stand beside her husband. She looked directly into his eyes before speaking. "This might be our only solution, Will; I'm not certain. But what I keep thinking about is what a driving force your dream for coal was all those months. Now we've seen the dream come true, but at the first hint of trouble we're talking about quitting, and I don't want to do anything hastily. Why don't we try the bond issue first, and if that doesn't work, then we'll sell out to the railroad. Okay?"

"I agree with Anna," Harvey said.

"So do I," seconded Harry Taylor.

"She does make good sense, doesn't she?" Will summed it up with a wisp of a smile dancing on his lips. "So, it's unanimous. We'll go with the bond issue."

Three days later the Johnson Coal Mining Company was incorporated with three directors on its board: William Whipple Johnson, Harvey E. Johnson and William Marion Allen. Will and Bill Allen each received a token one share of the stock for legal purposes, Harvey the remaining 9,998. This was indicative of the quintessential trust Will and Harvey had in one another. There was never any sign of rivalry or selfishness between the two brothers. The lopsided division of shares was simply an illustration of their extraordinary relationship.

The company letterhead showed a "J.C.M.C." coal car loaded with coal and beneath, the words, "CAPITAL STOCK, $1,000,000. FULLY PAID AND NON-ASSESSABLE."

The new corporation's first order of business was the issuance of $100,000. in bonds. The bonds were handled by a New York bank, but the bonds sold poorly. Soon it was obvious this last-ditch effort with bonds to save the mining enterprise would be of no avail. The move to sell to Jay Gould began.

A letter was sent to the nefarious financier.

Dear Mr. Gould:

We have 20,000 acres of prime coal land which we are offering for sale. Said land being located seventy miles west of Fort Worth, near Strawn, Texas.

At present, we have one mine shaft open and producing about 60 tons of coal a day at a depth of 62 feet which we sell to your Texas and Pacific Railroad. This is good quality bituminous coal. You will please note the findings of Mr. Jewett of St. Louis, in this regard. Our engineer, Mr. Weitzell, reports there are 3500 tons of coal to the acre. Therefore, we have 70,000,000 tons of coal underground. Also, you will please note a report by Mr. Cummins at my behest on the geological survey of the coal lands in Texas.

We are generously offering this company and mineral lands for $2,000,000. because we want to expand our cattle and horse operations. Your Texas and Pacific Railroad could get all the coal

it needs from these coal lands and still have surplus.
Respectfully,
William W. Johnson, President

Within a week Will received a telegram from Gould in reply:

Your sell offer coal lands ridiculous for unproven deposits based on one mine.

Jay Gould

But unbeknown to Will, Jay Gould had written a letter regarding the Johnson offer. The letter was addressed to Robert Dickey Hunter of St. Louis, an old friend of Gould's.

Dear Robert,

I received an offer to buy some coal lands from some Yazoo I don't even know. Letter enclosed. Since I know you are familiar with Texas, and in particular, the area around Fort Worth, you may want to look into this. I am not interested in mining coal. Let me know what you find, and remember, the Texas and Pacific Railroad will help in any way we can. Hope to see you next trip west.

Jay Gould

But Robert Dickey Hunter was already aware of the Texas coal operation prior to receiving Gould's letter; for he was one of the "moneyed men" Harry Taylor approached after Taylor's return to St. Louis. In fact, by the time Hunter received the letter from the financier, he had already seen the Johnson mine and was very favorably impressed. He had even written to Harry Taylor expressing his delight.

"...I inspected the company's mine in August, 1887, going down the shaft of the mine, which I examined with care. I found the vein to be about 30 inches in thickness, covered on the top with slate and underlain with mining fire clay. I regard the coal as of superior quality, suitable for steam and domestic purposes. I regard the property as very valuable. With necessary capital to sink additional shafts, and put on the market the coal which could be readily sold, I am satisfied the mine could be made to pay a profit of $2,000. per day."

Very Respectfully,
R.D. Hunter

Robert Dickey Hunter

Hunter, being a shrewd businessman, recognized an opportunity when he saw it. With promised help from Jay Gould, Hunter no longer saw any need to invest in the Johnson property, however. After receiving Gould's letter, Robert Dickey Hunter began making ruthless plans to take over the Johnson Coal Mining

Company. But it would be a six month tussle. A cat and mouse game; with Hunter the "cat" mercilessly playing with Johnson until Johnson was figuratively down to his last dollar before capitulating to Hunter's buy-out offer. Johnson would hold a life-time grudge against Hunter.

NINE

When William Harvey Johnson was born in the summer of 1887, Will and Anna felt they were once again blessed. And as before, they were overjoyed with their role as parents. Their new son was a fine, healthy infant, and although the couple had no cause for concern, memory of Marion's death hovered like a shadow in their thoughts. As a result, they were overly cautious in their handling of little Will.

Then in January, 1888, for the second time in three years, insufferable tragedy again jarred the Johnsons. Beloved brother Harvey became ill in early January, and died on the 28th. It was a devastating loss for Will. It was Anna's turn to be strong.

Understandably, after Harvey's death, Will suffered deep depression for several weeks and left the operation of the mine to the reliable R. S. Weitzell. Will had lost a brother, a friend, a confidant and a source of strength. Son "Little Will" and Anna sustained the grieving Will. But without Harvey, Will's energy and interest waned in the Johnson mine.

After his visit to the Johnson mine in Johnsonville, Hunter called on the T & P officials in Fort Worth, the same officials who had been alerted by Jay Gould to assist Hunter in his quest for the Johnson coal lands. If Hunter assumed control of the mining interest, would T & P extend the same courtesies and commerce shown the present ownership? Here was a portfolio on Hunter and his backers with financial statements and proposals for ensuring the coal needs of the railroad. With Hunter's great experience in the Colorado silver mines and his other successful endeavors, it was his opinion (and no slur intended on the present management of the Johnson Mine) that the present owner lacked the monetary resources to fully exploit the coal lands. If the mines were under the control of Hunter, a more fitting name for the enterprise might be "The Texas and Pacific Coal Company" to acknowledge allegiance to the prime user. To eliminate excessive coal dust and pea coal, as encountered in present deliveries, Hunter would guarantee clean coal by installing screens. He would use steam power and sink another shaft alongside the rail spur, a half mile to the north of the existing mine. All he needed was the assurance of the Railroad, and he would attempt to buy the Johnson Coal Mining Company.

But this flowery presentation to the T & P Division management was merely a courtesy. Robert Dickey Hunter knew he would become the chief supplier of coal for the T & P. Several years earlier, Hunter had resolved a particularly sticky problem with shipping cattle on the Missouri Pacific Railroad in Topeka, Kansas, another of Gould's properties. Since then, Jay Gould had been looking for an opportunity to return the favor to his old friend. If Jay Gould promised help, Hunter knew the coal operation was as good as his.

In March, 1888, Will received a letter from the T & P Railroad which threatened to take up the rail spur unless the management of the mines and the quality and the quantity of the coal improved. It was not by chance that almost simultaneously with the T & P letter; Will received an offer from Hunter to buy the mining company. True to form, Hunter's offer was penurious; $300,000. rather than the $2,000,000. Johnson was asking. Johnson was furious and a deep repugnance for Hunter ensued, but Hunter had done his background research and therefore had the upper hand. Hunter knew almost to the week when Johnson's money would run out. Hunter knew his first offer would be rejected, but he shrewdly took out two options which would hold the mine for Hunter until Johnson capitulated from lack of funds. For the first time since Harvey's death, Will took an active interest in the mining operation.

For several months Johnson and Hunter quibbled and quarreled over the terms of the sale. Johnson was slick, but he had never encountered an adversary like Hunter. Johnson wanted to remain a director of the company and to retain the name "Johnson Coal Mining Company" in reverence to Brother Harvey. However, by mid-September, Johnson ran out of money and could not meet the payroll. He was forced to accept Hunter's terms. Hunter bought eighty-eight percent of the shares of stock. Minority stockholder W. W. Johnson continued to disagree with the combative Hunter, and litigation was required to render a final severance. Will Johnson's dream was not entirely fulfilled. He finally sold for $317,500. which netted a quarter million dollars from his coal scheme. But this was a mere pittance compared to what Hunter and his investors stood to make.

Now the ruthless caginess of Hunter would show through. The pay of the miners was too high. The first task under the new owner was to break the back of the Knights of Labor Union and to get the pay reduced. This had to be accomplished before the organization of a new company, "The Texas and Pacific Coal Company", could be completed. Hunter issued an ultimatum to the miners: $1.40 a ton. The labor Union gave notice of non-acceptance and declared a strike. This was exactly what Hunter wanted; if the miners never worked for the new company, T & P Coal, which was not yet officially organized, then how could there be a legal strike against T & P Coal? To this effect, R. S. Weitzell, on October 1, wrote an official letter to Hunter:

> The miners are striking without reasonable cause. They should be paid off, their employment terminated, and you should have no further dealings with prior employees.

With a coal mine, but no miners, the Texas and Pacific Coal Company was legally organized on November 12, 1888. R. D. Hunter, President.

Johnson hated Hunter, but in the years ahead he secretly admired Hunter's visionary development of Thurber, formerly called Johnsonville. William Whipple Johnson, the "Father of the

Texas Coal Industry," got some measure of revenge on Hunter by developing competing coal mines near Strawn. His mine to the south of Strawn would be named Mount Marion, in memory of daughter Marion. And a cemetery east of this mine was called Mount Marion Cemetery.

TEN

Vic Belizza's work crew found St. Barbara's with dozens of years of dust and cobwebs but in fine structural shape, thanks to the care Joe Venutti had given it over the years. The church was beautiful in its simplicity, a fine example of late nineteenth century architecture.

As the group swept and scrubbed, Vic recalled his First Confession and Communion in the old church, and his thoughts traveled to three former pastors of St. Barbara's whom he had known: Fathers Kline, Deluca and Courser. Father Courser, Vic remembered, had a drinking problem. Vic stopped his work for a moment and reveled in the old church. The beautiful six foot statue of the Virgin Mother, given by the Gazzola family, was still in place. How sad it was, Vic thought, that the Ecumenical Catholic Church of today removed all statuary to appease the Jews into coming back into one church.

The altar was still intact which meant the church had never been profaned with the Novus Ordo, or New Mass. The churches of today did not have an altar; instead there were "Communion Tables" with the priests facing the people. Vic let his mind drift back to the past as he wondered what relic of St. Barbara's might be in the altar stone; usually a sliver of bone.

St. Barbara's still had its communion rail, although such rails were abolished by Vatican II. Vic had always drawn a certain comfort from the communion rail because it separated the not-so-holy, like him, from the altar where the holy sacrifice of the Mass took place.

The seventy-year-old pump organ, Vic knew, did not work; the rats and mice had chewed into the bellows leather. Vic's opinion was that the music, such an important and viable part of the old church was, today, unbearable. Now, there was no choir, just an off-keyed congregation which butchered the hymns that were mostly adaptations of Protestant hymns; a further attempt to lessen the difference in religions, and the thought saddened him. Was the church actually rejecting the composers who had devoted their entire lives to writing such soul-touching sacramental hymns as "Tantum Ergo," "Ave Maria" and the hauntingly beautiful Gregorian chants?

Vic smiled as he thought of a Latin Mass for the dead being said in this church for Gino Bertolli. Just like the church of twenty years ago, the one he knew so well, the one he drew comfort from. A Mass for the Dead, with the priest dressed in black vestments. Today's church called it the "Mass of Christian Burial." No black vestments, but gaudily colored as a symbol of happiness "...because we're imbued with joy that Brad is in heaven, at this very moment." That's what the priest said at a recent "Mass of Christian Burial" for a friend of Vic's. How did the priest know Brad was in Heaven? And try convincing the deceased's loved ones that it was a "time of joy." No, black had always been the symbol of death. And that's what it still should be, "A Mass for the Dead," a time of sorrow.

Throughout the morning, as the crew worked on the old church, several people stopped to visit, Catholics as well as non-Catholics, curious to know what was transpiring. In a small community such as Thurber Junction, religious activities were closely monitored, since there was little else to do. In a town where the Baptists and the Catholics dominated, each felt comfortable minding the other's business. Vic smiled again as he considered the number of years the Baptists in the community had been trying to get the precinct voted dry so that under Texas law, the sale of alcoholic beverages would cease. He doubted they'd ever succeed; too many descendants of Eastern European Catholics. And the Eastern European immigrants certainly liked their drink.

Vic was still thinking of this when they were surprised by a visit from Father Frank Hooper. Normally not so reticent, the priest today seemed exceptionally close-mouthed; probably dropping by to make a quick assessment for the Bishop. Vic did note with annoyance, however, that the priest addressed Mrs. Petrelli as Josephina. Well, at least, he was running true to form. And Vic noticed that not once, while Father Frank was looking into the sacristy, had he bothered to genuflect before the altar. But, then it was always obvious Father Frank cared little about showing respect for the Altar of God. In his Sunday sermons, Father often stunned the congregation by some blasphemous deed such as setting off a fire cracker, breaking dishes, cranking up a chain saw, hammering boards or blasting out rock music, all to emphasize a point. Such outrage in a place of worship? Thank God he never profaned this altar, thought Vic.

"Does the bell still work?" Father Frank called to Vic from the choir loft. "Let's try it," Vic said, dropping his broom and heading for the loft and the hanging bell rope. He could remember the pride Old Man Lorenz took in ringing the bell, a gift from the Italian miners in Thurber who had it shipped over from Italy. And Vic tried to remember the bell sequence that summoned the people. Was it fifteen, ten and five minutes before Mass? Vic reached for the rope and cocked his head toward the priest, "You wanna' ring it, or shall I?"

The color rose in Father Frank's cheeks. "No, we don't have to ring it. It might set off too much commotion in town if they hear a bell ringing in the middle of the afternoon."

"This town could use a good commotion," Vic declared, enjoying his moment of suggested domination over the priest. His hand was still on the bell rope and he was tempted to give it a good yank. But then the priest turned from him and the moment was gone. Vic smiled inwardly at the thought of Father Frank having to explain the ringing bells of St. Barbara's, but he dropped his hand and accompanied the priest out of the loft.

When the work crew finished, St. Barbara's was once again presentable and inviting to worship. Vic knelt at the altar and offered a prayer that the Funeral Mass be said in the church. Everyone was tired but proud of their work. The electricity still needed connecting. And the grass needed to be mowed, along with some weeding around the building. Maybe a little touchup paint here and there, and of course, they'd need to move in a small organ. But more importantly now: the Bishop's permission.

"He's driven into Fort Worth," Carmen Venutti told Vic when he called later in the day to speak with Joe. "Father Musser from California called, and then Joe called a monsignor in Aledo. His name was Kowalski. Anyway, Joe's visiting with him, and then Joe's got an appointment to see the Bishop at five o'clock. So Joe's got a pretty heavy schedule, but I'll leave a note you called."

Prior to his retirement, Monsignor Robert Kowalski served at Our Lady of Lourdes in Fort Worth. After thirty some years at this Church and several reprimands from the Bishop, the Monsignor had grudgingly changed from the Latin Mass to the New Mass. However, at Our Lady he still adamantly refused to allow the "sign of peace" handshake and would not permit the congregation to drink wine from a common chalice. And when Bishop Solezel demanded Monsignor cease reciting three Hail Marys at the end of each Mass for the conversion of Russia, the Monsignor glared at the Bishop, and in the most sarcastic tone asked, "Why? Has Russia already been converted?"

Although not nearly ready for retirement, Monsignor Kowalski finally decided to step down after one last swipe by the Bishop. It happened after the Monsignor refused Communion to a young couple, each wearing shorts and sneakers. The priest was livid that the two would have no greater respect for the Church, as well as the Body of Christ, than to dress in such an irreverent manner. And when he refused Communion, the couple stormed out of the church, climbed into a Mercedes and threw gravel in the parking lot as they sped away. The couple was from a wealthy family, and it was only a few hours before Bishop Solezel received a call demanding an apology from the Monsignor. But the Bishop went one step better: Not only would Monsignor apologize, the Bishop promised, but the Monsignor must do it from the pulpit.

The Monsignor did apologize from the pulpit, as the bishop directed, but the apology was followed by a sermon on modesty and dress in the church. At the end of the sermon, Monsignor Robert Kowalski, after forty-five years in the priesthood, announced his retirement. There was an outcry from the parishioners, and a fourth of the parish quit attending Our Lady. Many of those remaining openly criticized the Bishop, but the Monsignor was truly gone.

Since retirement, the Monsignor lived with his sister and her husband outside Aledo, Texas where the couple raised fruit and pecans. He stayed busy helping around the orchard and traveling to various locations to say the old Latin Mass for friends and relatives. In many ways, he learned his retirement was for the better, for he still provided the holy sacraments, and after so many years of priesthood, his face reflected the inner happiness that comes when a man has found peace with God and with himself.

"I'm glad Father Musser referred you to me," Monsignor told Joe when he arrived at the orchard. The two were sitting on the back patio sipping lemonade while talking and looking out over a field of fruit and pecan trees. "I grieve over Father Musser's emphysema. Father and I were in seminary together. We used to call him 'Rabbi' because he looked the archetype of a Jewish rabbi." The old priest chuckled as memories of his seminary days came drifting back into his thoughts.

"Well, as for your Latin Mass, let me tell you of some of the changes within today's church. In dealing with the Bishop, you'd be advised to not mention my name. I'm afraid I'm not one of the Bishop's favorites these days. In fact, what I'll try to do for you is get another priest outside the Diocese to say the Mass. That would save face for the Bishop." He paused for a moment and looked out at the orchard before continuing.

"I'll say the Mass as a last resort. As far as I'm concerned, you understand, I think the Latin Mass should be available to all who want it. It should not be dependent on the Bishop's whims, but you know these are troubled times for the Church, and while a few Bishops permit the Latin Mass in their churches, others are vehemently opposed, such as our own Bishop. We can see signs of the pendulum swinging back our way, and the Church will survive. The Ecumenical Catholic Church attendance is way down; money problems, seminaries, schools and churches being closed. But you've heard of the Pius X Society which has continued to train priests in the Latin Rite? Their churches and seminaries are full! They can't meet all the requests for the Latin Mass. Thanks to Bishop LeFebvre, Apostolic Succession will continue. However, we must remember Bishop LeFebvre is in his eighties." The Monsignor paused for a sip of lemonade.

"This is very interesting to me, Monsignor," Joe admitted. "I didn't know what was taking place within the Church, only that something wasn't right."

Monsignor Kowolski continued. "On the other extreme, we have the 'Sede Vacanists,' people who hold the belief the Chair of Peter is vacant because our last Popes have committed heresy. And while I don't agree with them in all aspects, they do have a point. For example, they feel it was heresy to change the Mass, a violation of the priests' Modernist Oath and the Pope's Coronation Vows. It might have been heresy when Pope John Paul II held joint services with Muncie of the Church of England, and the Pope has also participated in other non-Catholic activities. Why, there have been some misguided American Bishops who threaten excommunication for anyone attending a Latin Mass. Of course, excommunication can only come with the approval of the Vatican, and the present Vatican hierarchy may lack power to censure because there may have been too many doctrinal violations by the hierarchy itself. There's a recent letter from Cardinal Oddi to one of the faithful which says the Latin Mass does indeed fulfill the

Sunday obligation for attending Mass." The Monsignor paused again and studied Joe's face. "Please forgive me, Mr. Venutti. I tend to ramble at times, but this is a matter very dear to me."

"Don't apologize, Monsignor," Joe answered quickly. "You have no idea how delighted I am to have found a priest who tells it like it is. Lena Bertolli will be so pleased to know Gino Bertolli will have the Latin Mass."

"Well, still you must not encourage me. I'm afraid I could go on and on. Now, about St. Barbara's; if the Novus Ordo, the New Mass, has ever been said in that church, or if the altar has been changed in any way, then strictly speaking, I could not say the Latin Mass there. The church would have to be consecrated again."

"You don't have to worry about that," Joe replied happily. "I've been around that church all my life, never missed a service, and I can definitely say there has never been a New Mass said there."

"Good!" the Monsignor responded. "Now, about the Texas Historical Society's interest in the church; should you pursue the matter, I'd advise you to get St. Barbara's outright, or not at all. Don't settle for joint partnership with the Diocese. That way you can assure the building and the altar will remain the same, historically accurate. Also, you won't have to have the Bishop's permission every time you want a Latin Mass. Deal directly with the Historical Society and on your own terms, but leave the Bishop out of it."

"Believe me, I intend to," Joe assured the Monsignor.

"And should the Historical Society not be interested, don't give up. Talk to the Pius X Society about taking over the church. If there are enough people to support a Latin Mass, then the Pius X group might be the way to go, with or without the Historical Society, but don't mention that to the Bishop," the Monsignor warned. "Convince him it's for the Historical Society, which isn't a lie because that's what we're looking at now. Good luck whichever way you go. Call me tonight and let me know what the Bishop says about having the Mass in St. Barbara's. **'Benedicat vos omnipotens Deus, Pater, et Filius, et Spiritus Sanctus. Amen.'** "

Joe grinned broadly when he recognized the old Latin blessing and he responded with the Sign of the Cross. As he left the Monsignor, he knew he would need all the help he could possibly get.

On his drive to Fort Worth and to the Diocese offices, Joe's thoughts remained on the next hurdle. Would the Bishop grant the Latin Mass for the Dead, he wondered. If not, then what; the funeral home or the legion hall where the Mass could be said with a temporary altar? But dammit! Here's a dying man's last request, shouldn't that count for something?

If the Bishop refuses outright, should he change his Will as he'd hinted when Monsignor Flippin was giving him the run-around? To Joe's way of thinking the Vatican II changes were hastening the end of the Roman Catholic Church. He remembered when Vatican II had first come about; one writer reported that Pope John XXIII had undone in four years what it took the Church 2000 years to build up. Joe could also recall the photo of Pope Paul VI and the Protestant ministers who helped devise the New Mass. Protestant ministers telling Catholics how to worship! Was it the liberal European Cardinals who had stacked most of the Vatican II committees to get control of the Church, Joe wondered? But he had never been fully aware of what took place within the Church. All he knew was that something wasn't right with today's Ecumenical Catholic Church, and it had never really satisfied his spiritual needs. In a small community such as Thurber Junction, Joe realized the people were somewhat insulated from events that affected people in larger cities. And until now, like thousands of other Catholics, Joe had obediently followed the instructions of the priest and the Bishop, but not any more.

Joe pulled the car into the Chancery parking lot. Would Gino

Bertolli have requested a Latin Mass in St. Barbara's if he had known of all the commotion it would stir up, he wondered. Then recalling Gino's heritage, Joe knew the answer. Absolutely! Gino Bertolli's father, like every immigrant who came to Thurber, struggled continuously for acceptance and assimilation into the American way of life. And it was Gino's father who led the fight for the miner's union in Thurber; a long drawn out bitter fight. Hell yes! Gino would have still wanted the Mass had he been precognizant, Joe realized. In fact, right now, his soul was probably cheering him on! Joe smiled at the thought, crawled from the car and headed toward the Diocese offices for his meeting with Bishop Solezel, the dyed-in-the-wool spokesman for Vatican II.

As he waited in the reception room, Joe felt sweaty palms and a dry mouth and uttered a prayer. Was this, he wondered, going to be a critical juncture in his spiritual life?

While Joe waited, Monsignor Flippin gave the Bishop a quick briefing on the Venutti matter. "Your Excellency, the Diocese has been named beneficiary in the Venutti Will. His worth is about two million, and according to Father Hooper, Mr. Venutti and his wife have made substantial contributions in the past and have many times displayed staunch support for the Diocese. As I mentioned earlier, the problem is a Latin Funeral Mass for his friend, Gino Bertolli, in St. Barbara's Church in Thurber Junction or Mingus as the place is now called. That church has not been used for some time now. The parishioners in Mingus attend Mass in Strawn. Anyway, Mr. Bertolli made a request and Mr. Venutti is honor bound to fulfill it. Here's a copy of the Venutti Will, Your Excellency."

The Bishop scanned the Will and then said, "Why don't you sit in on this, George? I may need more information from you."

Joe was studying wall portraits of past Bishops when Bishop Solezel and Monsignor Flippin appeared. "Mr. Venutti," the Bishop exclaimed, extending a hand of welcome. More out of years of habit than respect, Joe stood, genuflected and kissed the

Episcopal ring before shaking the Bishop's hand. "It's my great pleasure to meet you and express our appreciation for all your spiritual and financial support of the Lord's work. Father Hooper tells me of your invaluable assistance in his parish, and now I understand you are burdened by a problem. I hope we can be of help to you, who has been so much help to us." The Bishop placed his hand on Joe's shoulder, gently guiding him toward his office, while at the same time bestowing upon him a smile of such benevolence that Joe felt immediate suspicion.

Joe's first impression of the Bishop years before had not been favorable. The man had always reminded him of Pope Paul VI; slightly built, tonsured head and a fixed, resigned smile. And even now Joe felt uneasy, more of a wariness which he now seemed incapable of shaking. The Bishop's flattery did nothing to help.

"Your Excellency, an old friend, Gino Bertolli, passed away in California," Joe began when the three were seated in the Bishop's office. "He will be buried in Thurber, where he was born, and he's requested a Latin Funeral Mass in St. Barbara's. We, of course, must have your permission, not only for the Mass, but for the church as well. It's been over twenty years since services were held in St. Barbara's."

"Who did you have in mind to say the Latin Mass, Mr. Venutti?" the Bishop queried.

"Well, Your Excellency, I was hoping perhaps you could name a priest," Joe responded---Monsignor Kowalski's warning still fresh in his mind.

The Bishop, with his fixed, insincere smile, looked directly into Joe's eyes as he declared, "We haven't said a Latin Mass in this Diocese in many years, not since I was appointed head of the Diocese. Most of us, Mr. Venutti, view the old Latin Mass as little more than a bit of nostalgia from a time passed. What we can do for you is say the current vernacular Mass in Latin. We do this in some of the colleges; it helps those students studying Latin. Would this be agreeable to you?"

Joe felt his face flush. "No, Your Excellency, it would not," Joe stated with far more courage than he felt at this moment. "Please understand, it's not for myself I make this request, but for an old and very dear friend who can no longer speak for himself. Gino Bertolli wanted the traditional Latin Funeral Mass, and I'll do everything in my power to see he gets it. I know, Your Excellency, there are Latin Masses in different parts of the country under the Pope's Indult, and I know there are Latin Masses in this Diocese, said by Pius X Society priests; of course, not sanctioned by you, but nevertheless, theologically valid."

The Bishop's expression grew stark, as if his face had suddenly been reworked, chiseled out of granite, to remain forever cold and immovable. Then just as quickly, the benign smile returned, and His Excellency nodded agreement. "Of course, you are right, Mr. Venutti. We, however, have not felt there is need for the old Latin Mass within this Diocese. From what my priests tell me, the majority of parishioners are pleased with the New Mass in English. The Mass has never changed; the essentials are still there." The Bishop leaned back in his chair and studied Joe. "Is the Historical Society interested in St. Barbara's, Mr. Venutti?" he asked, abruptly changing subjects and throwing Joe off guard.

"Well, ah---yes," Joe stammered, hurriedly trying to regroup his thoughts.

"Selling the old church to the Historical Society has its advantages," the Bishop continued. "For one, it would relieve us of the burden of upkeep while placing us in a good light."

Upkeep! Joe thought sourly. **I'm the one who takes care of upkeep, not the Diocese!** "Yes, I've mentioned to the Historical Society my willingness to purchase the church from the Diocese, restore it to A-1 condition and donate it to them. The Society would place a historical marker and take care of its future upkeep.

In the past dozen years, Your Excellency, I've spent over four thousand dollars on that building. Since the Diocese obviously has no further need of it, I believe it would benefit all of us to simply turn it over to the Historical Society. It's a fine example of late nineteenth century architecture, and it would be a pity to let it disintegrate out of neglect."

"A fine idea!" the Bishop exclaimed. "But there's no need for you to buy it. We can continue ownership and give permission to place their historical designation on it, especially since they're willing to take over the upkeep. I understand your town, Thurber Junction, which is now called Mingus, has a lot of history and was, at one time, a thriving city."

Joe knew the Bishop was simply trying to skirt the issue, the Latin Mass, but knowing diplomacy was still called for, answered the Bishop in as pleasant a tone as he could muster. "That was Thurber, Your Excellency; the Junction was just a suburb of Thurber. St. Barbara's was built in Thurber about 1892 and moved to the Junction in 1936."

"Oh yes, of course. You're ahead of me on history. But tell me, how are things in the Junction today? Do you suppose they'll ever return to mining? Coal, wasn't it? Or sulfur?"

"Coal," Joe said dryly, growing impatient at this impromptu history lesson because he knew the Bishop's mind was already set against the Mass, and it would be pointless for Joe to press the issue any farther. Rising from his chair, Joe stated, "Well, I've taken too much of your time already, Your Excellency. Please understand, I could never rest easy if I didn't see to Gino's last wish. He must have his Latin Mass. We'll find a way to do this final thing for him. Thank you for your time."

The Bishop, surprised by Joe's sudden termination of discussion, quickly replied, "Believe it or not, Mr. Venutti, we understand your plight, but let's hope by attempting to bring back an archaic tradition, you are not damaging the better good. We must maintain consistency in our Catholic beliefs throughout the Diocese. We can help you by sending out a priest to say the current approved Mass in Latin. Won't you at least consider this option?"

"Thank you, Bishop Solezel, but no. It would not be what Gino wanted, and I'm sorry, but it's not the same no matter what you say. Your Excellency, you're telling me that the Latin Mass which served our ancestors, our parents, Gino Bertolli and me for years and years is no longer any good. I thought the word of God was forever and that the Latin Mass was in perpetuity." Joe hesitated for a second and stared down at the floor. Then he raised his eyes to focus on the Bishop once more. "About St. Barbara's," he said, "I'll give the Diocese two thousand dollars for the church, and when the papers are signed, the Historical Society can have it. Thank you for your time, and I'll be in touch after the funeral."

Joe knew from the look on the clergyman's face he was not ready to conclude the meeting. Joe had the upper hand, and the Bishop could see two million dollars slipping out the room with Joe. As Joe turned to walk out of the office, Monsignor Flippin called out to him.

"Mr. Venutti, wait a moment please." The Monsignor was clearly flustered by what had taken place in the room, and now he seemed intent on smoothing over everything. "Your Excellency, pardon me for intruding, but I believe I might have a viable suggestion."

"Yes...Monsignor?" Bishop Solezal expectantly asked.

"Well, while it is true we must maintain consistent Diocesan doctrine, perhaps we could help Mr. Venutti by providing a list of our retired priests. He then could contact and select one of these priests who might be willing to say the Latin Mass. Of course, you understand, Mr. Venutti, we have no knowledge of which priest might be adhering to the Latin Mass. You'd just have to go down the list and ask them."

"Splendid!" cried Bishop Solezel. "What a splendid idea. Don't you think so, Mr. Venutti? Then you can set up an altar in the funeral home or some meeting hall and have the Mass you desire. This would solve everything; it's the least we can do for one who has helped us so much." The Bishop moved around his desk to stand beside Joe, a pleased look on his face.

Well, whoopee crap! Joe thought as the Bishop beamed over his own indulgence. Didn't the idiot realize that's what Joe had planned if he met with refusal? So where did the Bishop get the notion he had solved all of Joe's problems? Joe glanced over at the Monsignor and instantly knew the man was lying. Of course they knew which priests were saying the Latin Mass; they'd be damn poor administrators if they didn't! It was at this instant when Joe Venutti, who had never in his life questioned the actions of a Bishop, a Monsignor or even a parish priest, knew his spiritual life would now take a new direction. Because of Gino Bertolli and the lack of compassion within the Church to grant this man one last Latin Mass, Joe knew he'd devote the rest of his life, as well as his money, to reestablishing the Latin Mass within the Church. He'd fight the ultra-liberal, ecumenical, Vatican II, antichrist Catholics until the day he died. Bishop Solezel, Monsignor Flippin and Father Hooper included.

Joe forced a smile on his face, and sarcastically replied, "That's okay, Your Excellency, we'll manage fine. Thanks anyway."

He quickly left so they wouldn't call him back. He hadn't mentioned his Will. Let those two modern day "spiritual leaders" in there think they still have my Will, he told himself. He would use his Will as a lever in getting St. Barbara's. But once the church was safely in his hands, he'd negate that damned Will as fast as he could!

Frustrated and furious as he headed back home, Joe realized he'd already let Gino down in one way; no funeral in St. Barbara's. At least there would be a Latin Mass and that was some consolation. As he drove along, he thought of what still needed to be done. First, call Monsignor Kowalski to let him know about the meeting with the Bishop. And the funeral director, Al Lyons, to tell him they would need the funeral parlor chapel for the Mass. But that shouldn't be a problem, and although the chapel was small, Gino had been gone so long, there probably weren't too many around who still remembered him. Joe doubted that more than fifty would attend the funeral.

As soon as Joe arrived home, he called Monsignor Kowalski.

"Don't worry, Mr. Venutti," the Monsignor assured him when Joe recounted all that had happened. "I expected as much. I have a priest in mind for you from Marble Falls. I'll give him a call, and if he can't say the Mass, then you'll have me as a back-up. My sister's grandson will serve the Mass. He serves for me here, and I think he'd enjoy the drive out."

"Monsignor, you have no idea how much we appreciate all you've done. Your encouragement has given me new inspiration, but I hope you don't get into any kind of trouble over this. No danger of excommunication or anything, is there?"

The old priest scoffed at the notion. "What, me; an old retired duffer? I'm sure the Vatican has more pressing concerns. Besides, I was ordained to say the Latin Mass. God gave me that right, and no one, not Bishop nor Pope, can take that away from me."

"After the funeral, Monsignor, I'd like to sit down with you and talk more about what's been going on with the Church."

"Fine, Mr. Venutti, I'd enjoy it. Now, let me write down directions to your place. Stay on Interstate 20, take Thurber exit at tall brick smokestack, two miles north, a house with brown composition roof and a chain link fence. That's your home."

Joe's next call was to Al Lyons, and that was when he learned of the padlocked gate at Thurber Cemetery. "Damn!" he swore over the phone. "What next?"

ELEVEN

Funeral Director Al Lyons called Peacock Energy the first thing the next morning. The switchboard operator had trouble understanding the problem and switched to three different offices before settling on Mineral Leases as the right office. An assistant informed Al that, indeed, his office did handle the Thurber land, but that he had no knowledge of the padlock, and that the boss was not in right now, but "If you'll leave your number, I'll see that Mr. Gardner promptly returns your call."

"Okay. Ask Mr. Gardner to call Buck Buchannon at Thurber. This is important because we've got a burial in the cemetery on Saturday, and we need to get in now to dig the grave. So if he can give me a quick call and give us the combination, we should have no further problems."

Al called ranch owner Buck Buchannon next.

"Hell, Al, I already cut the damn chain," Buck told him in the same gruff voice in which he always spoke. "After you left yesterday, I kept thinking about it and got madder and madder, and finally I just drove over there and cut the damn thing. To hell with those SOBs! You've got enough on your mind, so you just go dig the grave and let me handle Peacock."

The Thurber Cemetery had always fascinated and distressed Al Lyons. It was a repository of dreams and hopes, a tribute to America's generosity. Within the cemetery lay a communion of several cultures blended to sameness by death. When Al walked among the forlorn graves he was reminded of the many different ethnic groups buried there: Americans, Blacks, Mexicans, Italians, Poles and a dozen other nationalities. The more prominent Protestants were buried in the well-tended Davidson Cemetery between Thurber and Strawn. There were several attempts throughout the years to clean up the old Thurber Cemetery, attempts, Al knew, which were usually spurred on when a far-off relative appeared from time to time and was unable to locate a family grave. Some money would be donated, and a new cleanup effort made, only to soon fizzle out because it was too expensive and too big a job.

The cemetery was enclosed by a four-strand, barbed wire fence. Immediately to the right of the entrance was the "African-American" section. Here lay some 150 graves of blacks who lived and worked in Thurber. The center and north sections of the cemetery contained immigrant Catholic graves, while the south and west portions held the remains of Protestants. There were over 1000 graves, but only about 300 of these had markers. Some were surrounded by brick fences, rotted pickets, rusty wire, old iron bedsteads, or outlined with rocks. Some were marked by only a rock at the head and foot of the grave, but most had no markings at all; a depression in the earth was the only indication of a burial. In one area, twenty graves had been indicated by neatly aligned white metal crosses, but no names or dates; an attempt to acknowledge the unknown dead, Al supposed. It was a pitiful assortment of graves.

The grounds were overgrown with mesquite, weeds and prickly pear cactus. Around many graves varmints had burrowed, searching for roots and grubs. It was sad to think of the many immigrants buried there, so far from home and family, and what those families would feel if they could view the devastation by nature and time.

Sometimes Al would read a tombstone and wonder about the person underneath. "Guido Garbraldi, 1885-1909." Twenty-four years old. Where in Italy was he born? Was there a grieving signorina or signora left behind in his hometown that would never join him in America? Or was he jaunty, handsome, a flirt, with an eye for all the ladies? Did he play bocce? What were his hopes? What did he think of America? Today, seventy-seven years after death, Guido Gabraldi was long forgotten, his grave never visited by family or friends.

Al's father had told him that during the Thurber years, there were many strange sounding causes of deaths declared on death certificates: hypertrophy of heart, spasmodic croup, peritonitis, flux, sepsis, fecal impaction, inanition, paresis, catarrh of stomach, dropsy, irritation of brain, toxemia, congestion of brain, jaundice, milk poison, dilation of heart, blood poisoning, consumption and insanity. Did one actually die of insanity, Al wondered with a wry smile. He also remembered hearing of the flu epidemic of 1918 and 1919. The prescribed antidote was Epsom salts, and the price of that remedy soared to a dollar a tablespoon. But surprisingly, there were not many graves marked with one of those years as date of death. Al had heard the sulfuric content of coal and coal smoke might have provided an aseptic atmosphere.

Al Lyons had no trouble locating the Bertolli plot, but he was puzzled by the surveyor's stakes and flags in the northwest part of the cemetery. And truck tracks running over graves? No time for Al to figure this out now. The burial plot was surrounded by a low brick fence. There were two graves, with room for four more. Al measured out the grave and made a list of instructions for the Bobcat operator. Before he left for Dallas-Fort Worth Airport to pick up the body, Al called Buck Buchannon. "You hear from Peacock Energy yet?"

"Nope. The bastards aren't too good about returning phone calls. Why? You find any other problem?"

"No, but I did see something peculiar up there; a bunch of surveyor stakes and flags in the northwest corner. Got any ideas?"

"Sure don't. You suppose it's got something to do with that gate being locked?"

"That's what I was wondering, Buck. You might ask Peacock about it when you talk to them."

"I certainly will, even if I have to drive to Dallas to get a hold of that SOB Gardner. Right now I think I'll just drive up to the cemetery and have a look-see for myself."

"Okay, Buck. I'll get back with you later. I'm on my way to the airport." Al Lyons had to make two more quick calls. He needed to get obituaries into both the Abilene Reporter-News and the Fort Worth Star Telegram because ex-Thurberites scattered throughout west Texas depended on these papers for the news. Although he needed to give them only the basic facts, Al knew how the obituaries would read:

> Gino Bertolli
> Ex-Thurberite
>
> Thurber Junction/Mingus. Gino Bertolli of Modesto, California died Wednesday of a heart attack in Modesto General Hospital. He was 78.
>
> Rosary will be recited at 7:30 p.m. Friday in Strawn Merchandise Funeral Home in Strawn. A Latin Funeral Mass will be at 10 a.m. Saturday in Strawn Merchandise Funeral Chapel. Burial will be in the Thurber Cemetery.
>
> Mr. Bertolli was born in Thurber Junction and moved to California in 1935. He was a retired machinist and a WW II Army veteran. He was the son of Giovanni (John) Bertolli who helped organize the Miners' Union in Thurber.
>
> Survivors include his wife Lena of Modesto, California; daughter Maria Kennedy of Sacramento, California; son Leo Bertolli of Lodi, California, and four grandchildren.

When Buck checked out the surveyor's work in the northwest part of the cemetery, he was fuming mad. Just as he thought, Peacock Energy was up to no damn good, and no telling what the bastards had in mind. Tire tracks right across some graves! Was there no limit to Peacock's insensitivity, Buck wondered.

He drove quickly back to the ranch, swearing there'd be hell to pay when he got hold of Gardner. His anger grew as the sweet-talking Peacock secretary told him Mr. Gardner was still out of the office.

“Well, give me his boss, or the damned president of the company, anybody who can give me some answers!” Buck roared into the phone.

“Who may I say is calling?” the secretary asked, her tone of voice never changing an iota.

“You just say that madder-than-hell rancher from Thurber. Whoever you get, if he’s got any sense, will know who you’re talking about.”

Buck waited far longer than he cared to, with canned music filtering through the receiver doing nothing to soothe his rage.

“I’m sorry, sir,” the secretary came back on after a few moments. “There’s no one available at the moment to help you. I will have your call returned, however...”

“Okay, little lady, you just do that. Right now, write down in that log book of yours that at 10:47 A.M. on this date, Buck Buchannon called and that he was highly put out because no one in Peacock’s entire building had enough gumption to accept the responsibility of taking his call. You write that down, ma’am, and I’ll be waiting for a call.” He slammed the receiver down.

The cemetery was actually located in two counties, the southern portion being in Erath County while the northern part lay in Palo Pinto County. Buck’s next call was to Palo Pinto County Commissioner for that precinct, Rip Collins. But Rip knew nothing of any flags or surveying going on in that area. Buck next called Erath County Commissioner George Danner. He, too, was unable to help.

State Representative Stan Goforth of Stephenville was the next recipient of a call from Buck. They were classmates together at Tarleton State College, long before it became a University, and the two were still close friends. Stan knew that Peacock Energy and

Exploration was trying to push a special bill through the legislation about unused public lands, but as far as surveying around Thurber, he knew nothing. He would give Peacock a call to find out what was going on.

The next call went to United States Senator Phil Burton, but the Senator was in Washington. However, an aide would call Peacock Energy and then apprise Buck of the response.

While Buck was still seated at his desk wondering just who the hell to call next, Mr. Gardner of Peacock Energy and Exploration returned his call.

"How are you today, sir?" Gardner asked in his most mellifluent voice.

"Plenty damned mad!" Buck shot back. "What the hell are you trying to do up at Thurber Cemetery?"

"I'm not certain I follow you..." Gardner hesitated. "The cemetery you say..."

"Bullcrap, Gardner! You're in charge of this damned land out here. Don't act like you're all of a sudden stupid. You know damned well what's going on, and I'd sure like to know, too. You understand?"

"Perhaps, Mr. Buchannon, if we can talk in a more conciliatory tone..."

"You can talk in any damned tone you like, Gardner," Buck interrupted. "As long as you're giving me answers while you're doing it. Or maybe you'd rather wait to be conciliatory when I bring charges for desecration of a cemetery!" he declared accusingly.

"Mr. Buchannon, if you could be more specific..." Gardner stalled while Buck became more and more furious.

"You know damned good and well I'm talking about that padlock on the cemetery gate and all your damn surveyor stakes in the northwest corner of the graveyard. If you don't, then you've either got a helluva case of amnesia or you're dumber than spit! I'll tell you what. You get one of those high priced, crooked Peacock lawyers of yours to explain cemetery desecration to you. That might either jog your memory or smarten you up a bit." Buck didn't give Gardner a chance to respond. Once more the receiver was slammed into the phone cradle. Buck Buchannon had about all of Peacock Energy and Exploration he could stand. He'd like to pull all the damned tail feathers out of that lousy Peacock.

After time to calm down and to think through the matter, Buck called his attorney in Stephenville. "How do I go about filing grave desecration charges?"

The attorney explained and then promised to send someone out to take pictures and get a complete description of the alleged desecration by late afternoon. "Good," Buck said. "I want the charges to be against that bastard Joseph Gardner, Peacock Mineral Leases, and Bill Youngblood, VP of Operations. And also, put George Dunlap on there. He's president of the whole damned sorry corporation. I wouldn't want to leave him out."

Following that phone call, Buck drove along I-20 to where Slim and some hands were patching up a fence a car had smashed through. "Take a couple of men and get a couple hundred bricks and several sacks of cement, Slim," Buck instructed. "I'm going to have a helluva lot of fun laying out my gravesite in Thurber Cemetery."

"Fun? In a cemetery?" Slim asked incredulously, almost afraid to learn what his boss was up to now.

Later, after Buck had marked out a square plot in the northwest corner of the cemetery, making certain a few survey flags and stakes were included within the newly marked boundaries, Slim realized what his boss had in mind.

Gravesite, Thurber Cemetery

"Doesn't this look like a dandy place to be buried, Slim?" Buck asked. "Right here, overlooking the valley the way it does. Why, a man'd be happy to have this as his final resting place. Put up a couple layers of brick around here, Slim, and don't worry about a foundation. And be sure you don't disturb these flags and stakes, or those others over there. The lawyer will be here this afternoon, and he'll want to see all this, exactly like it is. Especially that stake stuck in that grave over there. I've already taken some Polaroids of the tire tracks across the grave," he indicated with a wave of his hand. "In this new grass, the tracks stick out like a sore thumb."

"I can see now what you mean by fun," Slim said, a grin planted on his face. He turned to give instructions in Spanish to the Mexican hands.

The next morning Joe Venutti read Gino Bertolli's obituary in the newspaper. He wondered if the Bishop ever scanned the obituary column, and what his reaction would be when he saw this. "Latin Funeral Mass" spelled out for all to see. It might disturb His Excellency to realize that such "heresy" within his Diocese was plainly broadcast by the newspapers. And what would people think when they read that the Mass would take place in a funeral home chapel instead of a church?

TWELVE

Joseph Gardner was clearly disturbed by the previous afternoon's one-sided conversation with Buck, and it still showed as he walked into the office of Peacock Vice President Bill Youngblood on Friday morning. He had not slept well, and his face was drawn.

"What's going on, Joe?" Youngblood asked. "You look like hell. You sick?"

"I just wish I were. That bastard Buchannon out at Thurber is screaming about grave desecration and bringing charges against me. He's p-oed because I didn't tell him what we had planned out there. If only that damned fence crew had moved the fence when I told them to! But no! The damn fence at Desdemona was more important!" He fell into a chair and sighed heavily.

"Grave desecration?" Youngblood asked incredulously. "Hell, Joe, you haven't been out there in several weeks."

"No, but the survey crews have. A lot of graves are unmarked and overgrown. Of course, I told them to be careful, but you know what survey crews are like. And I did tell them to put a lock and chain on the gate."

"But hell, Joe; you knew you were walking a fine line when you did that. You can't deny access to a cemetery."

"Sure, I knew that. But that old cemetery could be classified as abandoned," Joe Gardner said wearily. "We checked with the funeral home, and the last burial was six years ago. Nobody goes up there anymore. Hell, Bill, we had to grade the road before we could even get up there with a pick-up. The chain was temporary, just to keep anybody from going up there until we got the fence moved. Once the fence was moved, we'd take the chain off."

"From what little the secretary told me, they're having a burial up there, after all these years. The guy from the funeral home couldn't get in, and he called Buchannon. Now, Buchannon's raising all kinds of hell."

"Well, we better damned well smooth this over quickly, and nobody better hear about us even thinking of moving graves. A fence is one thing, but graves are another."

The conversation was interrupted by a secretary on the intercom. "Excuse me, Mr. Youngblood. Mr. Dunlap would like to see both you and Mr. Gardner in his office immediately."

"Damn!" Youngblood swore aloud. Joe Gardner looked as if he might vomit.

Peacock's president, George Dunlap, was a brash, imposing Tennessean who preferred being thought of as a transplanted Texan. He glared from behind his desk as the two men entered his office. "Well, gentlemen," he began after they were seated. "It looks like the feces has just hit the propeller out at Thurber. I've been on the phone all morning with a state representative and a United States senator. Quite a morning!"

"Joe and I were just discussing the matter," Youngblood said. "You getting any flak? That rancher Buchannon is threatening us with cemetery desecration charges."

"Have you spoken with our attorneys?"

"No, not today. But I did talk with them prior to sending a survey crew out there. They told me there are no records of land being deeded for a cemetery and neither the county nor T & P Company records show any burial or cemetery associations. They even cited Vernon's Civil Statues that says cemetery lands had to be described and recorded and declared for interment purposes. This was never done for the Thurber Cemetery. We figured we could move the fence in forty feet; if no repercussions, we'd come back later and move those seven unmarked graves that would be outside the new fence. But now..." Gardner's words faded into silence as he realized the futility of ever justifying his actions.

George Dunlap shoved a newspaper across his desk at the two men sitting before him. "It might have just gone off without a hitch, too," he said, as he pointed to the obituary. "Except for this; a fellow named Bertolli died in California, but the family's going to have him buried in Thurber." He scowled at Joe Gardner, as he added, "So you see, Gardner, Mr. Bertolli is just as responsible for all this mess as you are, but Mr. Bertolli, however, is dead. You only wish you were. He can escape blame, but you, unfortunately, cannot." Dunlap watched with silent perverted pleasure as the color drained from Joe Gardner's face. Both men waited for further direction.

"We don't need any bad publicity so we need to get a quick handle on this. The two of you get right out there. I want you to be in Thurber by early afternoon and take someone from legal with you. I want our asses covered."

Dunlap coached Youngblood and Gardner on what to say. The agreed story line would be simple: just a preliminary survey, a feasibility study for recovering Thurber's vast coal reserves by gasification means. This would require a large amount of water and a lake would be built somewhere in the area, but no mention would be made of a dam connecting Cemetery Hill and Italian Hill. Recreation, fishing, new industries and jobs would be stressed. Studies have not been completed and decisions need to be made. Then the gasification process could be explained if necessary: "Since Thurber's coal seams average thirty inches in thickness, digging is not profitable. We'll use available natural gas to heat water to steam which is forced into coal beds. The coal melts and will be extracted by suction to make a variety of coal related products: pharmaceuticals, plastics, dyestuffs, agro-chemicals, resins and paints. The carbon gases will be captured and injected into oil and gas wells to increase production."

"Grave desecration?" Gardner inquired.

"We're not aware of anything of that nature. Our attorneys are checking it out, but if there is, it's absolutely inadvertent," Dunlap answered. "By the way, I thought the fence had been moved already. What's the reason for the delay?"

"The fencing crew's been tied up at Desdemona, building a fence around the two compressors there. They intended to move to Thurber as soon as they finished up there. Shouldn't have been more than a couple of days, but then Buchannon got into this uproar, and all hell broke loose..."

"Too late for regrets now, Gardner," Dunlap chastised. "Just get to Thurber and do what you can to mop up this mess."

State Representative Stan Goforth of Stephenville had a degree in civil engineering and had considered working for Peacock after graduation in the early 1950's, but instead, he became interested in politics. He had fond memories of the Thurber locale; for when he was a student at Tarleton State, Thurber Junction/Mingus was the closest watering hole, and Stan had let few weekends pass without a sojourn to that little town. And on most of these visits Buck Buchannon was his drinking buddy, and the two, even today, still talked of drinking and dancing at the honky-tonks in Thurber Junction/Mingus. Because of his friendship with Buck, Goforth had no compunction about using his political standing in demanding to see Peacock's plans for Thurber.

THIRTEEN

Had it not been for Robert Dickey Hunter, Thurber or Thurber Junction would have never come into being, and hundreds of immigrants would have looked elsewhere for their beginnings in America. Hunter chose the name "Thurber" to honor one of his close friends and investors in the coal deal, H. K. Thurber, a wealthy New York wholesale grocer. The Texas coal industry was begun by the Johnsons, but it was Hunter who saved and reinvigorated this newest venture in Texas' economy. Hunter knew what had to be done, and it had to be done Hunter's way.

Hunter had optimal qualities for hammering his company into a novel, flourishing empire. He was visionary with toughness and a blunt demeanor, characteristics gained from having to protect his cattle herds from outlaws, Indians, schemers and crooked lawmen and officials.

Hunter made his fortune by buying Texas cattle and driving them to northern markets. On one drive his cattle were marked for quarantine by a dishonest lawman. Hunter plied the lawman with drinks while Hunter's foreman drove the cattle across the border. In another instance, Hunter bought dozens of I.O.U.'s at a discount, promissory notes given by the tight-fisted, legendary cattleman, Chisum. When Hunter bought one of Chisum's herds, he paid Chisum with these I.O.U.'s. But no hard feelings, for Hunter later saved Chisum's fabled "Jinglebob" Ranch from bankruptcy.

When Hunter went into coal, his St. Louis cattle brokerage firm and associated holdings were worth $6 million dollars. From his Lindell Boulevard mansion in St. Louis, Hunter hobnobbed with the famous and mighty, the rich and society. But he knew how to subsist in a cowboy's environment, campfire grub and a saddle for a pillow.

Hunter came to America as a ten year old from Scotland. At

eighteen he had his own farm in Illinois. At twenty-six he wander lusted to the Colorado mines in Leadville and Denver. He made some money and sent for his fiancée from back home. The high altitude climate was not agreeable, and Hunter moved his family to the warmer climate of Texas in 1867. He became involved in cattle buying, made more money, and moved his operation to St. Louis. Over the next twenty years he attained great wealth because of his shrewd cattle-buying ability, but he continually looked for opportunities to make more money. Harry Taylor kindled Hunter's interest in coal, but it was Jay Gould who paved the way for Hunter's takeover of the Johnson Coal Mining Company. After taking over the Johnson venture, Hunter eagerly looked forward to the greatest challenge of his life.

He moved his family to Fort Worth into the fashionable Mansion House until he could build suitable quarters at Thurber. He went seventy miles west into the midst of the Palo Pinto Hills and set up office and a bed in the Johnsonville commissary. He was ready for battle. The first opponent: the Unionists.

Hunter was a short, sturdily-built man. Close cropped white hair, a mustache and a goatee. A defiant look. The right eye showed evidence of past conflict. He was partial to white shirts, and often, white trousers, and these accouterments seemed out of place in a dirty coal mining camp. Conflicting adjectives described Hunter, depending on which side one stood. Opponents called him antagonistic, feudalistic, ruthless and feared. In truth, the man had strong utopian ideas. But his methods of building his empire and model city were misunderstood. First, the Knights of Labor and their strikers had to be crushed and coal production increased. Then Hunter would build houses, utilities, churches, saloons, stores and entertainment facilities. A self-contained model city with everything company owned, and importantly, wages would return to company coffers. Under Hunter, Thurber would grow to a proud, happy, prosperous, bustling city which provided thousands of jobs for all nationalities.

After becoming familiar with his territory in this crude settlement, Hunter called in strike leaders in November, 1888 shortly after his company was organized. To the strikers, Hunter appeared to be no more than a dapper little gentleman, for it was easy to miscalculate the ability of this dandy in white standing before them. So easy, that the cocky unionists were hardly aware of the brewing storm before they were struck full force by the dynamic whirlwind that was Robert Dickey Hunter.

As the several strike leaders arranged themselves within the confines of his commissary office, Hunter remained standing and silent behind his roll-topped desk and calmly gazed upon the group, impervious to all. At first the Union men assumed the poor little man was so overwhelmed by the raw power of their presence that he was afraid to speak. But as the minutes passed and still no spoken word, the silence took on the cloak of discomfort. Noticeable tension filled the air, and scuffling of chairs and shuffling of feet began. Fed by fear that comes with facing the unknown, the tension finally reached its crescendo and could no longer be borne. Then in a voice which boomed with authority and belied his small stature, Hunter spoke to the roughs before him. "I called you here to let you know I'm the new head man, and to tell you how it's going to be from now on. Today, right this minute, we're starting fresh. Everything here will be brand new. I'm even changing the name of this place to Thurber, which is the name of a friend of mine. I guess you all know my name by now. I'm Hunter. I run the Texas and Pacific Coal Company now located in Thurber, Texas. And boys, I hate to tell you this, but while you may think you're still on strike, technically you're not. Not against me or my company." He threw them the semblance of a smile and gave them time to absorb this bit of information.

"What you mean? Course we're strikin' agin' you," one of the men yelled out. He was a huge, dirty-looking man with a tinny voice and rheumy eyes, and he quickly turned to the others in the room for support.

"How can you strike against my company?" Hunter smirked, with amusement glinting in his eyes. "You've never worked for me. Kind of difficult to strike against an employer you never had, isn't it?"

Uncertainty rumbled through the room like a wave before a new spokesman reared up and glared at Hunter. "That's crazy!" he protested. "This is still the same mine; we're still the same miners, and it's still the same kind of back-breakin' work. The strike ain't never stopped by damn!"

Hunter examined his fingernails several seconds and then smiled benignly. "Sorry, but you're wrong. You never received pay from me, so you don't work for me. Never have. That means that right now you're trespassing. So I'll tell you what I'm going to do. I'm going to give you exactly one week to get your shacks, your belongings and your butts off my land. If you're not gone by then, I'll call in the sheriff. And so help me God, I'll see every last one of you in jail! That clear? Any questions?"

"You cain't do that!" one protested vehemently. "It's agin' the law to take away a man's house. You cain't put us out in the cold with no place to stay!"

"The hell I can't! Just watch me!" Hunter assured him. "I can do just about anything I please because this show is all mine, and don't you forget it." He paused for a moment and then bestowed a condescending smile upon the angered group. "But let it not be said Hunter's not a fair man. I'm willing to give you another chance." He stopped speaking and waited for the murmurs to subside. "You stop this striking crap business right now and get back to work. I'll pay a dollar-fifteen a ton. That's only if there's no more union business. And I'm going to start screening the coal. There's no profit in pea coal for me, so I'm damn sure not going to be paying for it. That's the only way this coal operation can survive. And you have my promise on this one thing: it will survive!"

Hunter leaned back against his desk and removed a long cigar from his shirt pocket, bit off the end, moistened it with his lips and struck a match to it. He inhaled deeply as if to savor the moment and then exhaled slowly to watch the silvery plume of smoke waft toward the ceiling. For several long, agonizing seconds he studied the cigar as though he had no more pressing concern, while around him the mumbled threats and complaints were like one continuous sound. Not one striker spoke aloud to break Hunter's reverie. Finally, he directed his attention to the men before him, the same expression an animal might have for a smaller, cornered quarry. "I've taken over this concern for one reason: to make money. And the only way I can make money is to follow the plan I've outlined for you. You can take my offer, earn a good wage and remain here. Or you can continue this strike nonsense and the only thing you'll be getting is the hell off my land."

"It still ain't right," one of the strike leaders protested, his looks urging the others to chime in with him. "We was barely gettin' by at one ninety-five a ton. Now you're sayin' we gotta cut back further. We'll have to work like damned niggers! You'll be makin' all the money, and we'll be starvin'!"

"He's right!" cried another.

"You cain't do it!" another man yelled. The air was filled with threatening tension and the sounds of the miners' outrage reverberated from the walls. With each passing second, the strikers before Hunter became angrier and more menacing. But it was not fear that filled Hunter's thoughts, for Hunter feared no man. It was sheer and consuming rage; fury that these ruffians would so easily allow themselves to be ruled by greed instead of reason. As the sounds of protest echoed around him, Hunter slammed his fist down against the desk top.

"Dammit to hell!" he bellowed. "I'll make a dollar look as big as a wagon wheel before I'm through with you! Go back to looking at a mule's ass! See how much you make then! I've had a belly full of you loafers. You're not worth a dollar-fifteen. You're not worth half that! Just get off my land and take your damned shanties with you!" He abruptly sat down at his desk, facing side-wise to the strikers. He reached way back in the middle drawer, his fingers searching. The men calmed down as they contemplated the intimidating movements of Hunter. Then the ominous "click" of a trigger cocking and sounding as loud as the voice of God in the breathless room. Hunter never pulled the pistol from the drawer, for he never had any intention of using it unless attacked, but it got the message across that he would not be intimidated and that he meant business. Hatred mingled with fear as the strikers stumbled through the doorway.

"We ain't through with you yet!" one of the braver strikers yelled once outside Hunter's office. "You're a lily-livered sonovabitch, and you're gonna pay!"

"Like hell I will!" Hunter yelled back.

Standing outside Hunter's office were two company guards with Winchester 73's crooked in their arms, ready to restrain any offensive force. The strikers hurriedly dispersed. "Like hell!" Hunter shouted again. "Come back and make me, if you think you can."

The Knights of Labor officers were in a precarious position. While sympathetic with the miners' threats of violence against Hunter, the officers knew they were vulnerable if Hunter were harmed. They hastily called a meeting to explain the officers' predicament. "Now look here, we ain't havin' no killins', cause sure as hell, us officers of this Union gonna be picked up for murder or attempt at murder. So we on record as havin' nothin' to do with that." The speaker was ridiculed down and hot argument ensued. The men broke into groups and continued to bicker on how to get back at Hunter. If they did not respond to Hunter, or show they were not cowed by him, their labor Union and strike were surely dead. But when it came to taking action, not only did the Knights of Labor officers vacillate; the strikers did too.

Hunter, on the other hand, was not one to vacillate. As he had threatened, after a week's time, he began to evict miners from his property. With sheriff's deputies standing by to back him up, Hunter's workers tore down or dragged the miners' shacks off company land. The miners and their families regrouped on acreage owned by the union and located east of Thurber. Even then, hunger might have forced capitulation had not a local farm union provided food, thus allowing the impasse to drag on.

As the stalemate continued, more guards were hired to protect the T & P Coal Company property and the little Scotsman who ran it all. Hunter expected retribution from the strikers, and retribution was being planned by a few hotheads. Five of the strikers, led by a weasel-faced henchman called Jonesey, spent the next few weeks devising an attack to cripple Hunter's mining enterprise. For several days, Jonesey and his men watched Hunter's guards until they knew the routine.

It was decided that from the hill east of the mine shaft, three strikers would direct gunfire at Hunter's office within the commissary. While this was going on, Jonesey and another man would sneak up on the confused guard at the mine shaft, knock him out, and throw dynamite down the shaft. They were all to run southward to rendezvous at Deer Creek where they would hide out until the commotion died down, or until Hunter vacated Thurber.

It seemed a perfect plan, but the perpetrators underestimated Robert Dickey Hunter's ability to counter such acts, for Hunter had encountered Indians and robbers often in the past, and he had a contingency plan for Thurber.

On the night of the attack, the three men began firing at the commissary building. Jonesey and his partner swept down upon the guard at the mine shaft to give the guard a sharp but misdirected clout on the shoulder. Before the match could ignite the fuse, however, all hell broke loose. Men were whooping and firing at the hill and towards Jonesey and his pal. The charge was being led by that dandy little Scotsman with a pistol in each hand clad in nothing more than a snowy-white nightshirt.

The five assailants fled southward to the planned rendezvous at Deer Creek. Early the next morning they killed two deer. By 10 AM, posing as a hunting party, they carried the deer into the striker's shacks on the east side of Thurber.

FOURTEEN

Immediately following the attempted violence by the strikers, Hunter requested the state's help. Texas Ranger Captain S.A. McMurry and ten Rangers were sent in to protect the newly developed Texas and Pacific Coal Company. Still not satisfied, Hunter added further protection by erecting a barbed wire fence around nine hundred acres surrounding Thurber. Locked gates were installed, and day and night guards patrolled the fence perimeter.

But the need for protection would soon be a moot issue if Hunter were not successful in finding replacement miners to work for the company. With the Knights of Labor members unwilling to work, there remained only a dozen or so miners in the employ of T & P C C, and coal production was a piddling eleven tons a day. Hunter needed miners if he were to hold on to his newest enterprise.

As soon as the Texas Rangers were acquainted with the problems in Thurber, Hunter traveled to the coal fields of Brazil, Indiana. There he recruited over a hundred miners, almost half of them black.

It was not long before word traveled back to Texas that Hunter had hired new miners. The Knights of Labor were furious. Hunter had ordered them off his land, and now he recruited new people to take their place while they were near starving! Plans were made to meet the train and give the new miners an unfriendly reception. It wouldn't take long, the unionists assured themselves, to convince the Indiana boys that Texas wasn't the place for them.

But, once again, the union men underestimated their adversary. Just as word of Hunter's new miners had traveled back to Texas, so had word of the Knights of Labor's planned greeting gotten back to Ranger Captain McMurry. The Indiana miners were supposed to change trains at Fort Worth. But McMurry had Hunter and his new recruits switch trains in Dallas and then travel straight through to Thurber Junction instead of making the scheduled stop in Fort Worth. The Knights of Labor men, waiting at the Fort Worth depot, were once again duped by Hunter and McMurry. Hunter laughed all the way into Thurber Junction.

However, before the new miners were even settled, unionists made enough threats to scare off fifty of the recruits. Only the blacks agreed to work. This raised the total work force to near ninety, and coal production was upped to a hundred tons a day, certainly a great improvement, but far short of the coal needed. And Hunter praised the blacks in his first annual report to the stockholders.

Hunter sent his son-in-law, Edgar Marston, to Pittsburgh to recruit more workers. Flyers were distributed in the streets. "Work in warm Texas!" they read. "Plenty of work in the coal mines of Thurber, Texas, 70 miles west of Fort Worth. Good working, living conditions. Fine weather. Paid rail travel to Texas mines. See Mr. Marston at the Fairmont Hotel."

In the nineteenth century, Italy continued its centuries-old political and social mess with skirmishes and wars, treaties and counter-treaties and plots and coups. Italy was the birthplace of Machiavelli, and rightly so. Only seven percent of the people had electoral right and representation in government. There was forced military conscription for dubious causes. Italy was agrarian, but only the large estates made profits, while sharecroppers and tenant farmers grubbed out a bare existence. There was an agricultural crisis in the 1880's with a drop in output and prices, particularly grains. The government put a tax on grains which devastated the poor who relied on bread as the main staple in their diet. Thousands of Italians fled this background to seek higher social standards in America.

One of these immigrants was Luigi Bertolli. On the day that Marston's flyers littered the street in front of his rooming house,

Luigi had been in America almost two years. He was single, with a strong back and well-developed arm muscles from working the grain fields of Italy. After clearing immigration, Luigi found work as a stoker in one of the steel mills. The work was hard and the hours long but Luigi was grateful for his job. Until that moment, when he saw Marston's circulars, he'd not thought once of any other kind of work. The steel mill, after all, enabled him to live simply but in freedom in America. Consequently, several times since arriving in America, he had beseeched his eldest brother Alfredo to give up farming and bring his family to America. But steadfastly, Alfredo refused, saying that at the age of forty-eight, he was too old to be starting over. And passage to America for himself, wife and three children would take more money than he could ever earn.

Despite the constant refusals, Luigi had not completely given up hope that one day Alfredo would join him, and on this particular day, as he picked up one of the flyers windswept against the curb, the hope was rekindled. Carefully, Luigi read each word of the flyer, struggling with his English until he got the gist of the flyer's message. Then, he raced up the street to grab another sheet before the wind could carry it further away.

Minutes later, Luigi was in his rooming house, knocking at the door of the manager, Lorenzo, who had come to America several years before, grateful for the relatively easy job of managing a rooming house with mostly Italian immigrants.

"Please, a favor, Lorenzo," Luigi spoke in Italian as he thrust the flyer into his hand. "Translate in Italian for my brother, Alfredo, so he will come to America."

The manager smiled and said, "Still hoping Alfredo will come to America, eh, Luigi? You never do give up, do you? Well, give me a minute then, and I'll see what I can do." Luigi watched as Lorenzo's pen scratched across the paper, making each word understandable to Alfredo.

This done, Luigi ran up the stairs to his fourth floor room where he carefully placed one circular in the suitcase at the head of his bed. The other circular he placed in an envelope along with a letter which once again expressed his desire to have his brother and family in America with him. Finished with that, he ran seven blocks to the post office where he mailed the letter to Alfredo Bertolli in San Gimigiano, Tuscany, Italy. Then he waited and prayed for a favorable response.

Two months later, Luigi Bertolli received a reply from Brother Alfredo. Alfredo said he was still too old and too accustomed to his own way of life to join Luigi in America. But how about my son Giovanni who had just left the seminary? Would Luigi mind if Giovanni were to join him in America?

Mind? Luigi was ecstatic, and two months later Luigi Bertolli and his nephew Giovanni were on a train bound for Texas and the Thurber coal mines.

As a new arrival in America, Giovanni was too much in awe of his surroundings and too unsure of his own abilities to realize just how much he had going for him. He was only eighteen, robustly healthy, and unencumbered by romantic ties. He was also handsome, had an accommodating, smiling personality and a passable fluency in English, learned while studying for the priesthood, a worthy ambition which Giovanni readily admitted was more his mother's than his own. He had just recently discerned he was not cut out to be a priest and had left the seminary only two weeks before Luigi's letter. Little did he know how useful his study of the English language would be in his future life. Giovanni Bertolli might have found work in several cities in America, but instead, he was delighted to be traveling with his Uncle Luigi to Texas where they were begging for coal miners. "Not to worry, Giovanni," his uncle assured him. "No experience necessary. Just a strong back and a not-so-strong mind, like me," Luigi laughed.

But when they got off the train at Thurber Junction, they wondered if they had misunderstood the advertising flyer which brought them to Thurber. According to the rough-looking characters standing on the platform, miners were not needed. "If you're lookin' for work, they ain't none. Best git back on the train and go back to where you come from." He was a big, meaty man with a flat face and hair the color of dirty hay. Tobacco spittle ran down his chin, and as he finished speaking, he pursed his lips and took deliberate aim, spitting a stream of tobacco juice which landed in a puddle near Giovanni's feet.

Giovanni stared down at the pool of brown liquid and then back up at the stranger. Though the man's accent and wording were strange, Giovanni's seminary English was enough to get the man's meaning. Still, he thought it best to feign ignorance. He glanced at Luigi, who was standing nervously beside him, and then smiled shyly at the big man and his partner.

"Scusi?" he asked softly.

"Aw crap!" the big one exclaimed, this time spitting another stream of juice near Luigi's shoes. "Some more damned forners! That sonovabitch Hunter cain't get no real men to work fer him, so he gits these ignorint fools cain't speak no American!"

"Now boys," the big man repeated his threat, "If you're smart, you'll git back on that train."

"Yeh," his partner echoed. He was much smaller than his friend and apparently used to standing in his shadow. It was the first and only word he spoke, and even then, he seemed unsure, furtively glancing at the big man for approval and then backing once more into the shadow cast by the other's bulk.

Giovanni studied both of the men for several seconds, and then turned his eyes to Luigi. Neither said a word, but the look they exchanged was enough. They came too far to be run off by bullies.

Giovanni looked at the big man and said very plainly, "Excuse me, we go now." Then he and Luigi turned toward the dusty trail running southward.

A huge fist reached out and grabbed Giovanni's arm. "Lookee here, boy!" the ruffian leader shouted. Giovanni's free hand had already curled into a fist when the sound of another voice boomed out.

"Back off, Willard, or I'll run you in," the new voice ordered, and in an instant, the grip on his arm relaxed. He turned and saw a man on horseback approaching the platform, his face lost in the shadow cast by the wide-brimmed hat he wore. The silver glint of the badge on his breast pocket, a pistol strapped to his side and a long-barreled rifle on his saddle, was an unmistakable sign of authority.

"Just funnin', Ranger," the big one said, his voice less powerful with each word, and he began backing away, his partner close behind.

Giovanni looked up at the horseman and said, "Thanka you!"

"Thurber?" the horseman asked.

"Yes. Thurber, Texas coal mine," Giovanni answered, beaming. "Me and Uncle Luigi, we work!"

"Follow me," was the laconic reply. Then he turned his horse southward, away from the platform which represented Thurber Junction. As they picked up their suitcases and began walking, the Bertollis felt the vastness surrounding them.

"Texas," Giovanni whispered in a voice filled with wonderment. They were ready to begin a new life thousands of miles from Italy.

The land might have been Texas, but the mining camp they walked into thirty minutes later was Little Italy. Giovanni and Luigi were not the only Italian immigrants who responded to Marston's advertisement. And though it was near sundown when they arrived, and the miners had worked a full day, the arrival of two new countrymen seemed reason enough for a celebration. Out came the food and wine, and soon singing ensued. The recently constructed bunkhouse shook with revelry.

Giovanni Bertolli

The men talked, laughed and carried on. Giovanni gave recent news of Italy, and those who had been longest in Thurber gave a run-down on living and working in the mining camp. The Italians were not the only nationality who responded to Thurber's need for miners. More bunkhouses, similar to the Italians', housed Polish workers, and in others lived American and English miners not affiliated with the Knights of Labor.

When asked about the bullies at Thurber Junction, a quick history, Italian version, of the angry unionists was given, but assurances were passed to the newcomers like tidbits. "Not to worry about Union men. You stay in camp where guards and Rangers watch us, you safe."

"No need to leave camp, anyway," another miner said. "We have everything we need, except women. And they come soon when Thurber is settled."

"Yes," said another, "and my sweet Rosa will be the first one here. Too long without her in my bed. I'll gladly put up with her screaming just to have her arms around me once more."

"But, Carlo, why must we all have to put up with Rosa's screams?" the man next to him asked, poking at his friend's arm as he spoke and giving an exaggerated wink of the eye to the others. It was apparent to all that the two men shared a close friendship. "Wait until you hear Rosa's screams," the teaser continued. "No mine shaft is deep enough to escape Rosa's screams, and that is when she is in a good mood!" Everyone burst out laughing, and the speaker affectionately rubbed his friend's head with his outspread hand, grinning broadly at the discomfiture of the recipient.

Giovanni looked at his uncle and smiled. Only that afternoon he wondered if they had made a terrible mistake in coming to this far-off place. But right now, Thurber might not be too bad. It was beginning to feel like home already.

FIFTEEN

In April, 1889, Boleslaw Koplewski of Bremond, Texas, wrote to his cousin Piotr Wasieleski in Sierpc, Russia-Poland:

Kochany Kuzyn Piotr:

You ask of Texas. We work hard with cotton, hay. Good soil, but sometimes bug and dry. Same with other countrymen by Marlin, Texas, Panna Maria and St. Hedwig, Texas. In America you own land. Eight years work with share crop, Tatus (papa) buy land soon. Father Goleski tells of coal mining work in Thurber, Texas, America. Two days northwest Bremond. Coal digging no more hard work than farm. I soon am twenty one. You and brother Pavel come Thurber, dig coal. Together we work, have big fun.

Sincerely,
Boleslaw

But Boleslaw's letter was unneeded persuasion; for the Wasieleski brothers were eagerly awaiting migration, but money was the problem. Wujek (Uncle) Antonni, who had been six years in Baltimore, Maryland, wrote of work opportunities in America. But Uncle Antonni was now married and was not able to help his nephews with passage money. For three years now, the Wasieleski family had scraped and scrimped for sixty gold talers for each son's travel cost. Papa Wasieleski decided both sons must travel together to America. There were ninety-seven talers, still a little short of the required one hundred twenty.

Poland was second to Italy in the number of mine workers at Thurber. And like Italy, the Poles also faced harsh social conditions. For centuries, Poland had been overrun by countries from every direction of the compass; yet, the Poles retained strong ethnicity and would not allow their homeland to become extinct. The majority of Poles were peasants who belonged to the land, and they would tell their masters, "You may own us, Oh Lord, but we own the land." They had to work a certain number of days for their master. Very seldom were they allowed to own a house, and permission was required to move to another village. In 1795, Poland was partitioned into three parts by Russia, Prussia and Austria, and this partition lasted until WWI. Under this domination, native Poles faced cultural and economic discrimination. In 1863, the Poles rebelled against the Russians, but this uprising was crushed, and even harsher repression followed.

In the fall of 1889, the two Wasieleski brothers, Piotr and Pavel, finally had passage money and were able to leave their beloved but dismal and repressed country for the coal mines of Thurber, Texas.

In Thurber, Piotr became Giovanni Bertollli's mining partner and lifelong friend. The two were a study in contrasts. Piotr, on the one hand, was a short, powerfully-muscled young man with a quiet demeanor. Giovanni, in contrast, was tall and rawboned, with a face seamed with laugh lines. His quick smile and easy manner drew people to him. It was neither Giovanni's outgoingness nor Piotr's quietness that caused other miners and company hierarchy to take notice, however. It was, instead, the fact that the two together could dig more coal on any given day than any other pair in Hunter's employ.

From their first meeting, Piotr expressed an interest in learning the language of his new country and Giovanni was eager and happy to teach him. The two quickly became good friends at work and play. Giovanni even taught Piotr the game of bocce ball so the young Pole could join him during the Sunday afternoon games.

It was not long before their names were Americanized; Giovanni became John, and Piotr was changed to Pete. Neither objected to the name change, for each longed to be totally indoctrinated into the American way of life. But they, in turn, were implanting a definite part of their homeland in the American soil they treaded upon daily.

As new miners trickled in, Hunter's enterprise was gradually succeeding. He had come through the worst fighting and threats and worries relatively unscathed. A second mine was opened a half-mile north of the first shaft. It soon became apparent to Hunter he would need help in managing his growing company.

For that help, he chose William Knox Gordon, a young, brilliant civil engineer from Virginia whom Hunter had originally hired to survey the land between Thurber and Dublin for a railway. Hunter was able to discern qualities in Gordon's character which he admired, for W.K. Gordon was as gentle and compassionate as Hunter was brash and irrepressible. Yet, Hunter perceived that Gordon's gentleness was tempered with emotional steel. Hunter also liked the way Gordon handled people, a talent Hunter had never quite mastered. And it wasn't long before he began to admire the young engineer's physical strength. Shortly after Gordon began work for Hunter, he invited the Scotsman to join him in a workout with a punching bag; for Gordon, a daily ritual of which he was quite fond. After watching Gordon exert himself with the punching bag, Hunter waited for an explanation of why a daily contest with a sand-filled bag.

"It gives me an outlet for my frustrations." Gordon explained. "I can work off tension this way, and usually, if I have a problem, after a few rounds with this fellow, I'll come up with a solution." He grabbed the bag and hugged it in an affectionate manner. "It also develops my muscles, so if I'm ever called on to back up my words with my fists, I can. You'd be surprised just how much confidence that knowledge can give a man, Mr. Hunter."

But then there was a great deal about William Knox Gordon which not only surprised but delighted Hunter. As he watched the younger man deftly handle the awkward bag, he hoped their association would be a long and fruitful one.

On the first warm Sunday in March the year following the

arrival of the Bertollis, Hunter and Gordon were out riding, looking over possible mine sites and the proposed location of a new rail spur extension. They were surprised to come upon a group of forty or fifty Italian miners gathered in a rough circle around some wooden balls, all yelling and arguing with one another to such an extent that no one noticed the arrival of their employer and superintendent. The argument seemed to be in the placement of eight wooden balls in relation to a smaller wooden ball. The mine officials watched in silence for a moment as the words continued and even increased in intensity. Then, one of the miners noticed Hunter and Gordon. It was John Bertolli, one of only a few in the group who could speak English. He removed his cap and half-bowed in a timorous greeting. Immediately, the others around him began to quiet down.

"Gooda day, Mister Hunter. Mister Gordon," John greeted. "How can we helpa you?"

"What's going on here?" Hunter immediately demanded. The last thing he wanted was miners fighting among themselves. "What started this ruckus?"

John Bertolli laughed. "No trouble except for lose. Lose, buy birra. Lose, no drink. Is old Italian game we play, Mr. Hunter. Called bocce. Much words but no fight. Musta put bigga ball close bambino ball---baa-ling. Twelve maka game. Birra for win."

Since it was only a game and not a fight, Hunter immediately lost interest and turned his horse to leave. Gordon, however, dismounted and walked into the circle of men where he carefully examined one of the balls. It was rough-cut and so unsymmetrical it was obvious it would wobble when rolled across the ground.

"Where'd you get the balls?" he asked Bertolli.

"From bigga wood, sir."

"Big wood?" Gordon questioned, trying to understand what was meant. "You mean timbers? Mine timbers?"

"Yes sir, timbers," John agreed.

"I'll be durned," Gordon said under his breath, marveling at the extent to which man would go to entertain himself. He looked back down at the scattered grouping of balls and the men surrounding them. "Looks like great fun. Tell you what, you teach me to play bocce ball, and I'll get the boys in the carpenter shop to make you up some better balls. You want them this size?" he asked, picking up one ball and placing his fingers around it to judge its size. "About five inches in diameter, I'd say. And the little one---what did you call it? The baa-ling? About two and a half inches."

Gordon looked up at Hunter, still astride his horse. "Cypress wood ought to be good, don't you think, Mr. Hunter? It's a good hard wood."

"Probably so," Hunter replied in a disinterested tone. "You about ready to move on and let these men get back to their game?"

"Just a minute, Mr. Hunter, if you don't mind?" Gordon looked up at his boss and then turned back to John. Placing his arm around John's shoulder, he drew him slightly away from the others.

"You speak pretty fair English," he told the young Italian. "I need an interpreter from time to time. You might just fit the bill. I've seen you around the camp, but I don't remember your name."

"Bertolli, sir. Giovanni, er a---John Bertolli. Me onnerstan' and reada English. Speaka not so good. E'study seminary Old Country, Italy."

"Really? That's interesting. How do you like Thurber, so far?"

"Itsa fine, sir. Justa fine. If only..." John suddenly realized he was talking to a superior and should refrain from complaint, and he blushed for having come so close to making a serious blunder.

"If only what, Mr. Bertolli? We want to make Thurber as enjoyable as we can for the workers." His tone was one of reassuring warmth and concern, and John felt more comfortable.

“Yes sir,” John said. “Mabbe we hava padre for Cattolica Mass. Mabbe not so much fight. Umbriaco. Dronk.”

“A splendid thought!” Gordon enthusiastically responded. “Let me see what I can do, John. Perhaps we can get a priest from Fort Worth. If I’m not mistaken, the Bishop in Little Rock, that’s in Arkansas, has this territory. Let me write to him.”

“Yes sir, thanka you, sir,” John said quickly, his voice filled with gratitude.

“Now, is there anything else we could do to help you boys at work or play?”

John could hardly believe his good fortune. Not only was the “bigga boss” willing to arrange a Catholic Mass, but now he was even asking what more he could do! The young Italian, so used to oppression, gathered up his courage, and taking a deep breath, paused before speaking. He wanted to make certain it wasn’t all a dream.

“In Old Country, we maka pane, ah...bread. Outside baka, what you say oven. Lika this.” John gestured with his hands indicating a mounded igloo-shaped oven. Spreading his arms, he showed the approximate size.

Gordon chuckled. “All right, John. An oven’s no problem. We’ll send some cement and rocks over and you boys can build the ovens you need.” He then led John back to where the other men were still standing and added in a louder voice, this time addressing all, “Enjoy your game, gentlemen.” Then he turned to John and said in a voice for all to hear, “Mr. Bertolli, it’s been my pleasure talking with you. If you need anything else, just let me know.” He then reached out and gave John a hearty handshake.

John watched in silent astonishment as Gordon walked back to where Hunter was holding his horse, remounted and rode away with Hunter. Mr. W. K. Gordon, the superintendent, had called him “Mister Bertolli.” And in front of all the men! Not once since coming to America had anyone called him "Mister." And now, to have Mr. Gordon say it in front of everyone! Never had John felt so proud.

Gordon was true to his word, too. Within a few days cement, sand and rocks arrived near the bocce ball court, and the men, under John's direction, constructed a dome-shaped oven for the wonderfully delicious Italian bread they all craved. And before the week was out, Mr. Gordon told John that he had mailed a letter to the Bishop of Little Rock. John anxiously awaited a reply.

The following Sunday, as the men gathered for another bocce ball game, Gordon appeared with two sets of bocce balls. "Okay, John," he said in a lively tone, handing both sets to the Italian. "Now, it's your turn to make good on a promise. Teach me the game of bocce ball."

To John's delight, the "bigga boss" soon mastered the rules of the game, as well as the necessary overhand release to give the ball proper spin and control. By the end of the day, Gordon even managed to make a tricky "stick shot" to knock out the rivals' ball and stick his own ball in its place, thereby winning the game. And in the course of one Sunday afternoon, W. K. Gordon managed to win the friendship and trust of the Italian miners.

In spite of the arduous work in digging away at a twenty-eight inch seam of coal while lying in a prone position, the Italians and Poles easily adapted to the work and to living in Thurber. Life in Thurber was immeasurably better than it was in the Old Country. More importantly, America gave hope; digging coal was merely the beginning. The miners averaged only about forty dollars a month, but out of this, many were able to save passage money for family or friends to join them in Thurber.

The Italians were a happy group, always singing, laughing, drinking, playing bocce ball. The Poles, too, enjoyed their new life after the harsh existence in Poland, but their exuberance was more subdued than that of the Italians. There were long lasting celebrations, particularly for weddings. There were church feasts, card games and dancing to polka and waltz music.

With three sets of bocce balls, two new courts were laid out, and the bread oven adjacent to the courts became the meeting place for the sixty-some Italians in the summer of 1890. Soon after the bread oven was completed, the savory aroma of Italian bread wafted through the Thurber breeze. Nothing tasted better than steaming hot, thick-crusted Italian bread with butter, cheese or salami, for the hot bread brought out the full flavor of the food. To satisfy the demand, bread had to be baked several times a week. Mesquite wood was burned inside the oven. When white corn meal, sprinkled inside the oven, turned brown, the oven was at the right temperature. The mesquite ashes were scraped out, and an oar-like paddle was used to insert the shaped dough into the oven. Leftover dough was twisted into smaller rolls to make the crunchy, hard-crusted "cornutti."

Somehow, W.K. Gordon always seemed to know when the bread was ready to "come out" of the oven, for his appearance was too timely to be coincidental. He liked a thickly-sliced heel. Sometimes Gordon stayed for a game of bocce ball. It was a pleasant respite from his duties, and he always left with a loaf of bread under his arm. He enjoyed the cheerful, animated Italians and he knew the success of the company was largely dependent on these hard-working, fun loving men from the Old Country. On one Sunday afternoon, W. K. Gordon, chomping on a generous slice of bread and with a wine glass in one hand, walked over to John Bertolli, who was talking with Pete Wasieleski. "Ah, John," Gordon began. "What was it you said? 'Fresh bread and old wine?' I never knew bread could taste so good! I'm glad you built the oven."

"We thanka you, Mr. Gordon. Now eat much bread. Need more oven." John laughed. Then nodding at Pete, John made the introduction. "Mr. Gordon, my gooda friend, Pete Wasieleski."

"Glad to meet you, Pete. That's Polish, isn't it?" Gordon asked.

"Yes sir, Mr. Gordon," Pete responded in an understandable but heavy accent.

"I've come with good news, John and Pete. I got a letter from the Bishop in Little Rock, and he does have this territory. When I wrote him, I told him we have mostly Italians, Poles and some Mexicans. But he wants to know how many of each and how many women and children. We only have three wives and seven children on company property. From the books, I counted sixty-three Italians, twenty-seven Poles and thirty two Mexicans. Since the Mass is in Latin, I don't see why nationality should be important."

"Oh, yes sir, Mr. Gordon. The Mass is Latin, but the Padre, he hear Confession, and speaka sermon. And mabbe somebody wanna talk Padre."

"Well, of course, John. I simply wasn't thinking. In my church, the Episcopal Church, everything is in English. You and Pete have to keep me straight on all this," Gordon acknowledged, swallowing the last of his wine and then cutting himself another hefty slice of bread as Pete handed him one more glass of wine.

"You keepa eat bread, Mr. Gordon, we need more oven," John said in a jesting tone.

Gordon smiled and said, "You keep making bread like this, and you can have all the ovens you want." He paused for another sip of wine. "But back to the Mass. Since we have more Italians, it would probably be better if we asked for an Italian-speaking priest to begin with. Then, later, a Polish-speaking priest, next a Spanish-speaking priest and so on, on a rotating basis. What do you say to that?"

"Yes sir!" John exclaimed, while Pete said nothing, just nodding his head in agreement. "And please, Mr. Gordon, have Padre come Satday. Many Confession. Needa plenty time. Pete here, take hafa day, have many bad sin!" he laughingly teased as he slapped Pete on the back.

“I’ll ask the Bishop. You know Mr. Hunter wants to build a church, but of course, we’ll have to ask the priest about the design. For now, probably the best place for Mass would be in the warehouse behind the grocery store. You two take a look at it and let me know if it will do. And when the priest comes, I’m counting on you and Pete to meet the train and get the word out on the Mass and Confessions and all. I’m putting you two in charge of it, so let me know what you need.”

“Yes sir, gladly!” Both men nodded affirmatively.

“Good. Now I must be on my way. Anything else you can think of before I go?”

For several undecided seconds, John and Pete looked at each other. Then John cleared his throat and asked, “Mr. Gordon, sir. We lika musica. We singa alla time. Make orchestra. You know? Sassafono. Tromba. Daniel Raffael direttore. Many maka musica.”

“Music! A great idea!” Gordon exclaimed. “And a band would certainly liven up this place. Dances, concerts, holiday performances. It would give the men another diversion, too. Mr. Hunter will like it. We’ll call it the Hunter Band. We’ll buy the musical instruments. John you speak with Daniele Raffael. I’ll take care of the rest. And thank you both. Now excuse me, or I’ll be late for a meeting with Mr. Hunter.”

“Yes sir, Mr. Gordon. Gooda day!” the men echoed, as Thurber’s superintendent left. A minute later John nudged Pete. “Why you no tell me? Aska Mr. Gordon for store to get Italian salami.”

William Knox Gordon
Courtesy Thurber Historical Association

"You aska too much, and Mr. Gordon say 'No more. That John Bertolli wanna too much, I no giva him.' "

John threw back his head and roared with laughter. "No be worry, Pete. Mr. Gordon lika us. He no say 'No more'. Next time I aska for salami. You see."

But all of these little amenities to improve Thurber's living conditions would not have been granted if Thurber had not been "gentled down" by Ranger Captain McMurry. By July 1890,

Robert Hunter could boast of "kicking hell" out of the Knights of Labor. The Knight's membership and power had dwindled to insignificance. Labor was forced to reorganize, and the Knights joined with the Progressive Union to form the nationwide United Mine Workers. For the next several years, the UMW concentrated on organizing in other states before turning to Texas, after the turn of the century. The Knights had been beaten, but a few hotheads and trouble-makers still lingered around Thurber. On occasion, these "hard cases" tried to stir up racial disorder. In 1890 there were about seventy black miners in Thurber. The trouble was with the native-born Americans who came from confederate states. Just a few decades ago, the Negroes were slaves, but now they were earning equal pay as white men. The foreign born and Negroes were friendly to each other, for the Italian and Poles knew little about the Civil War and slavery. Captain McMurry arrested several men for "threatening bodily harm and property damage," and after that, the local guards were able to handle the situation for several years until the UMW moved in after 1900.

SIXTEEN

The Italian miners could get genuine homemade Italian salami by slipping through the barbed wire fence to Mazzano's store and saloon just outside company property, but the men had to be careful not to cross the fence too often in the same place because the grass would be worn down and the company guards would closely watch this spot. If the guards caught a miner buying outside the Thurber compound, there would be a cursing, confiscation of purchases, name taking and a stern warning. But this did not deter all Italians from buying outside the "bull pen," as Hunter's enclosure around Thurber was called.

After being caught a few times by company guards, some men were reluctant to risk crossing the fence again. It was for these men that John Bertolli hoped the company store would sell salami. Of course, the salami in the store would have to be shipped in from New York, but it would never equal Mazzano's homemade salami.

Franco Mazzano and his family were urged by a cousin to come to Thurber in the summer of 1889. Franco, wife Clara, and their two young daughters, eight and ten years old, were the first Italian family to arrive in the new town of Thurber. Hoping to encourage more families to move in, Hunter constructed a three-room house for the family. Clara was beside herself with joy. An entire house to themselves! In Italy she was only able to dream of such a wonderful circumstance. But in America, in Thurber, anything seemed possible. The dream was short-lived, however; for in the spring of 1890, Franco seriously injured his back while working in the mine. It soon became evident he would be unable to return to mining, and the Mazannos were asked to vacate their beloved company home. But the Italians looked after their own, and small money contributions were made. Although Hunter never learned of it, W. K. Gordon donated thirty dollars of his own money to help the Mazanno family. Enough money was raised to purchase a one acre lot which adjoined company property north of Italian Hill.

Initially, a one-room shack and an outhouse were built for the Mazzano's, but the construction of a larger domicile became a project of major significance within the Italian community. The project began to take on religious connotations when building lumber, varying in size and quantity, began to mysteriously appear on the Mazzano property overnight. Though many were questioned, no one knew of its origin. It was Clara who, after many unanswered questions regarding the lumber, threw up her hands and declared the lumber must have floated in on angel's wings because no mortal man had knowledge of it. It was humorously mentioned among the men that each time a new supply of lumber was found in the Mazzano yard, a like amount had disappeared from company building sites. But this fact was never mentioned to Clara, and the men continued to tease her about her "heavenly" lumber.

On Sundays a dozen Italian miners would put hammer and saw to turning the "angel's" lumber into a home for Franco and Clara and their daughters. W. K. Gordon loaned the workers two teams of mules with fresnoes to dig a small pond. A few yards from the pond, a well was dug for seep water, and next to the house a cistern was dug and lined with rocks and cement. Clara would need plenty of water for washing and cooking.

Since Franco could no longer work in the mines, the new home was not only to provide living quarters but also space from which to derive income. Quite naturally, a small restaurant, saloon and grocery store evolved from the largest room. Franco was so depressed and worried by his back injury and his inability to return to mining, he had difficulty in recognizing his good fortune, for the injury of his back forced him from laborer to small businessman, a transition which he would have never achieved on his own. Fate, physically painful as it was, gave him an alternate means of providing for his beloved Clara and his daughters. Within two years of their arrival in the United States, the Mazzanos were living the American dream of owning a house and a business. Luckily for the couple, the timing was right, for their small found a touch of home within Mazzano's.

Clara Mazzano, in her mid-thirties, was not an unattractive woman, though she would never dream of flaunting her sexuality before these young men. But she was talkative and cheerful and the men enjoyed her teasing banter. Franco was quieter and kept himself busy with the lighter work of the place: tending bar, cleaning and helping Clara in the kitchen. The men found him to be a patient, understanding listener who could relate to their hard work. The young miners had little money to spend, but the business provided a small, steady income, twice what Franco could make in the mines. And as more miners moved in, the business grew accordingly.

If the personalities of Franco and Clara were not enough to draw Thurber's Italian miners over the company's barbed wire boundary, the food and stocked delicacies would have done so. Clara, like most Italian wives, was an accomplished cook, and her repertoire of delicious Italian dishes included polenta, ravioli, arrosta polla, tortellini, cannelloni, minestra, spaghetti and a half-dozen other tasty flares. The stocked foods included homemade Italian salami, Clara's home-grown and canned Italian peppers, olive oil, and different cheeses and pastas. Since none of these items were available at the company store, the men found it good reason to visit Mazzano's. Although the miners were expected to buy their beer and wine at the company-owned saloon, the "birra" and "vino" always tasted better at the Mazzano place, and the intimate domestic surroundings added to the enjoyment of the drink. Thurber management might not like it, but Mazzano's fulfilled a need.

The miners spoiled the two young Mazzano daughters, and when John went to Mazzano's he taught the daughters simple

English words. Little did he realize that in several years he would be smitten by daughter Guiseppa who was ten years old at this time.

Every few months, John Bertolli would write up an order for the Mazzanos, addressed to a New York importer of Italian foods. And John was increasingly called upon to write or interpret personal or official letters for illiterate Italian miners. He continued to study and to improve his English, and he sought occasions to practice his English. And when Mr. Jay Gould made his first visit to Thurber, John was asked to introduce the Hunter Band.

The proposal for the Hunter Band was quickly approved by Robert Hunter, and W.K. Gordon rode up to John's quarters one evening to discuss this. "Well, John, that band idea of yours may come about sooner than we expect. If I go to Fort Worth tomorrow to buy the instruments, how long would it take Daniele Raffael to get the band organized?"

"Lika that!" John said with an exaggerated snap of his fingers. "No time Daniele Raffael maka orchestra. Gooda orchestra. You see. We talka Daniele. He tell how many instrumenta."

After introductions, and with John interpreting, the musician stated the number and types of instruments required.

W. K. Gordon discussed the time needed for the organization of the band. "Mr. Hunter was as impressed with the idea of a band as I was. In fact, Mr. Hunter may have been a little too impressed. He said a friend of his, Mr. Jay Gould, would be traveling to Thurber before the month is out, and Mr. Hunter wondered if the band could give Mr. Gould a rousing welcome. I told him I'd ask. I realize the boys work hard all day, and I wonder if they'd have time to practice after a day's work?"

John relayed this to Dan Raffael. "No worry. Maestro Raffael say band ready two, three week."

Gordon picked up on the term "Maestro." "We're counting on

it, Maestro Raffael. What instrument will you play, John?"

"No me. Play organo but no church musica Hunter Band."

Maestro Raffael and John stood silently as they watched Gordon ride away, but they could feel excitement and expectation surround them, for a new showpiece of Thurber was about to be unveiled.

In the early fall of 1890, Jay Gould made his first of several visits to Thurber. Gould's private rail car was parked in the middle of town, near the grocery store. This provided focus and speculation for Thurberites, but even the most curious failed to comprehend the power and reputation of the man inside the car. It was Gould's manipulation of the gold market which caused the "Black Market" panic in 1869. He had control of three northeastern railroads before his connection to "Boss" Tweed and a fraudulent stock sale forced him out. He later gained control of the Union Pacific, Missouri Pacific, and the Texas and Pacific Railroads. The Western Union Telegraph Company and New York's elevated railroad were also part of Gould's portfolio.

Jay Gould thoroughly enjoyed his visits to Thurber, which were agreeable respites from his usual pressured routine. Thurber was off the "main track", and he had a chance to unwind with his old friend Robert Hunter. Gould and Hunter were of the same mold: ruthless, opportunistic, driving, surly and blunt. They enjoyed each other's companionship, and Hunter liked to show off his domain and explain his progress and plans for other Thurber ventures. And Jay Gould took satisfaction in seeing Thurber develop into a profitable enterprise and in knowing that his T & P Railroad was responsible for the success of Hunter's little empire. John Bertolli removed the clean handkerchief from his breast pocket and mopped the sweat on his forehead. Nervously, he watched W. K. Gordon as he waited his signal, knowing that at any second the superintendent would nod his head and John would be forced to step up on the rear platform of the railroad car—and speak to the crowd.

At first, when Mr. Gordon asked John if he would make the band introduction since the band was his idea, John felt deeply honored. Now that the time had come, however, and as he watched the crowd before him---there must be three hundred---the ex-seminary student felt dismal dread. He had practiced and practiced, trying to eliminate his broken accent, but now he wondered if he would even find his voice. And if he didn't, how could he ever recover from the embarrassment? Most of those present were fellow miners and people from surrounding areas, but they would never forget the day John Bertolli stepped forward and had no voice!

John mopped his brow once more and shot a quick glance toward Maestro Raffael and the twenty Italian miners who made up the Hunter Band. Faces and hands scrubbed clean, hair glistening damp with oil, and plastered against the scalp, it was hard to believe these were the same men who each day emerged from a dark, deep hole, with facial features obliterated by coal dust. Now, shiny as their instruments, they looked happy and excited, ready to perform. John glanced back at Mr. Gordon, who was nodding his head. In an effort to calm himself, John drew a big breath and let it out with a whoosh. He then stepped up onto the train platform, waited for the crowd to settle, and began.

"Mr. Gould." He bowed slightly toward the guest of honor, then added, "Mr. Hunter, Mr. Gordon, and all people here. With big pleasure we show Hunter Band for first time. Thank Mr. Hunter for instruments. People many countries work Thurber. Many language. But music all understand. Maestro Raffael is direttore. Enjoy please. Thank you."

A smile as warm and encompassing as sunshine spread across his face as he realized he had completed the introduction without faltering! He looked out at the applauding crowd before stepping down. He had heard the band practicing in the evenings and knew even before the first note was sounded just how good they were.

And he felt pride as he looked in Gordon's direction and caught a smile and nod of approval.

The band began with a rousing Sousa march, "Washington Post March," and the crowd broke into immediate and enthusiastic applause. Who would have thought a small group of coal miners, the hands callused and coal ingrained, could so gingerly finger a delicate instrument, coaxing such beautiful music from its heart? But here they were, twenty muscle-toughened Italian miners, who not only won out against keen competition for an envied seat in the orchestra, but who also willingly consented to daily practice though still obligated to a ten-hour work day in the mines, six days a week. The results of such dedication were plainly evident. John watched Gould, Hunter and Gordon as the band finished the first rendition. All three were vigorously applauding. The Hunter Band was a tremendous success! Later it would make yearly appearances at the Fort Worth Stock Show and the State Fair, in addition to other special performances.

After thirty minutes Gould and Hunter retired into Gould's car, but the band played for almost two hours: marches, classical pieces, waltzes and current favorites. The music-starved crowd was wildly enthusiastic. And as a finale, Maestro Raffael led the band through "The Star Spangled Banner". As the strains of music fell over the crowd, John, along with the other immigrants present, stood stiffly at attention, some with hands placed in salute and some with tear-filled eyes, so thankful, happy and proud to be in America.

Following the performance, W. K. Gordon took John and Maestro Raffael into Jay Gould's opulently-furnished private car where Gould and Hunter were seated with drinks.

"Gentlemen," Gordon said, "allow me to introduce these two fine men. Maestro Dan Raffael, whose significant talent is responsible for the beautiful music which we've just heard." He looked in Raffael's direction, then placed an arm around John's shoulder and added, "And this is Mr. John Bertolli, one of our hardest-working miners, and the man whose idea it was that we form a band. So you see, gentlemen, the Hunter Band is everyone's band."

In a rare show of emotion, Hunter clasped each man's hand and smiled warmly. "Thank you, Maestro Raffael, Mr. Bertolli. Mr. Gould tells me that was as fine a music as he's heard anywhere in the country: New York, St. Louis, Kansas City---anywhere. And I agree. Now that we know what you can do, we'll be getting band uniforms, and we'll even build a bandstand. Please extend our thanks to all members of your fine orchestra. And Mr. Bertolli, thank you for bringing the idea of a band to Mr. Gordon's attention."

Later, still somewhat in awe of the personal attention he had received from Mr. Hunter, John translated what the mine owner had said for Raffael and the band members. Then, taking Raffael aside, he spoke his own feelings of gratitude.

"You performed a miracle, Daniele," John told the band director. "I was worried when Mr. Gordon said you had only had a month to get ready, but even after you said it could be done, I never dreamed it would be this good. The orchestra was magnificent! How did you manage to teach twenty men to play such fine music in such a short time?"

"I teach them nothing," Daniele replied. "You don't know Italians have genetic ability for music? It's in our blood, but even if it weren't, any Italian mother will see to it her son has a music teacher. Half the Italians in Thurber have some kind of musical training, if not instrument, then voice. My only task was to weed through and find the best. That, Giovanni, was not hard to do. So you see? Not a miracle, just typical Italians."

The year 1892 ended with over four hundred miners at work. Coal production was up to 440 tons per day and Number 5 mine had opened one mile west of downtown Thurber. An increasing number of miners' families began arriving from Europe. A three-room house could be built for less than $200 and these rented for $6 a month. For $18 a month, miners would get bunk space, two meals, a work lunch, and laundry service from families who took in boarders. It was very hard work for the wives, but it provided additional income and everyone benefited.

Water was a problem, and at first, Hunter shipped water in on rail tank cars. But as the population increased, Hunter built Thurber "Little Lake" near downtown Thurber to provide water. Soon the town outgrew this lake, and a new lake, Thurber "Big Lake", was built a mile east.

Hunter immensely enjoyed watching the progression of his idyllic community, and he and Gordon often took horseback tours of the area. On one such day on a warm Sunday afternoon in March, as the two made their circuit, Gordon remarked on the absence of activity at the saloon and the bocce ball courts. In front of one boarding house a group of men were solemnly gathered. Inside, the muffled strains of a woman's weeping could be heard. Gordon asked what the problem was, and in unison several miners replied, "malato." One of the miners went into the house to return with John Bertolli.

"Sickness of the lung. Vincente Bruno. Very bad. Need priest, doctor," John somberly said.

Gordon dismounted and went into the house to see for himself. Hunter remained atop his horse, seemingly unconcerned. When Gordon returned, he looked up at Hunter and said, "Probably pneumonia. I doubt there's much hope." Turning to Bertolli, he said, "There's a doctor in Strawn. We can send a wire quicker than we can ride, so I'll do that now. I'll also wire the Bishop to ask for a priest. I'm sorry John. I wish I could do more."

"I know, Mr. Gordon. But we try. Priest maybe too late. We say Rosary and 'Act Contrition', but Vincente, he need Extreme Unction, The Last Rites, with Padre."

The doctor did not arrive until late afternoon, and by then it was too late. Vincente Bruno was dead, the first death in Thurber, and no burial ground had yet been designated. Gordon approached Hunter with the problem.

"I wonder if he could be buried in the Gordon or Strawn Cemetery." Hunter asked.

"That's a long way for his friends to go. Eventually we'll have to have a cemetery here. hurber's the only place in America Bruno's ever lived or worked in. Be nice if he could be buried here," Gordon stated, clearly indicating where his sympathy lay.

"A cemetery has to be on high ground, and I've got plans to build houses on just about every hill," Hunter mused, more to himself than to Gordon. "But you're right; we'll need a cemetery sometime. Put it on the hill east of Number Two Mine. From now on, the place will probably be known as 'Graveyard Hill', or something equally morose."

"Yes sir, I guess so," Gordon replied dispassionately, displeased that Hunter should be so unemotional about the death of one of his employees. "But then, I suppose death usually is a bit morose."

The Italian miners did not work on Monday, the day of Bruno's funeral. Each considered it his sacred duty to give full tribute to his fellow countryman. And each man, in his own way, was deeply affected by Bruno's passing. Once again, the uncertainty of life had been thrust into consciousness, and thoughts of dying so far from friends and loved ones were disturbing and sobering.

At 10:30 that morning, John Bertolli was in Thurber Junction to meet the priest on the eastbound train from Abilene.

John stepped forward to introduce himself as the priest stepped from the train. "Good morning, Father, I am John Bertolli and I come to help you go to Thurber."

"Good morning, Mr. Bertolli," the priest said, extending his hand. "I'm Father Brickley. I hope I've not come too late?"

"Yes, Father, too late. Vincente Bruno, he die yesterday. We say Rosary, Act Contrition."

"Oh, I'm so sorry to hear that. This train is the first train east. Was it an accident in the mines?"

"No, no. Vincente die of lung sickness."

"Parli Italiano?"

John looked at Father Brickley and grinned affirmatively, and Father immediately began to converse in perfect Italian, much to John's delight. On the ride from Thurber Junction to Thurber not one word of English was spoken.

"Don't be misled by the name Brickley," the priest told John. "My father was a Britisher who worked in the embassy in Rome, but my mother was Italian. I was born in Italy and spent most of my childhood there."

"That's wonderful," John replied. "Maybe some day you can come to Thurber for Mass. There are many Italians in Thurber."

"So I've been told. In fact, this coming June, Father Fabrio, who also speaks Italian, and I will come to Thurber once a month. A new Diocese is being set up in Dallas and it will serve this area. Bishop Brennan will be consecrated next month to head the Diocese. I'm looking forward to coming out here on a regular basis."

"Me, too," John echoed, feeling pleased that another of his dreams for Thurber was about to become reality.

The Funeral Mass was solemn and very emotional. Several men openly sobbed. Boxes and barrels had been shifted around in the grocery warehouse to make a temporary chapel. John and another miner, a close friend of Vincente, served the Mass. Since there was no organ, the music was an accordion and a violin.

Several men made up a choir, and one did not have to be musically trained to appreciate that these voices were professional quality. When the tenor soloed on "Ave Maria", W. K. Gordon's eyes misted over. Never could he recall having seen an occasion of such somber beauty and pageantry.

Following the funeral, there was a holiday atmosphere. Tables were set up with an array of cheeses, salami, meat balls, fresh bread, wine and beer. The miners lined up; each had to say something to Father Brickley, in Italian, of course. And they hugged him or kissed his hand in a display of affection and gratitude. As W. K. Gordon watched the miners gathered around the priest, he realized there was more hunger for food of the soul than for the body.

Gordon accompanied the priest and John Bertolli back to Thurber Junction, and before Father stepped on the train, Gordon had a rough sketch of plans for a new church: a sacristy on each side of the altar, an upstairs church loft at the rear, seating for two hundred and enough land for the priest's house, a school and a playground. Gordon wanted the church located at the foot of what Hunter had so coldly dubbed "Graveyard Hill", but Father Brickley reminded him that Bishop Brennan would have final approval of any plans and sites.

Bruno's death pointed to the need of resident doctors, and several doctors were hired by the company. For $1.00 a month, a single man received medical services. The charge was $2.00 a month for families.

In the summer of 1891, Fathers Brickley and Fabrio began monthly Masses in the grocery warehouse at Thurber. The company-built Catholic Church was completed in the fall of 1892 and Fathers Litwora, Brinkley and Fabrio became the first mission priests. Since Hunter's company built the church, Hunter felt he should have the privilege of naming the church. He scanned the list of saints and decided on St. Turibus, whose feast day is March

23rd. Hunter liked the sounding similarity: Turibus---Thurber. But the miners wanted a Saint allied to their work: St. Barbara, patroness saint of miners. What could be more appropriate? And Bishop Brennan agreed on St. Barbara. St. Barbara served the parish well by listening to the prayers of families and miners in a dozen languages as they prayed for safety in the mines.

The Italians insisted the bell must come from Italy, and they took a collection to raise the necessary money. The bell gave a monotonic, dull bong, but it could be heard two miles away, its distinctive tone insistently summoning Thurberites to Mass. And each time John Bertolli heard its toll, he smiled; he was certain it could be heard all the way to Italy.

SEVENTEEN

When Piotr Wasieleski first came to America in 1889, he and brother Pavel visited their Uncle Antonni in Baltimore before proceeding to Texas. While in Baltimore, Piotr was introduced to a beautiful young woman, Cecelia Cichoracki. The Cichoracki family came to America from Rypin, Germany-Poland, a township just twenty kilometers northwest of Piotr's hometown of Sierpc, Russian-Poland. The immediacy of familiar locales provided conversation background, and it was not long before Piotr was smitten by Cecelia's delicate beauty and her ingenuous warmth.

Cecelia had been in America two years and worked as a seamstress in a Baltimore factory. She was persistent in her determination to master the English language and even tried a few English phrases on Piotr, but her words were absolutely incomprehensible to Piotr, and he was terribly embarrassed. As if she deliberately tried to show his ignorance! This was why Piotr, a few weeks later, was so insistent on learning English from Giovanni Bertolli. Piotr would show her the next time he saw her! If that time ever came.

Cecelia, noting Piotr's discomfiture, quickly switched back to the native tongue. "I'm sorry. I try to practice my English when I can. I must learn English. If not, people say 'dumb Polack, cannot speak English' and they don't like us then."

It was the first time, but not the last time, Piotr would hear the derogatory word, "Polack".

"I don't speak English, yet. Do you like me?" Piotr asked timidly, overwhelmed by the intimacy of his question.

Cecelia blushed, and her eyelids fluttered downward, momentarily hiding her eyes, eyes so blue and with so much depth that Piotr was reminded of the blue Polish skies at harvest time.

"Perhaps," she said, the sweetness of her voice granting lacy promise to the word.

Piotr felt a strange fluttering in his chest. "You will write me, then?" he asked. "In Thurber, Texas, where I go next, I know no one, except brother Pavel. If I write to you, you will answer?"

"Perhaps," she said again, but this time no lashes veiled the blueness of her eyes and her look was directed at him. Piotr knew instinctively her answer was not "perhaps," but "yes" and his heart leaped across the barricade of emotions.

For two years they corresponded in Polish, with words of English thrown in to try on each other. Each willingly conceded the possibility of a progression in their relationship. When Cecelia signed a letter in the English ending, "With Love", it was the first time she had used the term in either language. Piotr prayed to the blessed Mother of Czestochowa that no one would claim his dearest Cecelia before he could save the money to travel to Baltimore and make her his wife. His next letter contained his picture and a proposal.

Her reply was soon and in the affirmative, and Piotr was elated. With her letter, there was also a photograph of Cecelia, and now the young Pole's eyes filled with pride as he showed the small portrait to John Bertolli.

"Ah, Pete Wasieleski, you lucky man! She is most beautiful. When you marry?"

"Cecelia say July wedding. I talk pit boss. Tell I want two weeks for marry. Go Baltimore, Maryland. Marry Cecelia's church for proper wedding. Then come back Thurber."

"You talk Mr. Mitchell, company office," John instructed. "Tell him you need house. You and Cecelia, you family now. You need house." And then as afterthought: "But Pete, you need money for house, feed wife. You make forty-five dollars. You sure is enough for marry?"

"Ah, yes. But Cecelia sew. Make dress for neighbor, friend," Pete answered and affectionately threw an arm around his dearest friend's shoulders. "And someday, you marry, have house too. We neighbor, mabbe."

John shook his head and let only the shadow of a smile rest on his lips. "Some day, long way off," he said.

"But John, I see Mazzano girl smile for you. I can tell, she like you."

John's face turned scarlet, and he mumbled an objection. "But she is still a little girl."

"Not much little, no more, John. She grow fast. Not little all the life."

"Yes," John conceded, "she is blooming like a flower. And when she brushes against me, it disturbs me too much. I think maybe she do on purpose."

"Mabbe so," Pete said with a mischievous grin. "Mabbe John Bertolli find love."

"And Mama Mazzano would kill me if she know how Guiseppa bother me," John said, a frown on his face and disappointment forcing his body into a slump.

"What you do, forget her?"

"Forget, no. Wait, yes. Someday I make more money. Now, too poor. Guiseppa too young. I wait, but not too much wait by Mazzano place. I wait here where I no see Guiseppa too much. Mabbe trouble I see Guiseppa all time. Mabbe four, five years ask Franco for Guiseppa marry. But no worry now," John sighed, and then as if realizing he was dampening the high spirit of the moment, slapped Pete on the back. "Come, Pete. We go see Mr. Mitchell. Find you house."

The demography of Thurber was being shaped. The band of

coal ran westward and the newer mine shafts progressed in that direction, as did the train tracks to the mines. The hill to the west of the township was split by the rails. The Italians congregated on the north side of this hill, and the area became known as "Italian Hill." On the south side of the tracks lived the Poles, and this was "Polander Hill." The Mexicans lived still farther south in an area called "Stump Hill," and the blacks lived east of the Little Lake, near Number One Mine Shaft.

A newly built, three-room house on Polander Hill, number 538, was allotted to Pete. He paid the first month's six dollar rent, and he grinned broadly when Mr. Mitchell offered a congratulatory handshake.

In the two ensuing months, Pete worked harder than he ever had, even pushing his mining buddy John to work faster and harder, coaxing more coal from the ground than ever before. The extra dollars were needed for his trip to Baltimore.

Finally, the day of his departure came, and John went with Pete to Thurber Junction. "You tell pit boss I come back one week. He no give my job somebody else," Pete instructed John.

"Pit boss know, Pete. He know you good man. No worry. You bring back Mrs. Pete Wasieleski. We have big party," John promised.

It was a promise John kept. When Pete and Cecelia stepped off the west-bound train at Thurber Junction in July 1893, they were greeted by John and thirty other friends and well-wishers. From seemingly out of nowhere an accordion player appeared and began playing the traditional Polish Wedding March. As the music stirred the crowd, each man shook Pete's hand, and then kissed the bride. Then the newlyweds were led to a buggy decorated with colorful paper streamers. Two kegs of beer had been loaded in the rear of the buggy, and before the journey to Thurber began, there was a spirited round of toasting. A parade formed, with Pete and Cecelia's buggy in the lead, followed by the accordion player happily belting out polkas for the delight of the laughing, dancing revelers who brought up the rear of the caravan. All along the two-mile road from the Junction to Thurber, well-wishers came out of their homes to kiss the bride, grab a glass of beer, offer it in tribute to the couple, then take a big gulp and join in the parade. By the time the revelers circled the plaza in Thurber before heading toward Polander Hill, a hundred merrymakers were involved.

Once in front of their new home, Pete made a grand show of swooping Cecelia into his arms and carrying her across the threshold of No. 538, much to the delight of the crowd. Setting her lightly on her feet, Pete waltzed his new bride around the room as the wedding party crowded through the doors or onto the porch of the couple's home. Three hours passed before Cecelia was allowed a respite from dancing, with miners standing in line to dance with the bride. The nonstop dancing with the bride was a subtle prank to totally exhaust her on her wedding night.

One room was for dancing. In an adjoining room, cheap dinner plates were stacked up. For the privilege of dancing with the bride, each man would first have to break a plate by slamming either a dollar or a fifty-cent coin onto the stack of plates. As each man stepped forward for his turn at the plates, the room was filled with good-natured hurrahs and joking comments about the person's aim, strength or state of inebriation. The coins would be collected and presented to the bride.

In the kitchen a table was loaded with pierogi, cabbage rolls, kielbasa, dill pickles, pickled herring, beets, potato salad and pastries. A large Polish woman, Theophilia Galik, presided over the kitchen with a quick smile and a mandate that all eat their fill.

About 10 p.m. Father Litwora appeared to bestow blessings upon the young couple. A hush fell over the crowd as they knelt while the priest stood before the newlyweds, solemnly recited prayers in Latin and gave his blessing with the Sign of the Cross. Father Litwora was then led to the kitchen, where Mrs. Galik insisted he eat every morsel on the mounded plate she presented him. Between bites and sips of beer, the good Father chatted with his parishioners. He soon departed, and the music and dancing began again. There seemed to be no shortage of talented musicians in Thurber, and as one would tire or be overcome with drink, another would take his place. Around midnight wives began leading husbands home, for tomorrow would be a normal, or not so normal, day for some. Still, this wedding celebration was tame compared to some of the Polish celebrations which lasted for two or three days; Cecelia and Pete had endured their first wedding party a few days earlier in Baltimore.

The music and the partying of those "damn, crazy Polacks" could be heard all over Thurber, and even after the music and dancing ceased, the newlyweds would get no sleep that night for they were shivareed all night long. Every several minutes there would be a knock at the door, pebbles tossed at the window, a serenade, or rattling of pots and pans. It was a groggy Pete who went to work the next morning, true to his promise of being back to work the Monday after his wedding.

EIGHTEEN

In 1894 the population of Thurber was over one thousand. Coal production was 950 tons a day and there were four mines in operation. Perhaps Robert Hunter should have been satisfied with this progress, but satisfaction was a foreign emotion to Hunter, who had spent a lifetime questing for that which was not his. Hunter was not content unless he was "raising hell" somewhere with somebody, and it wasn't long before he found a new target: Jimmy Grant and his saloon.

Hunter was greedy and wanted all miners to drink at the company's "Snake Saloon." Grant's saloon was located east of Mine Number One and just outside of company property. Hunter had the Erath County sheriff raid Grant's saloon several times on frivolous charges. Grant, knowing that Hunter had control in Erath County, and that growth was westward, moved his saloon a mile north to Palo Pinto County and adjacent to Hunter's detested barbed wire fence, and along the Thurber to Junction road and rail line. This move made Hunter's blood boil and he swore again he would run Grant out of business.

The seething Scot decreed a crackdown on drinking, under the pretext that too much drinking was jeopardizing mine safety. This edict only served to increase Grant's business because no miner now would drink in the company saloon to be scrutinized or reported for drunkenness. However, Grant finally had enough and sold his saloon to Bruce and Stewart. But Hunter was not content with this, so he closed the road which ran in front of the saloon and built a new road a few hundred yards east. The reason given was that the old road was too close to the rail line, and the trains spooked the horses on the road in front of the saloon. The two saloon keepers filed charges against Hunter for closing a public road. But even with the road closed, the miners came in greater numbers to the saloon, glad to be getting back at Hunter.

Hunter was livid. If the miners had money to buy their drinks at Bruce and Stewart's, then by damn, they were making too much! He'd cut their wages back from $1.15 to $1.00 a ton! Then see how much they had to spend on alcohol! That would show them who was boss! He'd run his business or run it to hell!

Hunter had the miners over a barrel, and he knew it. The Union was dead in this part of the country, and it would be several years before the United Mine Workers could move south. There was no other work in the area, and the miners had little money of their own for most had been sending money back to families in Europe. For them, Thurber and company housing was home. And Hunter knew he could justify the pay cut by saying improvements and transportation enabled miners to mine more coal and make more money. The fifteen-cent pay cut, seemingly insignificant, was brutal, and this sowed the seeds of foment and resolve which would enable the miners to strike back at T & P Coal in several years. The Eastern European immigrants knew how to be patient. Had not Italy and Poland been repressed for hundreds of years and the people still survived?

W. K. Gordon was in a tight spot. Regardless of what he felt, he would always be loyal to his boss, Mr. Hunter. Still, he valued the affection and trust of the workers, and he could sympathize with them. He had great rapport with John Bertolli, who was a natural leader and spokesman for the Italians. Bertolli's comments and suggestions had been a tremendous help in managing the activities of Thurber.

John Bertolli felt trapped and betrayed by T & P Coal Company. He had been sending twelve dollars a month back to Italy and still saving eight dollars a month. He was now twenty-three. Who knows? In a few years when Giuseppa is older? But there was no way he could ever save enough money for marriage now, not with the pay cut. No matter how he analyzed this pay cut, it simply was not right. Before, he had not understood what the

Union was about, but after reading and talking about the Union, he now knew the Union was the only hope for better working conditions and more pay. He knew he would strive to bring about Union organization in Thurber. For now, his co-workers urged Bertolli to speak to Mr. Gordon, as if Bertolli could persuade the management to reverse its decision. He saw the coal oil lamp burning in Mr. Gordon's office and knocked on the door.

"Yes. Who is it?" asked Mr. Gordon.

"It is John Bertolli, Mr. Gordon."

"Please come in, Mr. Bertolli." Gordon was never known to be impolite.

"Mr. Gordon, sir. We have big trouble. The men ask me talk you. We no make too much money. Men no happy. Some send money Old Country, family. Some think marry. Mine buddy, Pete Wasieleski, marry last year. Now baby come, three mouths feed. Some men have the ladies they buy present. All is gone. It is bad."

Gordon paused, thinking of the right words. "Mr. Bertolli, thank you for coming forth. I regret the company had to cut wages. But we now have four mines working, and you must admit that with each mine we've opened, the machines and facilities have been improved so that now you can mine more coal under safer conditions and make more money."

Bertolli mulled this over before answering. "Yes sir. If make more money, why my pay five dollars less? New machines. But no make much money with pay one dollar ton. Men work hard for family, for marry, for lady he love. You know how hard is work. We dig by lay on ground, so short the coal," and Bertolli indicated with his hands a thirty-inch seam. "But we happy for work America. Good country. Now we are punish for hard work."

Gordon could feel the frustration and despair in Bertolli, and this bothered Gordon. "Mr. Bertolli. You know I value your friendship. You have been a tremendous help to me. I hope we can continue our mutual trust. Let's try the new pay rate to see if we don't come out about the same."

But Bertolli's mind was set, and he coolly answered, "Last pay I have five dollars less. Work hard. It is no just. I know the men, Mr. Gordon. You no get so much coal with men not happy, and I tell you, sir, I now understand the Union. Miners need help. Your company grow big, strong. Maybe Union grow big, strong, too. Maybe in five year Union make company see big mistake when cut pay. Thank you, sir. Good night."

Bertolli's words were true; in spite of an increased work force and the opening of two new mines, Numbers 5 and 6, coal production over the next several years dropped from 950 tons a day to an average 870 tons a day. The miners grumbled loud and long and asked for Union help, but the Union would be tied up for several years organizing miners in the northern states.

Saloon owners Bruce and Stewart wanted to reciprocate against Hunter for closing the road in front of their saloon so they encouraged miners to speak out against Hunter in the saloon, and it later would become a meeting place for the Union. Stewart once was distributing circulars in Thurber which advertised free beer at his saloon. He was caught by company guards, beaten up and thrown out of Thurber.

Hunter was a hated person, and he received a threatening letter at the Thurber Post Office:

Col. R. D. Hunter:

We have started an organization of avengers to kill tyrants, and if you do not open the road to the saloon we will kill you, you son of a bitch. And we have been chosen by the goodness of God to put down all monopolies, and if you do not discharge W. K. Gordon and that son of a bitch, Bob McKeinan, and that gray-haired bitch, Ben Matthews, we will kill you anyway. Open up the road to the saloon and discharge the sons of bitches and we will not hurt you. We are called by the Supreme Ruler to remove R.D. Hunter, F. Cronk, W. K. Gordon, Bob McKeinan and Ben Matthews and Andrew Remage.

Avengers

Hunter posted a reward notice and a copy of the death threat in Thurber and the surrounding area. It read:

$200.00 REWARD

I, the undersigned, hereby offer a reward of $200 for the arrest and conviction of the party or parties guilty of writing the following letter. The letter was dropped into the post office at Thurber about May 27, last. Parties were too cowardly to sign their names to same.

R.D. Hunter
President Texas & Pacific Coal Co.

In the Thurber mines in 1894, two hundred dollars was four months of hard labor. There was an informer. The letter writers were arrested and convicted in Federal Court in Waco, Texas.

On the earlier charge of closing a public road, Hunter was acquitted in county court. The court decided the road in front of Bruce and Stewart's was not a county or public road, but a private road.

Things were getting out of hand and Hunter again wrote for Texas Ranger help. He claimed that miners from other areas were being sent into Thurber as "walking delegates" to stir up a strike. This time, Texas State Adjutant General W.H. Mabry sent in only one Texas Ranger, Captain William (Bill) McDonald. McDonald was a shot-up, tough, cool individual. He was a top rapid-fire pistol man but preferred persuasion to force. The Captain reported to Mabry that most of the trouble in the Thurber area came from jealousy between Hunter and the owners of Bruce and Stewart's saloon. McDonald quietly sniffed about, all over town, "getting the lay of the land." He decided outsiders were being sent in to threaten the workers and to cause a work stoppage. At dusk one evening, Captain McDonald noticed kegs of beer being carried into the woods northwest of Thurber. Free beer attracted followers to listen to a fiery agitator who exhorted the drinkers and drunks to dynamite the mines and Hunter's office. This was a precarious situation because after more beer and urging from the speaker, there might be mob violence. McDonald calmly stepped out of the darkness into the firelight and shoved the speaker aside. "Now boys, I'm Captain McDonald of the Texas Rangers." he announced as he pulled his coat aside to show his badge. "We've got you surrounded. You'd best not listen to all that clabber because you'll be breaking the law, and I'll see you end up at the end of a rope. I know who you are, so you'd best break up this little shindig." The previous speaker had slipped away into the darkness.

The following morning Captain McDonald assured a group of miners that they had his protection, and nothing would happen if they continued to work. McDonald was right; nothing happened and things simmered down.

Hunter was acutely aware he might have made a mistake in cutting wages, but he'd be damned if he'd ever admit it! At a dollar a ton the Thurber miners were making about half of what the miners at Coalville made several years previous. Coal production was down, as were profits and miners' morale. W. K. Gordon was no longer invited to play bocce ball or to share bread. When miners saw Hunter or Gordon, they disdainfully turned their backs, and soon the back-turning was augmented by "raspberries" and "cat calls." When Hunter first heard these sounds, he made an absolute fool of himself; he jumped off his buggy, doubled up his fist, and challenged "you yellow-bellied, cowardly bastards" to step forward. Fortunately, no one did, because Hunter was in no physical shape to challenge anyone, much less a tough-muscled miner. The almost continuous stress and fighting since he took over Thurber had wearied and aged Hunter, who was now sixty-one. When no one stepped forward, Hunter angrily grabbed one man's arm and demanded, "What's your name?" The man wrenched his arm free and made sure his movement knocked Hunter off balance. "I'll fire every son of a bitch here!" he yelled as he staggered to keep from falling.

By now, a hundred angry, defiant men had closely surrounded Hunter and Gordon, lustily yelling threats and obscenities, and more men were rushing to join the disturbance. One blow, a wrong move or a rallying cry might set off a riot with widespread damage.

Hunter's behavior was absolutely reprehensible, but W.K. Gordon stood by his boss, ready to go down fighting if Hunter were attacked. Hunter finally realized what an impossible, dangerous predicament he had created. As he turned toward his buggy, defeated and with glazed eyes, the men refused to make way. The cool-headed Gordon quietly said, "Excuse us, please. May we leave, please?" The two drove off amid loud verbal garbage. This confrontation visibly shook Hunter who was flushed and weak, and he was ordered to bed by the doctor. After this incident, Hunter gradually placed most of his responsibilities on Gordon, so that by 1897, Gordon was practically running all of Thurber. This left Hunter free to concentrate on brick making, an enterprise which became as successful and profitable as coal mining.

In March 1897 the Green and Hunter Brick Company was organized. For several years now, when brick was required in his Thurber buildings, Hunter had to import bricks from LaClede Brick Company, St. Louis, Missouri. Green was president of LaClede Brick and a good friend of Hunter's, whom Hunter knew from his St. Louis days.

Shale for the brick came from "Steam Shovel Mountain", one mile east of Thurber. With eighteen kilns in operation, peak production was 80,000 bricks a day. Thirty-five different types of

Thurber brick were produced, but paving brick was the specialty, and before asphalt and concrete, Thurber bricks paved miles and miles of Texas highways and streets.

Very few foreign-born worked at the brick yard, for Hunter never was at ease with the "foreigners", and he treated them differently because most could not speak English. Apparently, his being born in Scotland did not qualify as foreign born in the Hunter scheme of things.

Hunter's health continued to decline, and he officially retired from management in 1899. But this did not mean he turned completely loose of his power, for he still had his say up until the time of his death. The man from Ayreshire, Scotland, died in November 1902, one year before the big strike and unionization of Thurber. Had he not died in 1902, the 1903 labor battle would have killed him.

Son-in-law Edgar L. Marston became president and W.K. Gordon was promoted to General Manager, but it was Gordon who became the dominant force after Hunter's departure.

Until his death, Hunter remained a paradox, on the one hand highly altruistic with his innovative, model city and living conditions. But on the other hand, he was scornful of the hard, dirty, backbreaking work of the miners and oblivious of their financial needs. Although Hunter did not care how angered the miners became over his pay cut, his keen sense of business survival warned him that further controversy could seriously damage T & P Coal. For the immediate future, if the price for digging coal were not upped, the company must find ways to soothe the miners' hostilities and to avoid more controversy. Consequently, the company began to provide many conveniences and improvements to life in Thurber. But again, there was a profit connection, and with each improvement the workers paid the price.

In 1895 rail transportation to the mines was begun at $1.00 per month, mandatory for all miners, whether one walked to the mines or rode the train. Also in 1895 Thurber became the first all-electric city in Texas, and the price was $1.50 a month for each house. Another company saloon, "The Lizard", was built on Polander Hill. A water filtration plant was added and water piped to the workers' home at $2.00 a month. In 1896 a seventeen-ton capacity ice plant and the largest cold storage vault in the southwest was built. Now the miners could ice down their beer at 75 cents per 300-pound block of ice. A slaughterhouse was located on the east side of Graveyard Hill. The meat could be stored in the cold vault, and the Italians now had a ready supply of meat for their homemade salami. A first class opera house was erected in 1897, and this was particularly pleasing to the opera-loving Italians. The Opera House would also be used for balls, plays, concerts, motion pictures, meetings and lectures.

Fresh milk was needed as more children were being born in Thurber, and a dairy was added east of Big Lake. Seepage from Big Lake gave moisture for a truck farm north of the lake. The Knox Hotel was built at the northwest corner of the square, and most of the company's important social events took place there. A Concord stage with four horses met all passenger trains at Thurber Junction, and this was the last regularly scheduled stage coach run in America. There was a weekly paper, "The Texas Mining and Trade Journal", which was used primarily for company propaganda and advertising. As Thurber approached the 20th century, it had everything a larger, modern city had to offer---except a decent wage scale, and it would take a Union to resolve this.

When Hunter retired in 1899, there was celebrating by the workers, for they knew they would do better under Gordon. While Marston had the title "President of T & P Coal", there was little doubt Gordon was the key figure.

As the population of Thurber increased, the company stores' sales correspondingly increased. In 1894 T & P set up a corporation to handle all Thurber merchandising; the Texas and

Pacific Mercantile and Manufacturing Company. Everything not connected with coal came under the purview of this corporation. The T. P. M. and M. Co. was in business to make a profit, and in this respect they were assisted by the barbed wire fence and company guards. The fence kept people from going outside to buy, and it kept peddlers from selling inside. Horse-mounted guards patrolled the fence line, and there were guards at the gates, but many Thurberites climbed back through the fence after dark with purchases made in Thurber Junction or Gordon. Even company management's wives would smuggle in merchandise by hiding it under their skirts. There was no objection to exiting Thurber's confines, but outside purchases could not be brought back into the Thurber compound. Mazzano's place continued to do well, and other Italian saloons and grocery stores were opened nearby and in Thurber Junction: Ronchetti's, Sealfi's, Corona's and Castaldo's. Merchandise and food were less expensive outside Thurber, but T & P wanted the monopoly to remain in Thurber. Mail order firms did well because the company could not stop or open U.S. mail.

The company promoted script for use as money. These coupons resembled theater tickets, were called "check" and were good at all company stores. An employee could borrow "check" against his wages, but once enmeshed in this system, it was difficult to catch up and get back on a cash basis. Again, this was to company advantage because the "check" advancement could be spent only in company stores, and the company avoided the problem of handling large cash sums. The foreign-born did not trust banks and there was no bank in Thurber. Many buried money in cans or jars in their gardens or backyards.

Pete Wasieleski was puzzled. He had saved money for his marriage and had no occasion to use "check". But twice within the last month, "Pete Wasieleski" had signed for $5.00 books of "check". Pete protested that the signature was not his, but the company would not write it off. Pete's friend, John Bertolli, came up with an answer and wrote a note:

To T & P M & M Co.

Pete Wasieleski never use check. After now, when he buy check he sign name "John Westfall" so nobody use name Pete Wasieleski.

Pete Wasieleski

During those first years when Hunter's dream for Thurber was becoming an actuality, the Scotsman was not the only one with visions of a brighter future. Four miles northwest of Thurber, in Strawn, William Whipple Johnson also had a dream: to get even with Robert Dickey Hunter for fleecing him of his coal lands.

With the money from his coal venture, Will built the finest house in Palo Pinto County and west of Fort Worth for his adored Anna. It was a large two-story structure with balustrade porches surrounding the house on both floors and embellished with fancy gingerbread trim. There were four brick chimneys and a wooden picket fence encircled the grounds.

While Will was forced to sell out to Hunter at a much lower price than he expected, Will was richer by a quarter-million dollars, and at the age of forty-five, he was wealthy by any measure. But Johnson was too money hungry and too energetic to sit still, and he was eager to strike back at that "bastard crook" Hunter.

Johnson's plan for evening the score with Hunter was simple: open competing mines in the area; siphon off Hunter's experienced miners with offers of better pay, and all the while, send rabble rousers into Thurber to stir up trouble.

Will's devoted Anna remained his trusted business confidant, a shrewd silent partner who advised him in his many, varied business schemes. Johnson's forte was setting up a business idea and convincing investors to put in their money. Most of Johnson's projects fizzled out or were sold before they became fully operational, but the foxy Johnson always seemed to come out better off than when he went into the project. Although Johnson had money to carry most of his enterprises to success, he was careful to never invest large sums of his own money, for some of Johnson's schemes were shaky. Johnson remained in almost constant litigation from his taking advantage of some investor, but strangely, even with the reputation of "skinning" investors, Johnson could always persuade others to invest in his companies.

With all the money they would ever need, a lovely home, community standing, a full life and with challenging business opportunities, the Johnsons could not shake their history of deep personal tragedy. For the third time in nine years, the worst possible disaster hit. This time, son William Harvey, at age seven, died in June 1894 of croup. Again, a heart-rending funeral illustrated the all-consuming love the Johnsons had for their children. A week before he died, the young boy portrayed a fairy in a school play in which he wore wings. The child was placed in the coffin with these wings. The funeral procession to and from church included the boy's beloved pony, Quebie, with empty saddle following the hearse. William Harvey's coffin was placed alongside his sister Marion's coffin in the mausoleum at the side of the Johnson home. Every evening Will and Anna would visit the mausoleum.

In the first fifteen years after selling his first coal company to Hunter, Johnson was involved in about twenty big-moneyed endeavors. He began with coal and ended with oil; anything that might generate money attracted Johnson. There were five coal ventures, not counting the Johnsonville mine, four other mining deals such as silver, copper, agate and galena, three lumbering projects, three railroads, a bank, a livery stable, a gas company, an academy for learning, cattle, land, horses and finally oil.

In January 1889, just three months after he sold his mine

interests to Hunter, Johnson was back into coal as one of the founders of the Weatherford Coal Company, whose mines became known as the Rock Creek Mines, thirty miles northeast of Thurber. The miners were paid $1.15 a ton, but there was no screening at Rock Creek, and this lured some experienced miners from Thurber. But Johnson did not stay around long enough to see large profits from these mines; he sold out six months later. His profits came from the sale of the land, and some of the investors sued Johnson for one-third of the profits from the sale of the land. T & P Coal wanted a monopoly on coal in Texas, and they bought out this competition in 1902.

The American Coal Mining Company was next in 1894. The coal deposits were east of Strawn and adjacent to the T & P Railroad main line. Johnson and an associate sold 2700 acres of land to the new company. Everything connected with this mine would be first class, the latest machinery and mining techniques. Even the living conditions of the miners would be better than those in Thurber. Johnson hated Hunter, but he admired Hunter's community development concept. The American Coal Company would build houses for the miners and control all commercial enterprises, and an innovative idea was the opportunity for miners to lease five-acre tracts from the company for the miners' gardening and livestock needs. There was difficulty in selling bonds, and when operating capital could not be raised, the company was sold to the Strawn Coal Mining Company. Again, Johnson manipulated to minimize his losses, and again, he became a defendant in another lawsuit. Once more Johnson jumped out too soon, for this mine became very profitable. This mine also attracted some Thurber miners, much to Hunter's ire. Two of the defectors were John Bertolli's Uncle Luigi, and Pete Wasieleski's Brother Pavel. Both men were single, and although housing was somewhat scarce in Strawn, the pay was higher, and there was no barbed wire fence around the town.

The Central Coal Mining Company was organized in 1897. In

a familiar pattern, Johnson provided 5200 acres for the new company, but this time Anna Johnson was the majority stockholder. And another familiar face, old friend Harry Taylor, was appointed to sell bonds for the new company. The president of the company, William Martin of Comanche, Texas, felt that eastern bankers were robbing the Texas investors, and officials quarreled. The bonds were heavily discounted, the capital never raised, and T & P Coal Company bought some of the land, but the Johnsons managed to hang onto 500 acres. Would Johnson never get revenge on Hunter?

Johnson's fourth coal venture, the Standard Coal Mining Company, was organized in 1900 with an initial investment of $100,000. Little effort was made to get this company moving, and it folded a few years later. So far, Hunter was in no danger of losing coal business to Johnson.

Although the Johnsons had not been financially hurt by these unsuccessful coal schemes, they decided that in their next undertaking, rather than be involved in financing and management; they would lease their coal lands and receive royalties there from. But the lessee of the Johnson's 500 acres, Ellis, became burdened with business failures elsewhere, and the Johnsons took over his mining interests. Surprisingly, this time the organization and operation of a coal mine went smoothly for Johnson. The company prospered, and finally Johnson had a very successful coal mine. The mine was named Mount Marion in memory of his daughter Marion, and the land east of this mine became Mount Marion Cemetery.

Johnson's Mount Marion Coal Mine, organized in the spring of 1902, was a "carbuncle on the ass", as Hunter would describe it, and with good reason. First, Johnson "stole" some of Hunter's experienced miners. Secondly, coal production from mines around Strawn, including Johnson's Mount Marion mine, steadily rose, while Thurber's production flattened out. Thirdly, Johnson did not have disgruntled miners and Union agitators pestering him.

Johnson was only too happy to accept blame for all of Hunter's accusations.

The "Walking Delegates", or Union representatives, who were harassing Hunter and his miners, came mainly from Strawn, to the delight and encouragement of Johnson. Johnson had no problem with the union, for Union Locals had quietly organized at Rock Creek, Strawn and Lyra. Any company which paid more than that "Skinflint" Hunter was all right with the Union.

In 1904 Johnson sold his interest in the Mount Marion Coal Mine to the Strawn Coal Company. He was now a millionaire, but he was not yet through with the "black rocks" which made his fortune. All available coal lands around Strawn were claimed, so Johnson turned to Coalville, the site of the first coal in the region. He purchased 4400 acres of the John Bird Survey, which was north of Gordon and seven miles northeast of Thurber. He built a fine large home, although not as ostentatious or as big as his Strawn home. There was a detached building for Johnson's office, two large barns and a mausoleum for the children's coffins. When the Johnsons moved to this new home in 1905, the children's coffins were carried in the back of their wagon.

For the next few years, Johnson planned and prepared for a coal mining community patterned after Hunter's Thurber, only better. A large lake was built to ensure adequate water. Roads were hacked through mesquite and shinnery, stock tanks and fences built, and a Hereford cattle herd developed to supply fresh meat for inhabitants of Johnson's ideal city. Wild Game conservation plans were devised and mine sites located. One barn contained hardware for construction of homes and buildings; hinges, bolts, door latches and locks.

But Will Johnson never followed through with this coal venture, because there would not have been as much fun in it now that his adversary Hunter was dead. Also, after Spindletop in 1901, the big money favored oil over coal, and Johnson finally put his money into an oil venture.

Mausoleum of Johnson Children

In 1908 the Palo Pinto Creek, which coursed through the Johnson land, overflowed its banks. The Johnsons awoke to see the wooden building which housed the children's coffins flooded and in danger of floating away. The black caretaker waded out with rope to anchor the building to a tree. He carried the two coffins to higher ground where a new flood-proof foundation for the mausoleum would be built.

In 1914 Anna suffered a partial stroke. The Johnsons rented a seaside cottage on the gulf at Corpus Christi, where Mrs. Johnson could recuperate. The prior occupant of the cottage had died from typhoid bacillus. Will contracted the fever and died in October 1914 at the age of seventy-one.

In spite of being around coal mines most of his life, Will Johnson never overcame his fear of being trapped and buried in a mine cave-in. Just as he would not permit the earth to touch his children's coffins, he was afforded the same consideration, and his coffin was placed in the wooden mausoleum between the two children.

When Anna Johnson died in 1922, native sandstone from the ranch was used to build an eighteen-foot square mausoleum on "Salt Point" which overlooked a shallow, placid, mesquite and cactus valley. Anna Johnson considered this the most magnificent view on the ranch. The mother's casket was placed on one side, the father's on the other side, the two children in the center, and the crypt was sealed forever. On one corner of the mausoleum there was a marble tablet with the inscription:

> "Residents of Palo Pinto County from the year 1880. Pioneers in the development of our natural resources. Leaders in all matters of material and moral progress. Their works do follow them."

Sadly, Anna Johnson and her only surviving child Fannie were never reconciled; consequently, Anna left her estate to her cousin, Cornelia Crocker, and Anna's Last Will expressed extreme bitterness toward daughter Fannie and Anna's sister Mattie:. . .

THIRD

> (...Gratitude is expressed to Anna's cousin Cornelia Crocker who cared for Anna in her last sickness, and who was ...) "all that an own daughter should have been; that my daughter Fannie Campbell has since infancy lived exclusively with her aunt, my Sister, Mrs. Martha K. Wellington, who resides in Denver, Colorado; that said sister is able to, and in all probability will, amply provide for my said daughter..."

EIGHTH

If there is anything left after all debts, legacies and obligations, Fannie Campbell would be the beneficiary.

NINTH

If all my obligations consume the estate "...It is my will and desire that my said daughter Fannie shall have no share or part whatever of my said property and estate."

TENTH

If Daughter Fannie Campbell opposed the probate of this will, "...she shall not in any event take or be entitled to any part of my property or estate..."

Mausoleum of Johnson Family

NINETEEN

Since 1894 the miners of Thurber had groused along on extremely low pay, but nothing could be done without Union organization. The $1.00 a ton for mining coal was misleading because of Hunter's screening method for weighing coal. When the mined coal was brought up it was dumped on a large screen which overlay another screen. The top screen had openings as big as a baseball while the bottom screen openings were smaller than the size of a walnut. The miners were paid only for the coal which would not fall through the top screen; this was used by the railroad. The coal which fell through the top screen and would not pass through the bottom screen was called "slack," and this was used for firing Hunter's brick kilns. Finally, the coal which fell through the openings of the bottom screen was called "nut" coal, and it was sold as industrial coal, mainly to Fort Worth breweries. It was strangely incongruous that the miners got nothing for the "nut" coal they mined, but they had to pay for the beer the "nut" coal brewed. When the strike came, the removal of the screens was a top priority.

By 1900 there were United Mine Workers locals in Strawn, Lyra and Rock Creek. By 1903 the UMW were ready to take on the Texas and Pacific Coal Company. Thurber's miners were more than ready for a Union, but organizing the men was an awesome task. Union organizers were severely dealt with in Thurber, for when they were identified as such; they were thoroughly roughed up by company guards and dumped outside the fence. Thurber was a closed city, and the guards around the barbed wire perimeter kept track of who came and went. The Pit Bosses watched closely for signs of Union activity, and miners were summarily fired on the Pit Boss's word. Firing was not too serious for the unmarried miners, for there was work five miles away at the Lyra and Strawn mines. But at these mines there was limited company housing, and this meant living conditions were more expensive and below Thurber standards. However, for the married miners who were fired, the problem of securing family housing in a new location was a worrisome concern.

There were informers who reported suspected Union activity. And there was a communications problem with sixteen different nationalities. Primarily, bilingual Italian, Polish and Mexican organizers were required, and these organizers had to have cunning and courage.

The mechanics of organizing the miners appeared straightforward. Tell what the Union was and what it could do; but again, this was no mean task with the diversity of languages. Hammer away at the idea a strike would succeed only if there were unanimity. Stress that everyone must join and all must stick together as a powerful group, able to thwart any company strike breaking attempts. Workers could join the UMW at any time, and when there was a majority, the Union served notice it represented the miners. Throughout this organizing process, keep the workers agitated.

Bruce and Stewart's saloon, just outside the company fence, was a hotbed of Union activity. Two Union men from outside Thurber would buy drinks for the house and then loudly discuss between themselves, the Union and the issues. There were informers everywhere, and the miners had to keep distance between themselves and the organizers, but the Union message came through. The language used in the discussion would vary; sometimes Italian, at other times Polish, Spanish or English.

Another tactic of the organizers was "hit and run". An organizer would hire on as a miner, and for a few days in the mine he preached unionism in one of the languages. Then he was gone, before the company could deal with him.

Pedro Salazar was enlisted to help organize the Mexicans. He had no family in Thurber; all his relatives lived in Mexico. He was bilingual with only a slight Mexican accent when he spoke English. He was light-skinned and taller than most Mexicans, and the Union took him out of the mines at Lyra to help organize the Thurber Mexicans. As an organizer he was paid twice what he made as a miner, but the pay was not that important, for he was a strong believer in Unionism as the only means to help his Mexican brothers. Several times he had appeared with another Mexican Union man at Bruce and Stewart's to loudly discourse on unionism. Somehow the risk and the thrill of Union organization appealed to him.

Pedro Salazar was concerned with the indifference of the Mexican miners toward unionism, and organization of the Mexicans had lagged far behind all ethnic groups. Part of the difficulty, he realized, was because of the innate Mexican fatalism, "What happens, happens." Secondly, many Mexican miners had wives and families and could ill afford to be fired for Union membership. Salazar wanted to goad the Mexicans into more action, and he contrived a sortie to Stump Hill where the Mexicans lived. He knew the guards at Thurber's gates would recognize him as Union, so he slipped under the fence near the brick plant at quitting time. With his light complexion he passed as an American, and after he mingled and walked with the workers towards Thurber, he angled off toward "Little Mexico," west of Thurber's Little Lake. He loitered around the lake until near dusk and then sauntered among the houses. With each man he met in the streets, he quietly introduced himself and gave his Union message.

Because of his successes that night, Pedro stayed on Stump Hill much longer than he had intended, and charged by the success of the evening, he was less wary as he made his way back to the fence near the brick plant. He was not thinking of a confrontation when he was startled by a company guard who was patrolling on foot. "Stop right where you are!" the guard challenged. "Move toward that light from the brick plant over there," he pointed with his pistol which was barely discernible in the darkness.

“Certainly, friend,” Pedro acceded. “I’m on my way to see my sweetie over the hill there. Have a drink of whiskey.” He offered his pint bottle to the guard.

The guard ignored the whiskey and kept the pistol pointed at the organizer’s belly. “Calling on a woman in working clothes at ten o’clock at night? You work in the brickyard, here? You got anything to show where you work? Keep your distance there; I’m lighting this lamp.” The night guards sometimes wore a miner’s cap and carbide lamp. The guard turned the lamp’s water hand, struck a match to the lamp and put it back on his head.

Salazar produced several money coins, a Thurber script book and a fake letter which was carried for situations just as Salazar now faced. The letter was addressed to “Thomas Kelley, Thurber, Texas,” and the writing was in a small feminine script. The Union had given Salazar the name from T & P Coal Company records which it had covertly obtained. The Union used the name listing to check off workers whom they believed could be counted on.

“All right, throw it down there, and back off,” the guard instructed. The guard glanced at the name on the letter then drew a small clothbound ledger from his back pocket. The carbide lamp blinded Salazar, but his eyes were adjusting, and he could see the guard checking the ledger.

“It doesn’t check, Mr. Kelley, or whoever you are” the guard smugly stated. “So we’ll just march on down to Captain Lightfoot’s office. My book shows a Thomas Kelley, but he quit here two months ago. You are trespassing on company property and at this time of night you are suspected of stealing or maybe damaging company property.”

Pedro Salazar weighed his chances. He did not want to be clubbed about by the guards and thrown outside the main gate as an example. The pistol was held waist high and Salazar had not heard a cocking click of the weapon. Deciding quick action was his only defense; Salazar took three quick steps, jumped and kicked at the guard's pistol which sailed away into the brush. Salazar completed his body roll and scrambled to regain his feet, but the guard quickly pulled his lead centered night stick out and was upon the Mexican. A vicious swipe at Salazar's head made a "clunk" sound as the connection was made, and it was the last sound Salazar would ever hear. The night stick crunched the left upper jawbone and the temple, and the union organizer never regained consciousness. The guard dragged the body a dozen yards into the brush outside the fence, recovered his pistol, and pocketed the whiskey, letter, script and money.

The buzzards and odor on a south wind led to the body three days later. The Erath County Sheriff was called and gave an opinion: "Murder, victim and assailant unknown, no clues." No one was charged with murder and the company buried the remains of Pedro Salazar on Graveyard Hill. The Thurber Mexicans learned of the murder, and while they suspected the company guards, said nothing. Salazar's death, however, was the catalyst the Mexicans needed, and when the Union oath was administered several months later to Thurber's miners, the Mexicans were in the front ranks.

With Robert Dickey Hunter's death in 1902, the miners required another focal point, and shifted their ire to W. K. Gordon, whom they derisively called "King Gordon." Edgar L. Marston, Hunter's son-in-law, succeeded Hunter as president, but he was absent from Thurber much of the time, preferring to run the company from New York. W. K. Gordon was extremely capable; let him deal with the problem of growing labor unrest.

In 1903 there were four coal mines in operation: Number 7, 8, 9, and 10. When a mine's passageways extended too far, there was difficulty in moving shale and coal, and this mine would be abandoned and a new shaft sunk. Every dollar T & P got from the miners, through sales of merchandise or services, or even from miserly wages, meant more money for shareholders. But Thurber 1903 was greatly different from Thurber 1894 when miner's pay was cut. By 1903 the company had a tremendous investment in Thurber: houses, utilities, merchandise, buildings, equipment, ice plant, power plant, livery stable, dairy, truck farm and brick plant. The company could not chance a strike which might endanger their investment. The miners were now in the driver's seat, but the company would try to bluff and bull its way through as had been done before. The Union organizers stressed to workers the vulnerability of the company, but with many diverse nationalities, there was difficulty in comprehending the concept of vulnerability. John Bertolli, because of his bilingualism, understood the Union and vulnerability, and as leader of the Italians, he would be a key man in organizing Thurber miners.

It was a February evening in 1903. John Bertolli was deeply depressed as he walked back to Italian Hill after a delicious dinner at Mama Mazzano's. But even such a superb dinner as rabbit stew polenta could not elevate John's mental state. The problem was money, enough money to marry and to support the Mazzano's first daughter, Giuseppa. For five years they had put off marriage, continuously hoping and praying that better pay would be forthcoming, but the prospects for more money looked as bleak as ever. How much longer could he expect Giuseppa to wait? There were dozens of young men who would jump at the chance to marry the comely Guiseppa. But fortunately for John, his contemporaries had the same financial problems.

John Bertolli had been working in the coal mines for almost fourteen years, and he was making less now than when he first came to Thurber. His pay for the last several years averaged forty-five dollars a month, but he still faithfully sent twelve dollars a month back to his family in Italy, and there was little left. His mining buddy, Pete Wasieleski, with three little ones now, was able to get by only because his wife Cecelia sewed for neighbors and friends.

John could make more money if he moved to the mines at Strawn or Lyra, but no, he was obligated to carry out his commitment he had made before W. K. Gordon several years previously; that the Union would come in and make the company see its mistake in cutting pay. He would try to improve pay and working conditions through Union efforts. His friends looked to John for leadership and guidance; he would never let them down.

For five long years Giuseppa had patiently waited. Wonderful, loving Giuseppa! So beautiful and appealing! Black hair, tied into a bun at the neck, framed an olive-skinned, oval face with turned-up nose and laughing black eyes. Now she was twenty-three, nine years younger than John. It seemed ages ago when Giuseppa, as a ten year old, practiced her English words with John. The two Mazzano daughters attended Hunter academy, a Catholic school staffed by six Sisters of Charity of the Incarnate Word, and English was one of the subjects.

When she was sixteen, Giuseppa was fully physically developed, and John was embarrassingly, disturbingly aware of this, just as he had been aware of her smiles and flirting with him since she was fourteen. But John was nine years older, and Giuseppa was being girlishly silly! John was not knowledgeable in the ways of young ladies; for he never had an opportunity to be involved. First, the seminary; then in Thurber, there simply were no ladies his age. There were men who sometimes missed a day or two of work to ride the train to Fort Worth to be with a lady of the night. But that took almost two weeks pay, counting the missed days of work. John danced with older women, the wives of friends, when there were celebrations, or when there were dances at boarding houses. And that was as near to a woman as most Thurber men could get.

But all this changed when Giuseppa turned eighteen, and Mama Mazzano took John aside, sternly admonished him, and set him straight. "Giovanni," Mama used the Italian name as she began her discourse. "You are a stubborn jackass! My Giuseppa is of age now. Can you not see Giuseppa has the calf eyes for only you? Guiseppa say, 'Mama, why Giovanni no like me?' And I say, 'Because he is stupid blind!'"

"But Mama," John feebly protested, "I am twenty seven, nine years older than Guiseppa and..."

Mama interrupted, eyes flashing. "So? And my husband is twelve years older than me when I marry at eighteen. And a better man and a stronger man in bed you cannot find than my Franco."

John's face burned from blushing at Mama's frankness and he fumbled for words to cover his embarrassment. "But, ah, I have so little money for the lady friend...I, ah..."

"Bosh! Nobody is asking for marry now! Be a mule!" And she turned her back to walk away. "That's all right. There are plenty of men. We need Giuseppa for cooking and in the ristorante, and I will find someone for her, someone who sees when a girl likes him, someone who is not so fearful of a girl."

"But wait! You think it would be good if I ask Giuseppa to the dance at Auda's Boarding House?"

"Of course, and that does not take the money. I know, and Giuseppa know, the mines no pay so much. The times is bad."

"And you think I am not too old?"

"I give you my holy word, but I tell you something, Giovanni. Giuseppa is good girl. You try something bad and I will take the butcher knife and cut your gizzard out. The marry and bambino come later in two, three year when you can be sure. There is time. Have fun when young."

The five years of their betrothal were the happiest of times for Guiseppa and John, and also maddening, uncertain times. The joyous heights of being together, making plans and sharing in the simple pleasures. The delightful dances, the Sunday dinners with the Mazzanos. Religious celebrations, holidays and band concerts. An occasional opera and, especially, since both were conversant in English, a play by a traveling road company. A moonlit walk, and the passionate longing, hungry, panting, petting which greatly heightened their need for each. But fortunately, there were few opportunities for privacy, and Mama Mazzano seemed to intrude at appropriate times. To give Giuseppa a baby without marriage would have been an unspeakable happening. Of course, John would have done the honorable thing, and a marriage would have to take place. But there would still be the problem of supporting a wife and baby. No. They would wait, excruciatingly difficult as it was.

True, conditions were very unsettled in Thurber, but there were subtle events taking place, good or bad, and Union pressure was being felt. Nothing out in the open, yet. Many rumors. The company made a show of bloodied Union men being cashiered out of Thurber. Union organizers had to be courageous and dedicated in their beliefs. Was the company strong enough, or ruthless enough, to thwart the Union? Certainly, the company would not give in without a prolonged fight; Hunter had set the policy fourteen years earlier. How bloody the fight? Dynamiting, destruction, killing? A Pyrrhic victory?

Time and again, John Bertolli relived his worst scenario. He would be strongly involved in the fight to improve the workers' status, for this was an underlying compassion for the downtrodden, and a characteristic which probably led him to the seminary at the age of sixteen. Fifteen years later, this humanitarian trait was more urgent because there was a firsthand, desperate need. If the Thurber mines closed would there be enough work in nearby Strawn and Lyra for all the miners? What of Guiseppa? He wanted so much for her, but in Strawn inexpensive housing with electricity and running water was not conveniently available. And Giuseppa's help was required in the family business. The conclusion was always the same; John would do what had to be done. First things first. If he could help speed the Union's work, his ordeal might quickly and favorably end, and he and Giuseppa would immediately marry. If the Thurber mines shut down, and the miners had to relocate in another part of the country, the Mazzanos' business would not survive, and they would also have to relocate. No matter. If love is strong, it will overcome all. But does it have to be filled with such nagging uncertainties?

As Bertolli, downcast and deep in thought, trudged back toward the fence and Italian Hill, he was joined by another figure who addressed him in hushed Italian. "Hello. Joe Fenoglio here who joins another who has momentarily escaped the confines of the barbed wire."

"I am John Bertolli. I have heard of Joe Fenoglio. Happy to make your acquaintance. But you must be careful!" John warned. "Speak quietly! I have seen what the company does to men who speak Union!"

"Yes. But so far so good!" Fenoglio chuckled. "They have to find me out, first. It is a game. The Union will give doctor's help if I am hurt, but I have no fear. My belief in our cause is stronger than being timid. As things are now, we are not much better here than in Italy, but we do have glorious hope for better conditions in Thurber if we fight."

"Shhh! Not so loud, Joe!" Bertolli cautioned. "You are right, but how do you know I can be trusted? The company pays the guards for finding Union men, and the guards pay the 'rats' who tell of Union men. I could be one who would tell the guards Joe Fenoglio is Union."

"Ah, John. But we are careful. We make some mistakes. You heard of the Mexican who was found dead by the brickyard? He was one of us. We go slowly until everything and everybody is ready, and then zap! We will squeeze the company until we get the pay we deserve, but we must all be together or all will be lost. It is known that several years ago, you spoke firmly to Mr. Gordon about the Union, and we also know you would marry Giuseppa Mazzano tomorrow if the pay were more. No. You are one of us," Fenoglio confidently stated.

“You are right,” Bertolli sighed. “I am ready, and I must do what I have to do. But if I am discovered, I might lose more than my job, for I might lose Giuseppa. I must be especially cautious.”

“If the company finds you out, the Union will get work for you in Strawn, or Lyra, or Rock Creek. Or they even pay your train to Illinois, Indiana or Pennsylvania. The United Mine Workers are strong all over America,” Fenoglio boasted.

“If we are victorious, what will our pay be?” Bertolli asked.

“First we will demand they remove the screens. In Strawn and Lyra they pay the miner for all the coal he digs. They don’t use screens. What do you guess? A fourth of the coal dug is lost to the screens? And then if we ask $1.15 a ton, we ought to make a third more money. Just think! We can make seventy cents or a dollar a day more!”

“Whew! That is good!” And John instantly visualized what a third more pay would mean to the miners.

“Yes. Even enough for marriage.” Fenoglio played on John’s emotions. “Will you help us?”

“How can I help?”

“You speak English. You understand what the bosses and big shots talk about. When you hear them say something bad about the Union or some miner, tell me what they say,” Fenoglio instructed.

“Yes. But we must be very careful. If I give you this information, Joe, you must never tell where it came from,” reminded John.

“You are right, John. Just as I cannot tell you who is working with us. But I can tell you that the entire organization of the United Mine Workers of America is behind us, and we will not fail if we have a little courage. The company cannot afford a strike. We will win. Just think of how you could help all workers, your friends and their families and Guiseppa.”

John held the barbed wire while Joe bowed through the opening. Joe continued the conversation as he, in turn, held the fence for John.

"Another way you can help, John, is to talk to miners you know and trust and are sure of. Tell of our plans, but never admit you are working for the Union and never make a definite statement about the Union. Always say, 'You heard', or 'Somebody said', or 'You read'. This is for your own protection."

"Yes. I understand. We cannot be too careful."

"We need Polish organizers. If you know some Polish miner who speaks English, please talk to him."

John instantly thought of Pete Wasieleski, but then had second thoughts. "I know one man who speaks some English. I taught him myself. I'll ask him, but I'm not sure because he has a family."

"I am happy you are with us, John. I have no wife or promise of a wife. If I am caught, I can always go back to my father's farm in Montague, Texas, north of here, near the Red River. Oh, one thing more before we part. Tell your friends you heard that after work next Friday, there will be free beer and eats at Bruce and Stewart's. Our president, Pete Hanraty, will speak on the Union. We hope to have two or three hundred miners there; the more the better. I work in Number 9. I will see you next Friday. Good fortune and good night."

John talked with and listened to miners. He and Pete made a mental list of miners who could be trusted and who might join the Union. There was note also of suspected "rats" and who could not be trusted. But careful as John was, he was reported for "suspected Union activity" and was told to report to the Mine Superintendent.

John Bertolli was well liked by miners of all nationalities. The "rat" suspected of informing on John was forthwith shunned and harassed. His tools disappeared, his lunch pail crushed and chunks of coal thrown at his back. After one day of being shunned, for his own safety, the "rat" was removed from the mine. Other potential informers took heed.

John knew he would be dismissed, no ifs, ands, or buts. With nothing to lose, he bypassed the Mine Superintendent and went straight to Mr. Gordon, because he wanted to have one last word with Mr. Gordon. As he walked toward Mr. Gordon's office, two dozen angry miners walked with him and milled about when John entered the office. Through his door, Mr. Gordon could see this display of support. He feigned surprise at seeing Bertolli. "Well, Mr. Bertolli. What's going on here? The Superintendent says 'suspected union activity'. Surely there has been some mistake for you to be accused of working against the company."

"I say there is a mistake, Mr. Gordon; a big mistake by the company, not by me. In America the law says you know who talk against you. 'Suspected union activity' is no proof who speaks against me. Who is this? How much did your guards pay him?" Gordon flinched at these last words, but Bertolli continued. "Company make big mistake when Mr. Hunter cut pay in 1894. I tell you then union come. Now T & P get big pay cut. Big mistake when company have Judas tell what you like to hear. I never think of you that way, Mr. Gordon." John boldly spoke out because he figured he was through in Thurber.

Coming from a man whom Gordon respected, these words were shocking and painful to Gordon. But once again, as in 1894, Gordon was in the crossfire between company policy and workers. "We are under strict instructions to remain a nonunion town, Mr. Bertolli," Gordon firmly informed Bertolli. "We had enough trouble with the Union when we first opened fifteen years ago. We've done well without the Union..."

Bertolli interrupted. "Yes. You and your company have done well, Mr. Gordon, but the workers, no. It is not the natural life the miner lives. Many men want to marry someday, and I know seven men, me too, who would marry tomorrow, but they do not make plenty money for the wife. It is like the seminary, a life of celibacy.

But here, this is not our choice, and the workers make big sacrifice to make T & P big company. The miners grow impatient, and every day you lose miners to Strawn and Lyra." John Bertolli knew he bordered on impudence, and had it been anyone but him, Gordon would not have permitted such frankness.

Outside, the crowd of miners had grown and Gordon heard: "Bertolli go, we go!" and "Bertolli no work, nobody work!" and "T P no! Union yes!" This outburst disrupted Gordon and he paused to listen briefly and looked toward the door, but he remained calm as he continued to state the company's position. "You know we cannot permit Union men to disrupt our operations, Mr. Bertolli?"

"Yes, your guards beat them up and throw them out the gate." And again, Gordon cringed at the words.

"I know nothing of that; that is not company policy." Gordon denied. "We do dismiss workers who don't agree with our policies," Gordon passively stated, now groping for a face-saving way out. It was touchy, for if he terminated their popular leader John Bertolli, the miners outside could get mean. President Marston had again requested Texas Ranger assistance, but the Rangers had not yet arrived.

As Gordon paused to sort his thoughts, Bertolli intruded, by softly summing up the situation. "You must do what you have to, Mr. Gordon, and the miners will do what they have to. One miner makes no difference, for now there will be a dozen miners take his place." Bertolli waited for Gordon to say the dreaded words: "Vacate the premises."

After further pause, Gordon said, "You must not get involved with the Union, Mr. Bertolli."

"And again I say, Mr. Gordon, where is the Judas who has made such an accusation?"

"I will discuss your situation further with the Superintendent. And in the meantime, please see that your friends outside behave in an orderly fashion. The Texas Rangers very shortly will be guarding our interests. We will let you know of our decision, Mr. Bertolli." But nothing more was ever said by the company to John.

Outside the crowd was jubilant to learn Bertolli was still with them, at least for the time being, and they marched to Mazzano's to celebrate. Bertolli's incident served to bolster the weak-hearted, enhance the Union, and indicated T & P Coal Company was uneasy with even the slightest Union activity.

It was Sunday morning and John Bertolli's head hurt. He had drunk too much birra the previous evening in celebration after his confrontation with W. K. Gordon. Hurting as he was, he had to see his mining partner, Pete Wasieleski, to warn him of the accusation made for "suspected Union activity". Pete might be accused of the same, merely from his association with John. But Pete was not a leader like John. In accusing John, perhaps the company feared John's influence with the men and only wanted to warn him. But Pete, with a wife and three small girls, could not chance losing his job. Pete would likely be at ten o'clock Mass. Difficult as it was, John rolled out of bed, for he had to obey the Third Commandment: "Remember to keep holy the Lord's Day." He had never missed Sunday Mass in Thurber.

After Mass, John went to Cecelia and Pete. "Good morning Mrs. Wasieleski, Pete. We must talk, Pete. Something important. Oh, my head hurts, I drank too much."

"Come to lunch, now then," Cecelia invited. "We are eating 'zupa kartoflana', potato soup in English, and fresh bread. That will help your head. And I will make you some 'plaski' from the bread dough. Pete has to lay brick and I must sew two Communion gowns. So we eat early."

John relished "plaskis", thin pieces of bread dough fried in deep grease. "Ah, Cecelia. My head feels better already just thinking of 'plaskis'. Thank you."

The conversation was in English, and Pete and Cecelia were forever grateful to John for being able to speak the language. The English words which John taught Pete while at work were relayed to Cecelia, thereby enabling both Cecelia and Pete to speak and to write passable English. When they had time in the long summer evenings, Pete and Cecelia went to evening English classes taught by the Catholic Sisters. Polish was seldom spoken at home around the three Wasieleski daughters, for the parents wanted the girls to speak proper English.

With the availability of brick from the Thurber Brick Plant, all new company buildings and some structures and accessories were made of brick. After 1900 there was a building boom in nearby Thurber Junction. Pete had a natural ability for laying brick. Pete practiced at home and helped neighbors with sidewalks, cellars, cisterns, flower beds, wash houses and foundations. After several months he was augmenting his mining pay by laying bricks. Wife Cecelia, as an expert seamstress, was also busy sewing for neighbors and friends when three lively daughters would permit her the time. Although it was Sunday, Cecelia and Pete, after dinner with John, would work at their second jobs until dark.

At Pete's home, after a few gulps of beer, John's head felt better, and he told of being reported for Union activity and of his meeting with Gordon. "If they turned me in, Pete, since we work together, I fear they'll suspect you, too. You must not say or do one thing more about the Union. The company is worried, and the guards get a reward for each Union man they find. It will be sorry for a married man with a family like you to be out of work."

Pete was astounded that someone would betray John. "Who would report you, John?"

"Lenzinni and I, we talk about the Union's free beer at Bruce and Stewart's next Friday. I look over by the tracks, and Barton, you know the fat, lazy one who works with Jackson? Well, he was bent over, behind a car, like he was hiding. We think he is the one. Have you seen how he always tries to talk to the pit boss? The men will make Barton sorry; they have plans for him Monday. A man would be out of his mind to work against the Union because it's our only hope."

"God forbid, John, but if the company makes me leave, we will have to move to Strawn and live with brother Pavel and his wife. They have no babies, yet, and it will be crowded, but that is what we will have to do."

Cecelia set a plate of "plaskis" in front of John and announced, "We will eat in ten minutes."

"Thank you, Cecelia, this will make me well." Then to Pete, John commented, "I envy you so much, Pete. You have a wonderful wife, a happy home and three lovely daughters. If we get the Union, Giuseppa and I can marry, and perhaps someone will envy me," he grinned.

"Thank you, John. And I thank God for Cecelia. There is no greater joy than a caring wife and a healthy family. You will see. But it has been hard the last several years with poor pay. I don't get the wife and daughters everything I want for them. We need a bigger house. Already the girls need more room. I promise you I will let up with the Union business. Pete Galik is doing good work with most of the Polish miners. I will tell him of our talk."

After leaving the Wasieleskis, John headed for Mazzano's. Some of last night was not too clearly fixed in his mind, and he had a great need to ease his troubled conscience. He greeted Franco and Mama and kissed Giuseppa. "I must apologize for drinking too much last night," he addressed the family.

"Bosh!" retorted Mama as she quickly put John at ease. "Every man is need umbriaco when he have bad time! We worry you no have job. But all is good. Everybody happy, have good time. No be sorry."

Later Giuseppa poutingly told John, "You hold me too strong last night, and I have bruises where you pinch me, here." And she indicated her breasts. "And you bite my lip. I like better be gentle."

"Dear Seppa. I'm sorry. I will always try to be gentle, I love you so much, but I was happy and drunk because I would not be leaving you. You have never seen me drink so much. It is a sin. If the Union goes good, maybe in two, three months we can marry, make bambino."

These words changed the pout into a smile, and Giuseppa purred, "Oh, John, I want that so much!"

After a good night's sleep, John felt refreshed and ready for work, eager to watch for Union developments.

Texas Ranger Captain John H. Rogers and several Rangers appeared in Thurber two days later. It was the fourth appearance in Thurber for the Rangers. But the presence of the Rangers this time worked both ways; while the Rangers protected company officials and property, company guards were more restrained in using violence to stifle Union activity.

After work most miners usually stopped by a saloon for a drink to "cut the coal dust". The company's Lizard saloon on Polander Hill was convenient to most miners since this was near the place where most miners got off the train which carried them from the mines. But not this Friday evening. With the Union standing for free drinks and eats, Bruce and Stewart's was crowded elbow to elbow. Pete Hanraty, UMW District President, moved through the crowd, careful not to shake hands with anyone for fear of informers, but he bobbed his head to all as he loudly emphasized he was from the United Mine Workers of America. He banged his hand on the bar to quiet the crowd, asking for their attention, and then he paused until the murmuring stopped.

"I'm Pete Hanraty of the United Mine Workers of America. I won't take too much of your time---there's too much to eat and drink. We thank Bruce and Stewart for the use of this place. These boys are one of us and deserve your trade." Hanraty led the applause.

"I know we have many different nationalities here this evening, and it would be hard to arrange for several different interpreters. So if you don't mind, I'll speak in English. Because that's all I know, but I'm sure you will understand enough to make out what I have to say. Everybody can understand this." Hanraty held up a piece of cardboard with a large "NO SCREEN, $1.15 A TON" printed on it. This brought loud cheers and foot stomping.

"How about this?" Another piece of cardboard with "T & P" printed on it. With a great flourish, Hanraty scribbled through this with colored chalk. Loud boos.

"This?" Another piece of cardboard with "UMW" emblazoned on it. Loud cheers and applause.

"We want everybody here to join the United Mine Workers Union. This is the only way we can get our pay raised. T & P cannot afford a strike. But they will try to show us they are more powerful than us. If T & P shuts down the mines the Union will get you work in Strawn, Lyra or Rock Creek. And if need be, we are prepared to pay your train fare to other parts of the country for work. They may shut down the Thurber Mines for a short while, but we will call their bluff. We must be together and have courage. The company is afraid of us because they know what the United Mine Workers Union has done in other parts of the country. The company guards beat us up and have 'canaries' sing for them to betray their fellow workers. And I know we have some 'canaries' here tonight. And I understand some of you have questions you want to ask, but we have to be careful, or the 'canaries' will sing for the guards, or 'King Gordon', or Marston. And while I think of it, another thing we demand from the company is the removal of the barbed wire fence. Talk this over with your friends you know and trust. We are almost ready for the final push. Be patient and strong. Please join the Union when we ask you to sign. We will win! WIN! WIN!" And the responding cheer concluded his remarks.

When the canaries flew to the company officials, the officials did not take pleasure in what they heard of the meeting.

Pete Hanraty could make his fearless remarks because he was not employed by T & P, but UMW District 21 President Hanraty could back his talk up with extraordinary bravery, for a month later, disguised in full beard, mustache and sideburns, he applied for work at the Thurber Brick Plant. His "work" was to sell the brick workers on Unionism. Because most of the brickworkers spoke English, Hanraty had little trouble in getting his message across. Hanraty "worked" only a few weeks at the brick plant before leaving Thurber, but he did his "work" well, for when the time came to strike, the brick workers were ready.

Near the end of August 1903, William Wardjon, International Organizer for the UMW and unknown to T & P officials, came to Thurber from Illinois. A few days after he began working in the mines, he hurt his hand. Unable to work because of his hand, the bandaged hand gave him an excuse to wander about the mine selling Unionism and announcing a Labor Day rally to organize the miners. The rally would be held in Lyra, where Lyra's union miners hoped to give encouragement and support to Thurber's miners in joining the union. Also, in Lyra, Thurber's miners would not be under the surveillance of "rats" or company guards.

The atmosphere in Thurber was energized. There was an expectancy, an excitement; something was about to happen. Hanraty, Fenoglio and Wardjon stepped up their organizing efforts; the time seemed ripe for the Union to make its move.

W. K. Gordon tried to thwart the Lyra Union rally by promoting a company-sponsored Labor Day party. In the company paper and in distributed circulars, it was announced that on Labor Day the company would open up the exclusive Big Lake Club and grounds to everyone, something that had never been done before. Free eats, drinks, music, speeches, games and a look at the facilities where the company "big shots" spent their leisure time.

There were over a thousand people at the company's Big Lake picnic on Labor Day 1903. Most wandered the grounds out of curiosity to see where management played. Others came for the free beer and food. To counter this Thurber Labor Day celebration the United Mine Workers at Lyra had free beer and was ready to swear miners into a Thurber Local. About two dozen strongly "pro-Union" miners made the eight-mile trek to Lyra; the walk made easier by two kegs of beer on a mule-drawn wagon and some miners riding on the wagon.

With much pomp and formality, most of these miners were sworn into the Union, among them John Bertolli. All these miners present at Lyra that day were given a rousing, fiery pep talk by Wardjon, and twenty newly sworn-in Union men went back to Thurber to fire up other miners. After a few days, the majority of miners were ready to strike for Union recognition. Accordingly, on September 9, Union officials demanded the UMW be recognized as representative for the miners, that the coal screens be eliminated, that wages be upped, that the guards and fence around Thurber be removed and that eight hours constitute a working day.

In response, the company tossed out "crumbs"; $1.05 a ton, rather than the current $1.00 a ton, (but no mention of the coal screens), a nine-hour working day and a 7:00 a.m. train departure for the mines, rather than 6:30 a.m. Gordon followed this with a statement that Thurber would remain a non-union camp. Any worker disagreeing with this policy would be paid off immediately. Gordon's offer was an insult which incited the workers to march off. On September 10, 1903 a trickle of miners converged into a stream of 800 miners who flowed northward on the Thurber-to-Junction road, two miles to Thurber Junction, across the Palo Pinto Creek bridge, then northward to Rocky Creek, which was a mile north of the Junction and midway between Thurber and Lyra. Here, on this site, at the wooden bridge spanning the narrow creek, one of the most impressive but little known scenes in labor history took place. From Lyra, 200 union members marched eastward to

Rocky Creek to meet their Thurber brothers in a display of support. The Lyra miners on the north side of the bridge somberly watched as the Thurber Mexicans on the southeast side of the bridge, with hat in hand and the other hand raised, repeated the Union oath in Spanish. On the southwest side of the creek, the Thurber Italians, Poles and other nationalities repeated the oath in their languages. After loud cheers, miners from both camps mingled and excitedly talked with each other. Wardjon, speaking slowly, so interpreters could relay, congratulated the new UMW members and told them of plans to vacate the mines. The miners were to stay out of the mines until District President Hanraty told them to return to work.

Company officials dejectedly watched as the miners marched off to Rocky Creek. The mines were deserted and this was the day the company dreaded. Gordon issued an aggrieved statement: "The Union demands an unreasonable pay increase which amounts to $1.35 per ton. The company cannot grant this demand; it will go out of business first." The strike was on.

District President Hanraty called the miners together on Friday, September 11, in Grant's Town. Through interpreters, he told the miners they had won a great victory by being organized and that they should vacate company housing and draw whatever pay they were due. The Union would find jobs in nearby Strawn or Lyra or in the northern coal fields, and food and shelter would be provided for families and workers. He urged the miners to remain united and strong, and he stressed higher pay, being paid twice a month, and being able to freely shop in Thurber Junction and Gordon at lower prices than in company stores.

The company put on a show that, indeed, it would carry out its threat "to go out of business first." On Saturday September 12, 1903 the company began paying off. It took until noon Sunday to get everyone paid up. On Sunday the company train made a special trip to the mines to allow the miners to get their tools. The Rangers went along to prevent vandalism, but they need not have bothered because the miners were sober and orderly.

As the people began to withdraw from the city, an unreal, uncanny silence blanketed Thurber. All stores, industries and homes were closed. A column of pedestrians, wagons and buggies loaded down with possessions moved northward toward the Junction and Lyra, not unlike refugees escaping an advancing army. By Tuesday Thurber was abandoned. It was as if a plague had wiped out the city. Texas Ranger Captain Rogers and the Rangers feared the worst during the withdrawal, but were happy that no malice, drunkenness or rowdyism occurred during the departure. Some miners returned to Italy, fully believing this was the end of Thurber, and not comprehending how labor negotiations could reopen the mines.

John Bertolli was going to the Illinois mines for two reasons. First, if he stayed in Lyra or Strawn, he might have taken a job from some married miner who needed to be with his family. Secondly, Pete Hanraty, Union District President, had asked him to study the Union setup in the Illinois mines. The most troublesome task in leaving Thurber would be the separation from Giuseppa, and as the day of departure approached, the tears increased.

"Sweet Seppa, you must not cry. How can I tell you that in just a short while I will return and everything will be fine? The pay will be better, and we can be married."

"But John, what if the mines do not open again?" she sniffed.

"Then you come to Illinois and we can be married. Maybe your whole family will come. But have no fear; we must have faith in God and the Union. Do you think the company would close down forever the houses, mines and buildings with all the money they have spent?" he reassured her.

"No, but they could bring in more workers to take your place."

"If the company tried this, the Union would make strikes all over the country in protest and factories would shut down. This is why the Union is so important and powerful."

"Oh John, I cannot help crying. I must be brave like the other women whose men must leave them. I love you and will miss you and will pray for you." One last embrace and John ran for the special train which would take him to the Illinois mines and away from Guiseppa.

John's mining buddy, Pete Wasieleski, would go with him to the southern Illinois coal mines. Since the local mines could not absorb all the Thurber miners; some married men had to go to Illinois if they wanted to work. Pete's wife and three girls had a place to stay in Strawn with Pete's brother Pavel and his wife. One other family would also share Pavel's house, as it was not uncommon at this difficult time for two or three families to share the same house.

Pete had trouble explaining to three small daughters, Valerka, Lottie and Stella, why he had to put all his clothes in one suitcase. Pete's eyes were watery as he had the last few moments with his family.

"Cecelia, darling. It will be hard for you with three little ones, especially crowded in one house. I will think of you and pray we will soon be back together. Everything turns out for the best. That is God's way. Remember that. Soon I will return, and we will make more money, and the fence will be gone, and we can shop in Thurber Junction at the dry goods store. We can even buy you a sewing machine when we get the higher pay," Pete tried to cheer Cecelia.

"Yes, Pete. We will be fine. Do not worry for us. It is you traveling to a far place that has to worry. Please write soon. We will miss you."

"You girls mind Mama and when I come back I will have a present for you." A kiss for each and Pete turned away before the tears began.

T & P Coal Company spent $30,000 trying to bring strikebreakers as Hunter did before in 1888, but the Union was able to stop all but three men from entering Thurber. The three became known as the "$30,000 men."

About a week after the strike began, Edgar L. Marston, President of T & P Coal, came down from New York, finally realizing that his presence might be needed. In Fort Worth he asked for a conference with Wardjon and Hanraty and then issued a long, rambling statement to the press on the company's past troubles with organized labor. But he made no mention of the screening method of weighing coal, or of the drastic pay cut in 1894, or of the strength-sapping task of digging at a thirty inch layer of coal from a prone position, or any of the other irksome work conditions. In this obloquy, he gave a blatant falsehood: "There has been no dissatisfaction, grumbling, no upheaval nor strike from 1888 to September 1903."

He wound up his discourse with the usual: "The Union demands would mean bankruptcy. The company executives will man the mines as they had in the past." Another conspicuous lie.

In spite of those bombastic misstatements, when Marston met with Wardjon and Hanraty, he agreed to recognize the Union and its demands. The company was not about to consider bankruptcy, for there was money to be made even when the Union demands were fully met. Marston knew this, and the Union knew this.

On September 20, 1903, over 1000 men, miners as well as other Thurber workers, walked from Lyra and Strawn to a lifeless Thurber. But the Thurber Opera House overflowed for the first Union meeting ever held in Thurber. An important announcement was expected. Marston, Gordon and Union officials Hanraty and Wardjon arrived in Marston's private railroad car on the spur which ran through downtown Thurber, only fifty yards from the opera house. It was a very dramatic appearance. The important announcement was that an agreement had been reached between the company and the Union and that contract details would be worked out next week.

With removal of the coal screens, and $1.15 a ton, the contract meant a thirty-five percent pay increase, an eight-hour day, bimonthly pay, Union dues deducted from pay, removal of guards and fence, free transportation to mines and a payment of $25. to the deceased's family if accidental death occurred in the mines.

Thurber workers, other than the miners, were also organized at this time by C.W. Woodson, Secretary of the Texas Federation of Labor, and Thurber became the first city in America to be one hundred percent unionized with seven different unions recognized: miners, clerks, meat cutters, bartenders, carpenters, machinists and brick workers.

After the strike, and probably for the first time in America, the Union put its symbol on each brick: an impressed triangle with a letter "B", a "T" and another "T" at each apex of the triangle. The "B T T" stood for Brick, Tile and Terra-cotta workers.

On October 8, 1903, John Mitchell, President of UMW of America, granted a charter to the Thurber Local Union No. 2538. John L. Lloyd and William McKinnon were president and secretary, respectively, of the Thurber local.

Labor Day, September 7, 1903, began a memorable month in labor history, for the Thurber miners' strike was the first significant strike in Texas, and the activity during this period was consequential for the labor movement in the southwest.

Three years after the first miners Local was formed, John Bertolli helped organize a second and larger miners' Local for Italians when the first Local remained indifferent to the foreign-born miners.

TWENTY

In mid-October 1903, with the aftermath of the strike settling down, John Bertolli and Pete Wasieleski jubilantly, triumphantly returned from Illinois to loved ones in Texas. They jokingly referred to their journey as a vacation. After the joyous tears and kisses subsided, John showed Giuseppa the matching wedding bands he had bought in Fort Worth.

"Oh, John! How pretty!" squealed Giuseppa. "This means we can be married soon! When?"

John, straight-faced, teasingly asked, "Would next summer be too soon?"

Giuseppa's mood shifted to a pout about to burst into tears. "But, John! You said as soon as the strike was over we could be married! You know I want your bambino now!"

"Dearest Seppa. After being separated from you for two months, you know I could never wait until next summer. I want to make bambino with you now," he playfully, hungrily embraced Giuseppa.

"John! Don't make fun like that!" Giuseppa giggled. "We can talk to father Baker after Mass Sunday and as soon as Father Baker can pronounce the wedding banns we can be married. You come tonight and we plan the wedding. Mama and Papa have a surprise for you. Oh John, I've prayed the rosary every night while you were gone, and now my prayers have been answered." Giuseppa's tears began.

Pete had cloth dolls for each of his daughters and a bolt of cloth for Cecelia. The next day a wagon carried the Wasieleskis from Strawn to their house in Thurber. In a month's time, Thurber was nearly back to normal, the inconveniences of the strike forgotten, as the people reveled with more money and freedom in shopping.

Mama and Franco Mazzano had not one surprise for John, but two surprises. As a dowry, they would give Giuseppa deed to five acres on the Back Road to Thurber Junction. This was a half-mile from Mazzanos and close enough that Guiseppa could help each day in their business. The Mazzanos had acquired the five acres from Art Rumford as settlement of his bill at Mazzanos.

Art Rumford was in his sixties, a widower with no family; a hard drinking, roughhewn man who was one of the early settlers of the area. He owned four hundred acres on the east side of the Back Road where he raised and sold cattle to the Thurber slaughter-house. When Rumford got drunk at the company saloon in downtown Thurber, he often had fights with the guards at the gates; therefore, he did most of his drinking at Bruce and Stewart's or at Mazzano's. Rumford liked Mazzano's Italian food and the crusty, chewy Italian bread. Several times when he was too drunk to get home, the Mazzanos would let him sleep it off on the floor, looking after his money, putting a pillow under his head and covering him with a quilt. After several drinks, Rumford became careless with his money; consequently, the Mazzanos suggested a charge account for his eats and drinks. When the bill grew to eighty dollars, it was Rumford who proposed settlement by trading some of his land. "Hell, I got no family, just relatives in England. You folks are the closest family I got, and you been good to me. I'm getting old and I got enough money and land to do me. Thurber Junction will grow now that the strike's over. Think I'll sell the land along the road. Lots of folks wanting to move out of Thurber, own their own house. I know Giuseppa will marry soon, and John Bertolli's a fine man for her. What do you say; I trade you five acres for the bill I owe you? I'll have judge Ritchie draw up the papers." And the five acres became the homestead of Mr. and Mrs. John Bertolli, Thurber Junction, Texas.

Over polenta with field lark stew and their best wine, Mama Mazzano happily planned the wedding. She was thrilled that her

Giuseppa would at last be married to a handsome, outstanding man like John Bertolli, and she mentally compared John to her Franco in her marriage twenty-five years earlier. She was pleased the children would be American-born, and life would be much easier than she and Franco had known.

Mama Mazzano sprang her second surprise. "Eh, John. Where you and Giuseppa live? The T & P no hava house six room. You, Giuseppa maka many bambino, taka big, big house."

Embarrassed, Bertolli stammered, "The Company gave us number 774. That's not too far from here, next to Spagmolli. Three rooms are big enough for now."

Mama Mazzano felt the wine and carried the humor to its fullest, as she giggled away at John and Guiseppa's discomfiture. "For sure, John, you, Guiseppa have so much love, mabbe you maka two, tree bambino one time. Tree room house not so big." When her giggling subsided, she took another sip of wine and said, "You builda house on land by Meester Rumford. We giva money now, Giuseppa work here, helpa us til bambino come nine month. We helpa you, you maka much money now. Pay back when you have the money. Franco and me get old. Needa bambino maka young again, eh Franco? You needa garden, grape, cow, chicken, fresh milk for bambino, eh John, Giuseppa?"

The stunned John protested, for he had always paid his own way, but his future mother-in-law would have her way. The wedding date was Saturday, November 21, 1903.

The wedding gift from the Wasieleskis was that Pete would do the brickwork for the Bertolli home. Cornerstones, chimneys, fireplace, cellar, cistern and bread oven. As Pete laid the brick, he dreamed of the time when he and Cecelia would own land on the Back Road. Perhaps neighbors to John. Owning land in America! As much as one could afford! But Pete didn't want much land. Maybe enough so that each of his daughters could have a dowry of several acres. In Pete's native Poland, the majority of people were peasants, and it was the magnates or the King who owned all Polish land. Oh, there were some small landowners, who, through courage in battle, or service to the King or magnates, were given small pieces of land. These small plots were efficiently cultivated to earn money which bought a little more land. In Poland the small landowners strived to acquire enough land so that each son would be given land when he married. But Pete had no sons yet.

After the ordeal of the strike, Thurber was ready for a wedding celebration. John and Guiseppa's wedding would be the excuse for effusive festivity. Thurber would never see another Italian wedding like the Bertolli's. Father Baker announced the wedding banns on three successive Sundays, and the long-delayed wedding took place.

On Friday, the day before the wedding, the cooks gathered at Mazzano's. The main wedding dish of "rissotto," rice cooked in chicken soup, gizzards, livers, ketchup and cheeses, was prepared in a wash tub. Fifty loaves of Italian bread would be fresh out of several ovens tomorrow morning. There would be spaghetti, ravioli, cheeses, salami of several varieties, and the salad would be freshly mixed tomorrow morning. The delicious pastry, crostoli, took all afternoon to make. The dough was rolled out paper thin, cut in strips, shaped into a bow, fried, and then rolled in sugar.

Friday evening after work, John's friends steered him to all saloons except Mazzano's. First the Snake Saloon where W. K. Gordon, seeking to renew John's friendship with the strike over, bought the drinks and toasted the groom to be. Then Bruce and Stewart's, Sealfi's, Corona's, Castaldo's, Rochetti's and the Lizard. There was much ribaldry and toasting, for John Bertolli was well-liked, and all nationalities recognized his work with the union in improving working conditions.

"Hey, Giovanni! We count. Nine months after tomorrow, you have bambino!"

"No! No! Nine months and one day! Vino, birra, much umbriaco. Have sick wedding night. Sleep!"

"No more two-ton day, Giovanni. Too tired for dig coal. One half ton, mabbe."

"No be worry, Giovanni. We each put one piece coal on your pile."

"Be sorry for Giovanni's buddy, Pete. Now, poor Pete do all hard work. Giovanni too weak."

"Giovanni. You marry, thinka Giuseppa alla time. No maka money America. Go back Old Country."

As John and the wedding attendants stood under the circular archway to the altar of St. Barbara's, John was distracted by the thoughts which flashed through his mind. Unable to concentrate on the Wedding Mass, John thought of the first Mass said in St. Barbara's, of Fathers Brickley and Fabrio, of the two years he spent in the Seminary in Italy. How fortunate that he should have someone as wonderful and lovely as Giuseppa, and the thought that he and Giuseppa would be together that night sent ripples up his spine. He thought of a different life in Italy and of the hard work but good life in America. How grateful he was to be in Thurber and America and to own his own home and land. Would he be a good father and husband? So many friends and the hard fight for the union. Then Pete Wasieleski, the Best Man, nudged John to kneel, and John blinked his eyes to clear the reverie.

The wedding dance was at the Italian Dance Pavilion, one of the three open-air dance pavilions in Thurber. There were three bands, each in a different corner of the pavilion. Dan Raffael and the Hunter Band played the waltzes, and as soon as one band finished a song, another band would begin. Sometimes all three bands played together. When there was need for food, Mazzano's was a short distance away, and when hunger was satiated, more drinking and dancing at the pavilion followed.

John and Giuseppa were escorted to their new home sometime after midnight, along with much drunken singing and gaiety, and the singing and harassment of the wedded couple continued for the few remaining hours of the night. The customary shivaree was more boisterous than usual. Someone tied a stick of dynamite to a fence and lit the fuse. The drunken revelers scrambled, fell and staggered away from the fizzing fuse, barely gaining safe distance before the blast.

It was a raggedy, sick bunch at the late Mass on Sunday. John and Giuseppa made it to Mass in spite of no sleep, for John had never missed a Sunday Mass at St. Barbara's. The congregation snickered when Father Baker wryly remarked he was happy to see the newlyweds in Church, and then added there was plenty of food and drink left. "But please don't start until the Mass is over." Louder laughter.

When the guards were removed from the gates at Thurber, the suburb of Thurber (Thurber Junction), to the north, grew as businesses opened to cater to shoppers from Thurber. Among the first of the dozen stores to open in the Junction was a grocery/feed store by Joe Abraham and a dry goods store by Tom George. The two were Lebanese immigrants with Americanized names. Joe Abraham provided a convenient grocery service because he realized many mothers could not go out for shopping; therefore, he drove his buggy to Thurber each day where he delivered orders and took orders for delivery the next day.

Joe Abraham's business success again illustrated the many opportunities which America offered. Abraham knew the Junction would grow once Thurber opened up, and he bought land south of the main rail line, cleared it, and then sold it to businesses which he thought would help the Junction prosper. Abraham also foresaw the need for a bank because Thurber had no bank with its use of script for money, and he chartered the Thurber Junction State Bank in 1907. Joe Abraham was religious, compassionate and civic-minded, but he was too busy making money at a younger age to consider marriage. Finally, at the age of fifty he felt financially secure for marriage, but he made up for lost time, for in the next eighteen years he fathered eleven children, the last at his age of sixty-eight.

Immigrants were not totally accepted outside of Thurber, and native-born Americans kept their distance. In Thurber Junction, Anglo-Saxon Protestants segregated themselves by building homes and businesses on the north side of the main T & P rail line, and this part of town was called Mingus. Foreign born entrepreneurs opened businesses and built homes south of the main T & P rail line in Thurber Junction: Abraham, George, Taramino, Galik, Gazzola, Auda, Vietta, Nader, Meneghetti, Castaldo, Gobel and Angelo Reck.

As Thurber Junction continued to grow, a first class depot was built in 1906. The Junction, in addition to being a shipping point for a dozen coal cars a day, was also a coaling/watering/dining stop for trains. A rail car repair shop was opened a short distance south of the Junction on the rail spur to Thurber,

Pete Wasieleski continued with his after-work and weekend brick-laying and Cecelia continued to sew for neighbors. A son, Bolesaw, was born in 1904, and Pete was overjoyed that the name "Wasieleski" would be perpetuated. The only thing missing in the Wasieleski's life was that of owning land and a home. Their savings slowly grew, but not enough before all of Rumford's land on the Back Road was sold, and Pete disconsolately realized he would not own the land he desired.

A few times a month, on long summer evenings, Pete, Cecelia and the children would stroll the mile to the Bertollis for a pleasant visit and dinner. John and Pete, sipping on a bottle of wine, would look over John's garden, grape arbor and animals. The girls would play with the animals or fish in the pond. Cecelia would help Giuseppa with sewing and cooking.

Pete couldn't help but be envious of John's homestead. How Pete yearned for his own land! To feel the soil between his fingers! They said Texas was too hot and dry to grow anything. Bah! Give me some land and I will show them! Sometimes after visiting, Pete would be dejected because land seemed so far out of reach, and Cecelia would try to reassure Pete. "Sweetheart, there will be other land. I know the land on the Back Road was what we wanted, near the Bertollis, but perhaps Rumford will sell some land on the road to Gordon. If we just keep saving and praying, things will work out."

Pete would glumly reply, "Yes, I know you are right. But land is getting scarcer and costs more than ever. No matter how much we save, it seems we will never have enough. I'm sorry, Cecelia, but I must have some land to work! It's in my blood! Just to plant the corn with my own sweat and to see it grows! But I need to always be humble and remind myself of the terrible conditions we left behind in our dear Poland, and how fortunate we are just to be in America."

In the summer of 1907, Pete bricked a cellar for Joe Abraham. In casual conversation, Pete mentioned his need for land in Thurber Junction, and in particular, on the Back Road to Thurber.

Joe said, "Pete, I might be able to work something out for you. A man left town owing the bank three hundred dollars. There are about five acres and a house that needs work on it, but it's worth more than three hundred. If you can pay me four hundred, I'll foreclose on this. It's east of here, on the Back Road, next to Thornberg's. Would you be interested in this?"

"Yes sir! Only God knows how much I want to own my own land! Thank you!"

"Then, I have some long overdue personal loans on three adjoining lots, maybe four or five acres in all. Would you be interested in this, also?"

"Oh, yes sir! If I have that much money," Pete apprehensively responded.

"Pete, I will tell you Thurber Junction is growing, and that the land we speak of is worth the money. If you don't have the money, I'm sure we can work something out at the bank. I've delivered groceries to your house for several years, and you've always paid cash. You're one of the best brick masons around here, and I know how hard both you and Cecelia work. We need people like you in Thurber Junction. Let's you and Cecelia and I sit down and talk about this."

"Please, Mr. Abraham. Let us surprise Cecelia. Could only you and I talk about this?"

That evening Cecelia noted Pete's ebullience. "Piotr! Have you had too much beer?"

"No, Kochanie. Do I have to have beer to be happy?" Pete flippantly questioned. "I have a beautiful wife, three lovely daughters, a fine son, good health and we are American citizens. What else would I need to make me happy?"

"Piotr," Cecelia admonished, "I can tell. If it's not beer, then I know you have some good news. What is it?"

"No---Nothing. If I am happy, then it will have to be a surprise." And Pete began to hum his favorite waltz melody, "Beautiful Ohio". As curious as Cecelia was, she could not get it out of Pete. Her Pete could be stubborn at times. What Pete was hiding would have to wait.

A week later Joe Abraham presented a proposal which staggered Pete: ten acres in all, adjoining, with two houses for $700. Pete could repair one house and rent it to miners for "batching" privileges, and this would almost be enough to pay off a two-year bank note. Pete had almost four hundred dollars saved. Since 1903 the Wasieleskis had put aside eight dollars a month, difficult as it was, but now the sacrifices were well worth it. But even at that, they would be three hundred dollars in debt! So much money! Then add the interest! What if something should happen to Pete before it was paid?

"Insurance, Pete. For two dollars a month, if something happens to you, permanently crippled or death, everything would be paid and Cecelia would own it all."

But Pete had misgivings because this was the biggest, gravest decision he faced in America. The property was about a half-mile from John Bertolli's home, and Pete asked John to look over the place and advise him. John was emphatic that Pete should buy. "You will never get another chance for land like this. Mr. Abraham has done a big job in getting all this ten acres together for you. Pete, you make some money by laying brick, and the "batch" house will almost make the payments. Take this. If you don't want it, I'll sell my place to you, and I'll buy this," John urged Pete.

Joe Abraham cosigned Pete's note, and after Pete signed the papers, his eyes glistened as he hugged and thanked Joe Abraham. "Mr. Abraham, if you could understand what this means to me..." Pete shrugged his hands, at a loss for words. "In my country, Poland, I could never own land. Just think of it! My very own land! To do what I want with it and to grow what I want! Thank you! Now, I will run with the surprise for Cecelia."

At supper Pete staged a big act by wearing a long face and solemnly stating, "Our children need more fresh fruit and vegetables and milk and fresh air. Thurber is too crowded. They grow so fast."

Cecelia turned from the stove to glare at Pete. "What a change. From happiness the last several days to complaining about something we have no control over. I'm surprised, Pete," she sarcastically added. "You know fruit costs so much and the vegetables are not so good this summer. My! You are the cheerless one this evening! Where are all the smiles of the last several days?"

With Cecelia's lecture, Pete could not maintain his act, for he exploded into laughter and slammed his fist on the table. "Then by golly, we'll grow our own fruit and vegetables!" He began to jig around the table. "We did it! We did it, Cecelia! It's ours! All ours! Land! Cows! Fruit trees! Ten acres and two houses! Not one house, but two houses! Think of that!"

Supper was forgotten and Cecelia could not stop crying. The girls listened in wonderment as Pete described their new home and answered their questions.

All were too excited for supper, and it was put away for later. Pete took his family to St. Barbara's to see Father Merendino. Father was of Italian descent and possessed exceptional multi-lingual skills. In the "Thurber Journal" Father announced he was capable of hearing confessions in seven different languages; a perfect priest for Thurber.

"Good Evening, Father," Pete greeted the priest.

"Pete, Cecelia, young ladies and Bolesaw. The days grow shorter and the nights cooler. Good to see you and the family."

Pete was bursting to share his good news with Father Merendino, yet he wanted to appear casual, not boastful. "We have good news, Father," Pete announced, as he rocked back and forth on his heels. "Today, I am a landowner. Yes I bought ten acres and two houses in Thurber Junction, so we'll be moving there." Puffed up with pride, Pete then began to elaborate on his property, its location, why he selected it, the description of his houses, how he intended to use the property, but Cecelia shortly cut him off.

"What my husband came to ask, Father, is 'When you can bless the two houses and the land?'"

The good priest's face glowed with happiness, and he boosted Pete's ego by saying, "Gladly! Gladly! Why, Pete, you probably own more land around here than any of your countrymen. I can come after Mass next Sunday."

Cecelia said, "Father, we won't be completely settled in, but I'll make some pierogi for you. And we'll have Sunday dinner right after the blessing. We'll invite the Bertollis over for the blessing."

The family then went into St. Barbara's where Pete and Cecelia lit a votive candle and knelt in prayers of gratitude.

The following years were rapturous years, for there was love and joy in God, family, home, crops and neighbors and in virtually everything Pete and Cecelia did. Pete easily paid off his bank note before the end of two years. Pete's relatives in Poland, upon learning of his ownership of so much land, believed Pete was extremely wealthy, for they frequently wrote, asking for money.

By 1908 the building boom in Thurber and Thurber Junction was at a peak and brick layers were in great demand. Although digging coal was for the foreign-born, and brick-laying was for those of English or American descent, the company asked Pete to temporarily leave his mining job to help in the construction of the 130-foot-high smokestack for the power plant. Pete gladly accepted, for the pay and work was better than coal mining. When the smokestack was completed, Pete climbed the interior scaffolding to the top, pulled a bottle of whiskey from his pocket, took a big drink, broke the bottle on the smokestack, swayed and staggered on the scaffolding to feign drunkenness, then scampered down to the bottom amid applause, laughter and cheers of the workers and onlookers.

The Wasieleski family was further enriched by the birth of a second son, Casimir. Each Baptism or First Communion was the occasion for a celebration and dancing. In their new home there was now plenty of room to entertain.

Built in 1908, the 130 Ft. Tall Thurber Smokestack

True to his expectations, Pete's land became an abundant

producer of vegetables and fruit. In three years there were peaches, pears, persimmons and apples. During the hot summer, and before he got a windmill, Pete watered his garden with a tea made from cow manure and water. There was a hay field and a corn patch to produce feed for chickens, ducks, hogs, a cow and a horse named "Booster". "Booster" was a good all-round horse, and the family used him for plowing, riding, pulling a buggy and wagon and petting by the children. There was a smokehouse for curing meats and a cellar for storing the jars of canned fruits and vegetable. Indeed, the children got their milk, fruit and vegetables.

In 1910 Pete surprised Cecelia with a Fischer piano. Soon, all three daughters were playing the piano, expertly taught after school by Sisters of Hunter Academy. In addition to the regular courses, the Sisters of the Incarnate Word taught penmanship, sewing, etiquette and music.

The first hog was butchered at the first hard frost. After the hog was felled with a .22 bullet to the head, the throat was cut, and the blood collected for a blood sausage called "sczhatanenya". In addition to smoked hams and sausages, some meat was preserved by immersion in a lard barrel.

The fruit, especially the peaches, always tempted the children, even when in a green state, and they had to be reminded not to touch until the fruit turned color. Pete and Cecelia were gone one day when a neighbor came to ask for fruit for his sick wife. "No sir," the girls answered. "Mama told us not to touch the peaches." When Cecelia returned home, she was aghast that her daughters were so selfish. "For yourself, don't touch, but be good to your neighbors." And she picked a bag of peaches which the daughters carried to the neighbor with apologies.

Pete and Cecelia insisted the family speak English at home, so they might all become good Americans. Of course, when Polish friends visited, the talk was in Polish. Just as John Bertolli was a leader of the Italian community, Pete Wasieleski was a leader of the Polish community.

The letters Pete and Cecelia received from family in Poland indicated an extremely difficult existence in their native country which remained under the domination of Russia, Germany and Austria until after WWI. The Wasieleskis remembered their families and sent packages and money, but Russian and German postal authorities opened mail from America, and relatives seldom received the packages and money.

In late winter 1912, Cecelia was slow to recover from a cold and she was aware of a dull pain in her lower back, but there was time for illness with five children. After a month Cecelia finally agreed to see a company doctor who diagnosed her condition as relapse of the flu. But Cecelia was modest and did not tell the doctor of a watery, bloody discharge, she confided in Giuseppa Bertolli who insisted she see the doctor again, and this time Giuseppa would be with Cecelia to make certain the doctor did a thorough examination. The doctor said "female trouble" and prescribed laudanum if the pain became unbearable. Soon Cecelia was confined to bed, but no one mentioned cervical cancer in her presence. Whatever her illness, Cecelia sensed it was terminal.

In the evening after chores were completed, the five children would gather around Cecelia's bed and tell what they had done or learned at school that day. There were several melodies written for the beautiful prayer "Ave Maria" besides Gounod's and Shubert's classic versions, and each evening Cecelia would ask the three daughters to sing this prayer which seemed to comfort her. The Fischer piano was in Cecelia's bedroom, and when a daughter mastered a new composition she would play it for her mother.

As the end neared, Cecelia told her children that whatever happened to her she would always be with them. That if she ever returned after God called her, the children were not to be frightened, for she would be there to help them. The first son, Bolesaw (Bob), contended his mother did return once after her death. The return, apparition or dream was so vivid that Bolesaw, throughout his life, never wavered in his belief of seeing his mother return.

Each evening Pete would hold Cecelia and rub her back as they quietly talked. "Pete darling, I feel like I am deserting the children and you. The children are growing so fast. They need me, but I am helpless."

"No, Love, don't think that way. We are all in God's hands, and with our prayers you will soon be well. You have been such a good mother and wife we never have to worry about the children. They do well in school, they are well-mannered, and they do their work. All will be fine," Pete tried to assure.

"That is so nice to hear. God has been good to me, for letting me come to America, owning our own home and land and our children are good Americans and will not have to face the hard times you and I had in Poland. God and you and the children have given me so much joy. I would never change my life one bit. The illness I have now is nothing compared to the happiness you have given me." Pete's tears would come after Cecelia finally dozed off.

The blissful years of the Wasieleskis ended in 1913 when Cecelia died. Pete willed himself to overcome intense grief, for there were five children from ages six to seventeen who needed him. Cecelia remained Pete's one true love; he never remarried or even seriously courted another woman, and Pete, a widower at age forty-three, hardworking and propertied, would have been a prize catch for many women.

The Bertollis helped Pete sort out and organize a life without Cecelia. Pete's oldest daughter Valerka, almost eighteen, would soon marry. The second daughter Lottie, age fourteen, would have to leave school to manage the household and look after the three younger siblings. Giuseppa Bertolli frequently dropped by to help Lottie with cooking, sewing and washing. Adjustments were made, and life went on in Thurber and the Junction.

TWENTY-ONE

United Mine Workers Charter No. 2538, dated 8 October 1903, and signed by John Mitchell, President of UMW, gave Thurber miners authorization to organize. John Lloyd, President, and William McKinnon, Secretary, signed for the local Union. In addition to these two positions, there were two other local officials, Vice President and Financial Secretary. These four positions were desirable and comparatively well paying.

To complete the organization of the Union local, there was a Pit Committee, a Legislative Committee and Pit Representatives. These were appointive slots, part-time and non-paying, except when Union tasks required travel or leave from regular work. The function of the Pit Committee was to consolidate complaints from the Pit Representatives. When the Pit Representative and the Pit Boss could not resolve a difference, it was submitted to the Pit Committee for resolution.

It was a simple setup, and there was no need for Organization or Membership Committees, because every worker in Thurber belonged to a Union. If one worked in Thurber, he belonged to a Union, and a two dollar fee was automatically deducted from wages.

All officials and members of committees were American-born. A few Pit Representatives were foreign-born but spoke passable English. The four local officials were initially appointed to three-year terms by Pete Hanraty, District 21 President, and the local officials made all local appointments to the various positions.

In late 1906, the first Union election was held in the Thurber Opera House. All four incumbents were up for reelection, but only the positions of President and Secretary were opposed. John Bertolli ran for President against Lloyd, and Joe Mercatto, an Italian-American, ran against Secretary McKinnon. Like John

Bertolli, Joe Mercatto spoke and wrote almost perfect English. Mercatto's parents came to New York in the early 1880's and Joe had been educated in Catholic schools in New York. It seemed only appropriate that some of the local Union officials should be of Italian descent, because the majority of miners were from Italy, and more than three-fourths of the miners were foreign-born.

On election night the District President and District Secretary along with the four local officials, were on the Opera House stage to conduct the first election. The votes would be counted by the District Secretary and the local Financial Secretary. While the ballots were being counted, the Hunter Band serenaded members.

The ballots were sorted into two piles, and then counted, first for President. Then the procedure was repeated for Secretary. The results were written down, and a big show was made of placing the ballots in a locked box.

Local President Lloyd thanked the members for attending and announced that immediately after the results there were free drinks and eats at the Snake Saloon. District President Hanraty was introduced, and after a few comments, the election results were printed on a small chalkboard which was visible only to the first several rows.

President: John Lloyd	443
John Bertolli	303
Secretary: Wm. McKinnon	466
Joe Mercatto	294

"Meeting adjourned!" Election results were taken for granted, not seen or not comprehended at this particular moment and there was a thunderous dash to the Snake Saloon.

Pete Wasieleski, sitting next to John Bertolli, was stunned. "The vote is not right, John! Everybody I talked to said you were the one. I showed them how your name and Lloyd's name were printed. Even though many can't read English, they can recognize names." With that comment, Pete bounded up and onto the stage.

Amid the din of the exiting miners, Pete shouted, "Mr. President, can we see the votes for a recount?"

Local President Lloyd turned from District President Hanraty to face Pete. "Oh yes. Your name escapes me right now. Right on the tip of my tongue," he said as he stuck out his hand.

Pete ignored the extended hand. "Pete Wasieleski."

"Of course! How are you, Pete? This is Mr. Pete Hanraty, our District President."

"I met Mr. Hanraty three years ago when we were organizing," Pete coldly replied. "Can we recount the votes?"

"On what grounds, Pete?" Lloyd asked.

"Over half the miners are Italians, one-fourth are Poles and we all voted for Bertolli. We need to have some say in Union business. Bertolli and I saw the same thing in the Illinois Union; majority of members born in the Old Country, but never allowed to hold a Union position, regardless of education or English-speaking ability. Recount the votes with me and somebody else not a Union officer!" Pete demanded.

By now the ballot box had been carried off.

"If you're saying something's crooked, you'd better back up your accusation," John Lloyd angrily declared.

Pete stubbornly retorted, "I back my accusation with the vote box, but it has quickly disappeared."

Pete Hanraty intervened. "Mr. Wasieleski, there are Pit Representatives and the Pit Committee which handles complaints. If you will..."

"Sure! But we need a recount now!" said Pete as he slapped the table for emphasis. "And a committee would not meet for another month. We need something now!"

"Tell you what, Mr. Wasieleski. Submit your complaint in writing, addressed to me," Hanraty replied. "We keep the ballots under lock and key for two months. I'll personally check the ballots."

But Pete would not be placated. "Mr. Hanraty, something is wrong, and we miners from the Old Country know it because every time we make a complaint to the Pit Committee, nothing is ever done, and you still take two dollars a month from us. I think you might be sorry if you don't recount the votes and help us."

John Lloyd blurted out, "What kind of a threat is that?"

"This is America! We came here to escape just what you are doing to us! We'll start our own Union!" Pete shouted as he stalked off the stage before the two could respond.

In their haste to get at the free food and drinks, most of the miners failed to comprehend what had happened in the counting of the votes. They had assumed John Bertolli would be unanimously elected, for as they had logically reasoned, he was one of the leaders in organizing Thurber, and he had placed himself in a hazardous position in the fight for unionization. He was very popular with all nationalities, and he was the natural leader of the Italian miners who made up more than half the working force of Thurber. As word of the election results got around and in the ensuing discussions, the mood became angry.

Pete was trembling from anger as he rejoined Bertolli, Mercatto and several others. "I tell you, we are fools if we let them steal this election! I'm so mad; I think we should go right now and use muscle to take the box from them!"

John put his arm around Pete's shoulder to calm him down. "I know how you feel, Pete, but by now they've got the box under their bed behind a locked door in the Knox Hotel. If we went there, they would have us arrested. We'll do something because the present officers don't represent us, and they ignore us like we didn't matter."

"Yes," one of the miners spoke up. "Like the time the Pit Boss accused Piatri of taking his lunch bucket and cussed him out and gave him a bad place to dig coal for a month. We complained to the Pit Committee, and they did nothing."

Another miner spoke. "The Pit Committee never did tell us what happened when we told of the weak timber in Number Eight. I still think the lumber is rotten. Or, how about when LaBrea in Number Nine wanted a wet proof box to keep the dynamite dry? They never did get a dry box, and half the time they need to shoot two times because the dynamite is wet."

Mercatto said, "They still need to do something about the trains. When the engines are hauling coal, make sure they are back in time to take us home. No sense in making the miners wait an hour for a ride home. The coal can wait until tomorrow, but they think the coal is more important than us."

By now Pete had calmed down. "What makes me mad, too, the Pit Committee would not ask T & P for Good Friday a half day work so we could go to Mass. Or make it for those who want to go to Church. All the Union officers are Protestants, and they don't have Good Friday services like we do. If you want to work Good Friday, all right...What's the word for it, John?"

"Optional. Well, let's talk with more of the fellows, and get some feeling what we should do. We can use the Italian Pavilion as a meeting place."

The consensus at the meeting was there were too many grievances of the foreign-born being ignored, and all the immigrant miners favored a new Union which would be more sensitive to their needs. The Mexican and black miners would also join the new Union. With the present Union, there was also prejudice against the Negro miners, for the Civil War was still an issue, and miners from the Deep South remembered Hunter brought in

Negroes as strike breakers sixteen years previously.

John Bertolli wrote a letter to Pete Hanraty, President of District 21, UMW, to formally request a charter for a second Union which would be more democratic and better serve the needs of the immigrant miners.

The UMW did not want a second miners' Local in Thurber, and Hanraty wrote back that national President John Mitchell was of the opinion that a second Union would weaken labor's present strong stance in Thurber.

Hanraty's negative response was the answer which Bertolli expected. Bertolli's next letter went to the American Federation of Labor, which began in 1881 as the Organized Trades and Labor Unions of the United States and Canada. Unknown to Bertolli, the AFL membership was limited to skilled workers, and since miners did not fit this category, the AFL was not interested in sponsoring a Thurber, Texas, miners local, regardless of a possible eight hundred membership.

When the four local Union officials learned that a serious move was on for a second Union, they tried to smooth feelings. They went out of their way to meet with immigrant miners and appeared overly solicitous of the miners' welfare. Quite often now, the Union officers "set-'em-up" for the boys, but it was too late now.

Bertolli next corresponded with the Industrial Workers of the World, only recently founded in Chicago. The IWW was called the "Wobblies". In reply, the IWW declared they were for the common laborers and would be interested in sponsoring a charter for Thurber miners upon further negotiations. The IWW was aware of the plight of all laborers, world wide, particularly those foreign-born who were exploited in America. Unknown to Bertolli at this time, the IWW movement had undesirable ideological elements such as Marxism and anarchy.

In the meantime, the Italian miners began to assert themselves, and W. K. Gordon wrote a letter to Edgar Marston.

Thurber, Texas, Dec. 10th, 1906

Mr. Edgar L. Marston, President.
Texas & Pacific Coal Company,
New York, N.Y.

Dear Sir:

The output of coal for November reached 31,912 tons; it would have exceeded this amount materially, but for an idle day caused by the derailment of the forward section of the passenger train on the morning of November 12th, putting all mines idle...

Our mining force now consists of perhaps seventy five percent (75%) Italians, the other twenty-five (25%) being Mexican, Negroes, Poles, English etc. The Italians are becoming very restless and are desirous of kicking out of the traces and affiliating with some other Union body, I believe to be to be the Industrial Workmen of the World.

Last week, at No. 9 Shaft, the Italians headed by one, Frank Vittoria, refused to go below, claiming that one of the cages was in bad condition; the following day, which was Friday, they again refused to go below, claiming that the check weight man had been insulted by the company's weight man.

In the meantime, I wired Messrs. Mitchell and Hanraty of their actions and they instructed Vice President Edward Cunningham to come here immediately. On Monday the trouble had spread until the Italians in other shafts were involved; Cunningham arrived, but was absolutely unable to cope with the situation, and finally so expressed himself to me....I adjusted the matter by accepting the company weight man's resignation. It developed, however, during the agitation, that the trouble was not so much on account of the misunderstanding between the weight men, as it was to test the strength of U.M.W. of A. The Italians told me that their people had become tired of the union, as the latter had no regard for them, other than to receive their monthly dues...

Yours Respectfully,
W. K. Gordon

Gordon's comments about the IWW were true; a few days later, John Bertolli, Pete Wasieleski and Joe Mercatto took the IWW letter to W. K. Gordon. With the settling of the 1903 strike, Bertolli and Gordon were again on friendly terms, their past differences forgotten. In spite of appearances, Gordon never had any problem accepting a labor Union in Thurber, but as General Manager during Thurber's labor strife, he had to follow the policy of company directors. Gordon, physical fitness adherent, admired the muscular toughness of the miners and he knew that without the foreign-born miners as an inexpensive labor force Thurber would not have succeeded.

Gordon, through the years and often on his own initiative, had installed many safety features for the protection and welfare of the miners. Gordon understood that a safe, happy worker was more productive. In thirty years of Thurber mining, mainly because of Gordon's concern and several patents on safety devices, there were no cave-ins, no underground fires, no uncontrolled explosions and no deaths from the poisonous "blackdamp" gas. There were several fatal individual accidents in the various mine shafts but no large scale mine disasters.

Gordon listened as the three miners gave their litany of how the UMW had deliberately scorned the immigrant miners in Union activities. Pete made his assertion for a religious holiday on Good Friday, and as suspected, Gordon had never been approached by the Pit Committee on this issue. Gordon readily agreed to a religious holiday, for there was empathy for the fervent religious nature of the Eastern Europeans.

As the meeting concluded, Gordon said, "I certainly understand your feelings in this matter. Let me keep your letter and give me a few days. We already have seven different Thurber locals. Let me see if any of existing locals could take you in. We don't want any strikes or disturbances. Things are running just the way we want them to run." The three miners assured Gordon that they, too, did not want another strike.

When W. K. Gordon looked into the organization of the Industrial Workers of the World, he was aghast at the possible implications. He would never permit such an organization in Thurber! Since the dissenting miners could not be fitted into any of Thurber's existing unions, the UMW would have to grant a second charter. Accordingly, Gordon sent an urgent wire to John Mitchell, President of UMW, requesting he grant a second charter or the UMW would be in competition with the IWW.

In response, John Mitchell sent Pete Hanraty to talk with W. K. Gordon. Gordon gave Hanraty a stern lecture.

"Mr. Hanraty. There are many educated, English-speaking, naturalized Italians among our miners. Yet, these people somehow are not permitted in responsible positions or activities of your Union. They suspect fraud in the last election. Now, I know the mood of these miners because I've worked with them the past sixteen years. I have many friends among them, and I know they are not unreasonable. These people are proud to be Americans and they have faith in our democratic ways. So I'm not asking you, I'm telling you and John Mitchell these foreign-born miners must be represented or there might be serious consequences." He paused as he handed the letter to Hanraty. "This letter from the IWW says it all. We are not going to have another battle over who is representing whom." Hanraty glumly read the letter.

Gordon finished his lecture. "You go back and tell John Mitchell we want no more labor troubles here, but that there will be trouble unless he grants a charter for a second miners local. With twelve hundred miners, and a thousand of those foreign-born, there's room for two organizations."

Gordon's warning was quickly heeded, and Thurber, again was unique in that it had two miners' unions, each sponsored by the

UMW, and each respecting the other's "territory".

The Italian Local Number 2763, had several times more members than Local Number 2538, the English-speaking local. A dramatic demonstration of the democratic zeal of the Italian Local was shown when Bob Rogers, a black miner, was once elected president of the Italian Local. Rogers' father, a former slave, continued to work for his ex-master after the Civil War. The master, a benevolent Virginian, provided for Bob Rogers' education.

There were many effective officers of the Italian Local: Santi, Merico, Pasconi, Pogiani, Caniperoli, Garbolio and Martignago.

Lawrence Santi and Lee Merico represented the Thurber Mine Workers during legislative sessions in Austin, and they often spoke in support of many important pieces of legislation, such as child labor, mandatory schooling, free text books, industrial safety laws and worker's compensation.

TWENTY-TWO

After the strike of 1903 and with the formation of the Italian miners local, management and labor worked closely together and there were no serious troubles. Coal production continued to increase to a peak of about twenty-two hundred tons daily in 1915.

The thirty-inch seam of coal meant hard digging from a prone position. Pads were sewn into the hips and shoulders of the miners' clothes to lessen the uncomfortable impact of the cinders. The work was arduous, and only the thought of the fun times above ground made the work endurable.

Among all the nationalities in Thurber, the Italians were more lighthearted and fun loving. With the Italians there was the exuberance and joy of being an American: always a hustle and bustle, vitality, a purpose, a prank, voluble argument, something happening, a song. When the men were underground, the womenfolk, too, worked hard. Cooking, cleaning, sewing and washing for their man or the boarders. But evenings, Sundays and holidays were a time for play with a variety of diversions. Music was always in the foreground, or background. Dancing and drinking and flirting. Good bread, wine and food. Bocce ball, concerts, operas, school plays, traveling circuses, parades, stage plays, ball games and church services, particularly during Lent. Baptisms and weddings. "Work hard, play harder."

As the Bertolli family grew, Guiseppa and John became less involved with outside activities. As Mama Mazzano predicted, the bambinos were frequent, two boys and two girls. The last born, Gino, arrived in 1908.

On Christmas Day, Rico Visentine, his accordion, Bertolli and several others preserved an Old Italian custom of strolling house to house, serenading and then being invited in for refreshments and drink. Unfortunately, nine homes seemed to be the limit before drink and laughter interfered with the singing and navigating of the jovial group.

There were several brush-covered arbors outside the Snake Saloon, and on summer days miners would sit in the cool shade and breeze of the arbors and loudly argue or sing among themselves or with crews from other mines.

There were always a dozen bocce ball games on weekends. The loud arguments in this game seemed always to emanate from which ball was closer to the baa-ling', the small target ball.

"The striped ball's got it! Bet you a dime!"

"Hell, I don't want to take your money!"

The argument would continue as the measurements were made by using the foot to mark off the distances.

"You moved the baa-ling' with your heel! Let me step it off!"

"Like hell I did! You just want to argue! Get some sticks then!" And finally two sticks would be adjusted to make the measurement and settle the argument, but the argument would carry over into where one located the baa-ling', or what the score was, or how many steps one took in shooting. The arguments were in direct proportion to the amount of beer consumed, and the arguments were understood to be a part of the game.

The Italians made a delicious dish called "polenta" which was made from boiled corn meal. The boiled corn meal was poured into a flat pan, and when it firmed, it was cut into pieces with a piece of string. A stew called "padcho", which was made from small game such as rabbit, squirrel, dove or field lark, was poured over the polenta.

The field larks were caught at night using a carbide lamp and cow bell. Supposedly, the cow bell made the birds think nothing was about except cows. Grab the bird, pull the head off and toss it into the bag. Bertolli's favorite prank was to take a newcomer or visitor field lark hunting. W. K. Gordon took great fun in this trick and several times asked Bertolli to take Gordon's guests hunting. The visitor was instructed to keep ringing the cow bell while the others went off to head the birds toward the cow bell. At midnight, a lone cow bell could be heard ringing, the jokesters long in bed after having a drink and a good laugh.

The Italians wanted desperately to become a part of the "New Country." One way was to join clubs or lodges. There were two Italian clubs: Stella d'Italia and the Druid. The American clubs open to the Italians were the Redmen, the Oddfellows, and to a lesser extent, the Masons. Of course, the Catholic Church disapproved of secret organizations, but many Italians did not realize this until they were strongly rebuffed by an Italian priest, Father DeLuca. As a group of Italians marched into St. Barbara's, in colorful attire and regalia of their lodge to bury one of their brothers, Father DeLuca angrily told them to "Get the hell out! Get the hell out of my church!"

Father DeLuca was outspoken and controversial, and Father's chief annoyance was tardiness to Mass. Several Mexicans were never on time for Mass. Father saw them come in during the sermon or when he turned around to say, "Dominus vobiscum". He admonished them and begged them, but to no avail. One Sunday in the middle of his sermon, the Mexicans straggled in. Father paused, stretched his hands out pleadingly, looked heavenward and said, "Oh God, you give me jackasses, and I'll give you jackasses right back."

A second way of being a part of America was to own a share of an American company: buy stocks; but there were always crooked promoters who took advantage of the immigrants' inexperience in finances. The stocks would be low priced at fifty cents or a dollar a share, and at these prices the miners could afford a few dollars worth of stock. Oil was coming on and there were several crooked oil schemes such as the Texas United Oil and Refining Company and Beaver Valley Oil and Refining Company.

The biggest stock fraud which fleeced the Thurber Italians was perpetrated by another Italian from St. Cloud, Minnesota; S.C. Pandolfo, "President" of a nonexistent Pan Motor Company. Automobiles were exciting mechanical spectacles, and automobile companies were formed, and just as quickly, absorbed or dissolved. In the early 1900's over two hundred companies were organized. Ford's assembly line methods produced 15 million Ford Model T's between 1908 and 1927.

Pandolfo, flashily dressed and driving a monstrous Maxwell touring car, promised the gullible Italians quick riches. "Everybody will be trading his horse for an automobile. There is money to be made in America, and the easy way is to own part of the company."

"Just look at him," the miners talked among themselves. "Had he not been a factory worker himself a few years back?"

Bertolli was suspicious of the sporty, smooth Italian, Pandolfo, and he warned his friends when they asked Bertolli for advice. "Why has he traveled all the way down here, to Thurber, a thousand miles, to sell his stock? Pandolfo is probably touring the country, hitting Italian populations. There are many crooked stock schemes all over the country. I saw that when I was in Illinois. Before you buy, let us write the mayor of St. Cloud, Minnesota. If the company is good, you can buy stock later."

But Pandolfo's promise of fast riches was too strong an enticement. The elaborately embossed PAN MOTOR COMPANY stock certificate with a dazzling, four-door touring car pictured at the top was worthless. Pandolfo had bilked $5000 from the naive miners. The promoter from St. Cloud was convicted in federal Court and served time for his fraudulent methods.

The geological faults and upheavals which produced coal outcrops near Thurber caused serious water problems for northern Erath and southern Palo Pinto counties. Just twenty miles south of Thurber and thirty feet down, there was plentiful, potable sheet water. Yet, in the 235-feet-deep Thurber mines, troublesome water seepage problems were never encountered. Robert D. Hunter, President of T & P Coal, first solved the water problem by shipping water in by train. Then he built Thurber Little Lake, and when Thurber outgrew this, he built Thurber Big Lake which accommodated Thurber throughout its existence.

For John Bertolli, Pete Wasieleski and others living in Thurber Junction, water needs were more uniquely challenging. Each house in the Junction had a well, cistern or rain barrels. If a house had two or more acres and a drainage slope, ponds were dug next to wells to provide well water seepage. During droughts, two-hundred-gallon tanks of water would be hauled by mules, and later by trucks, to pour into cisterns and wells. Buckets and jugs of good Thurber water were also available when a trip was made to Thurber. There was a weak seepage of "hard" water about twelve feet deep in the Junction, but this water would not produce sufficient soap suds, and when drank, a physic resulted.

The closest approximation to indoor plumbing was a hand pump over a cistern on the back porch. Everybody drank from the same dipper, which was dipped into the water bucket, and the dipper was left floating on the water, or hung nearby.

Washing clothes, particularly miners' work clothes, consumed the most water. First, the women scrubbed the clothes on a washboard using lye soap. Then the clothes were soaked in boiling water over an outside fire, rinsed in another tub, hand wrung, then hung on a clothes line to dry.

Before wash facilities were installed at the mines, the miners went home dirty: faces, head, hands, arms and clothes covered with coal dust. At home the family had a tub of warm bath water waiting. Baths for the rest of the family were weekly events which took place behind the kitchen stove in a number two washtub.

Each house had an outdoor privy, located on the back property line. At night, indoor chamber pots were used and emptied each morning. Schools had "eight holer" outdoor toilets. A favorite Halloween prank was to overturn an outdoor privy.

Pete Wasieleski's boast that he could grow anything was modified to depend on the frequency and amount of rainfall. However, Pete and John Bertolli, both avid gardeners, solved some water problems by using the first windmills seen in Thurber Junction. A well was dug close to a pond and a trench ten feet deep, connecting the tank and well, was filled with coarse gravel. The windmill pumped the water from the well into a brick trough. The gardens were sloped so that water would feed from the trough into irrigation channels. The Bertolli and Wasieleski cellars were always loaded with canned beets, spinach, sauerkraut, peas, tomatoes, pickles, peaches and pears and several bushels of potatoes. Corn and oats were grown for the farm animals. After the oats were thrashed, the oat hay was piled in the barn with pitchforks.

From the milk of a Jersey cow, butter, buttermilk and clabber milk were made. The curds of clabber milk were hung in cheesecloth on a clothes line to dry into cottage cheese. The cottage cheese was used to make pierogi, Pete Wasieleski's favorite dish. Milk, butter and buttermilk were sold to neighbors, the milk usually in half-gallon lard buckets.

Joe Abraham again showed his strong business acumen when he sold land and loaned money to A. J. and Frank Teichmann to build a flour mill behind the Abraham store. The German millers' flour mill was the only one of its kind for miles around. This meant business for Joe Abraham and Thurber Junction, for the farmers brought in wagons of wheat, corn and oats to sell to Teichmann, or to have the grain custom-ground for their yearly needs. While the farmers waited on the grinding to be completed, they shopped at Abraham's, the dry goods stores, or had whisky at Goebel's or Taramino's.

Teichmann's Best Flour was inexpensive, good quality flour,

and practically all production of flour and corn meal could be sold in Thurber and local stores.

There were three main roads leading into Thurber: one on the west from Strawn, one in the middle paralleling the rail spur into Thurber from the Junction, and one on the east which was called the Back Road. The one and a half mile long Back Road was a microcosm of Thurber with a balance of nationalities living alongside the road. Of fifteen families living on the Back Road, there were seven nationalities represented.

The DeHahns, a French family, lived a quarter-mile from the Bertollis. Birdie DeHahn, the twenty year old daughter, sometimes acted peculiarly. She was a shy, quiet person who often visited Giuseppa. Giuseppa was content to chatter away while Birdie prferred to cuddle or play with Bertolli children. On bright, full moon summer nights, Birdie sometimes strolled the Back Road. In 1909 shortly after midnight, during a full moon, Birdie, wearing a white flowing nightgown, came into the Bertolli home and took Baby Gino. A short while later when Giuseppa looked in on the children, she shrieked, "John! Gino is not here!" John threw on his trousers and ran next door to the Engstroms while Giuseppa searched the house and yard. The Choates were awakened and joined the search. The DeHahn mother and father awoke to the commotion and saw that Birdie was gone. One group ran up the Back Road to the north, another to the south. They found Birdie near Gibson Branch crossing on the Back Road, humming and cuddling Gino. Giuseppa, crying with joy as she took Gino, said, "I knew Birdie would not harm Gino."

Birdie's mind continued to deteriorate and a few years later she was committed to an institution in Wichita Falls. For many years afterward, Giuseppa would send sewing and crocheting materials to Birdie.

TWENTY-THREE

The years from 1904 to 1920 were bounteous years for Thurberites. Families grew, and there was work security and contentment in belonging to a great nation. There were harbingers of difficult times ahead, but these were too subtle for the unsophisticated miners to grasp.

Ever since Spindletop at Beaumont, Texas, in 1901, the big money talk was oil. Some railroads changed from coal to oil prior to WWI. W. W. Johnson, who founded the Thurber coal mines, began studying oil investments in the early 1900's even though he was still deeply involved with coal.

Oil was found northwest of Strawn in 1914, ten miles from Thurber, and the rapidly-growing automobile industry made increasing demands for oil and gasoline.

In 1915 Thurber piped in natural gas from the X-Ray Field, ten miles south of Thurber, to fire the power plant and brick kilns.

W. K. Gordon, General Manager of Thurber, began drilling test holes for oil in 1912. He was convinced oil was in Thurber's vicinity and drilled test holes west of Thurber and some to the northwest, forty-six drill holes in all. There were several shallow wells with small amounts of oil and very good shows of gas, but at this time there was little demand for gas. Shallow gas-bearing sand at about 550 feet was named the "Gordon Sand".

Company geologists were sent to Thurber but were unenthusiastic about oil prospects. This did not impede Gordon's quest for deep oil, and a delegation from Ranger, Texas, fifteen miles west of Thurber, asked Gordon to drill in Ranger. The company grudgingly gave Gordon permission to lease mineral lands, and Gordon secured 300,000 acres in four counties for the T & P Coal Company.

The first well in Ranger, the Nannie Walker, hit strong gas but was abandoned. The second well, the McCleskey, looked like a dry hole and the company wanted to stop drilling, but Gordon told the driller to continue. When the McCleskey hit, W. K. Gordon was hunting with his son Billy near Hohhertz, fifteen miles northwest of Thurber. Father and son returned to their car, which was parked on the side of a dirt road, and saw a note stuck on the steering wheel: "The McCleskey blew in!" And Ranger boasted of "The Oil Field That Won WWI".

Every two years the contract between the UMW and T & P Coal was reviewed. The 1913-1915 contract paid miners $1.32 per ton. In the 1916 negotiations the company balked at a Union demand of a 5-cent per ton increase. The miners walked out for three weeks and the company gave in, but it was apparent the limit to coal profitability was being reached. The contract talks were held in the Worth Hotel in Fort Worth, Texas, in more restrained surroundings than might have been found in Thurber. Contrary to belief, John L. Lewis never appeared in Thurber.

In 1921 there was little demand for coal and the company reneged on its contract and proposed a reduction in wages. The Union declined, and the company locked out the miners and ordered them to leave company property. The popular misconception which the company promoted was that this was a strike, but in truth, the company broke the contract and locked out the miners.

The Union used surplus army tents to set up a tent city in an open field a half-mile north of Thurber. Some families moved in with those who owned homes in Thurber Junction, and John Bertolli and Pete Wasieleski each took in a family until the families relocated in Fort Worth. Most of the miners thought the eviction was temporary, that the Union would soon force the company to reopen its houses and mines.

In the beginning the UMW provided food for the evicted miners and families, but after a few months, this food fund dwindled, and the local officials, particularly Lawrence Santi, had to scrounge and beg food. The miners finally realized they were no longer needed, and they began to drift away to seek work elsewhere. The Thurber coal mines were closed after thirty years. Many miners returned to Italy and four hundred miners moved to the coal fields in Illinois.

Some Thurber coal continued to be mined until 1926; the non-Union miners who worked for these wages were called "scabs."

The shock from the 1921 lockout and shutdown of the mines all but obscured a small, violent sympathy strike in Thurber Junction. The sixty workers at the railroad car repair yard which was on the rail spur a quarter-mile south of the Junction, protested the Thurber lockout by striking against the railroad. Railroad detectives were brought in, and guards teemed all over the area. Harsh words and threats were exchanged. Allegedly, two striking rail yard workers, Clyde Graves and Bill Lorenz, went into Taramino's Picture Show in Thurber Junction, hustled out a detective and severely beat him. The two men were arrested and sprinted off to Fort Worth but were never charged. The railroad's response to this and to the sympathy strike was to permanently shut down the repair yard. This seemingly vengeful closing, along with Thurber's events, was a horrendous calamity for Thurber Junction, which at this time had a population of 1800.

The focus of the company shifted from coal to oil and the name was changed to Texas and Pacific Coal and Oil Company. Coal miners were no longer needed. A new breed of worker moved into Thurber; mostly white collar workers from the northeast. There was little need for foreign-born ex-miners to work in the oil fields or on pipe lines. Oil field workers were already trained and vital communication might be a problem with ex-miners who did not speak or understand English very well.

Booming, teeming Ranger had no housing facilities for T & P Company employees, and the workers drove from Thurber to Ranger and back each day. To house the new workers, the company built thirty four new, modern brick houses on Thurber's New York Hill at an average cost of $6000 each. This contrasted sharply with the few hundred dollars it cost to build the first houses for the miners. Some people rode a local train from Thurber to Ranger. With the exodus of the foreign-born miners, Thurber's character changed completely and was gone forever. Thurber was a different city. It was "Thurber" in name only. By 1930 most of the thousand wooden miners' houses were gone, either moved away or sold for scrap lumber.

When the company closed the mines in 1921, those who lived in company housing had only one choice: move on. For those who owned homes in Thurber Junction and who had large families, the decision was more difficult. With depressed conditions, their homes could not be sold, and there was no money for moving elsewhere.

Almost coincidentally with the closing of the mines, the Volstead Act became effective in January, 1920. This Eighteenth Amendment prohibited the manufacture, sale and transportation of intoxicating beverages, but the provisions of this act were not enforceable. This gave rise to violent, organized crime in larger cities, but to the hopeless, unemployed miners of Thurber Junction, Volstead was a Godsend and a way to survive. For the Junction folk, bootlegging became a family affair; there was no organized crime, and Roaring Ranger was a thirsty, valued customer.

But long before the Volstead Act, the Italians made wine and whisky for home use. The homemade wine was used as altar wine in St. Barbara's. John Bertolli had a productive grape arbor of special Texas varieties which were developed by T. V. Munson for the Montague, Texas Italians. John's old associate of the Union fight of 1903, Joe Fenoglio, gave John some clippings. For other wine makers, wild "mustang" grapes which grew abundantly along the country roadsides south of Thurber made good wine. But most of the Italians depended on carloads of grapes shipped in from

California, and the Italian kids with grapes in their lunch bags had many friends. The Italians used the leftover grape skins from wine to produce a "grappa" whisky which came off at about 170 proof. To the grape skins sugar and water were added to produce the drinkable ethyl alcohol. But with prohibition and an enthusiastic demand for the Junction whisky, the genuine "grappa" was made from raisins which could be bought in wooden crates or sacks from any local grocer. Grapes spoiled and were seasonal. The Junction "grappa" whisky differed from other bootleg whisky in that most "other" whisky was made from grain and mash. However, some of the local whisky was made from anything which fermented: peach skins, apples, pears and potatoes.

In addition to grappa whisky, bootleg beer was made. This home-brew was called "chalk beer" for the white, chalk-like sediment at the bottom of the bottle. Bottles, caps, a capper, rubber tubing, a crock, water, malt, yeast and sugar were the essentials. Cans of malt, "Bulldog" or "Blue Ribbon" brand, as well as bottle caps, could be bought at any grocery store. One brand of malt even gave a circumventive recipe on the can: WARNING "Do not mix the contents of this can with five gallons of water, four pounds of sugar and four cakes of yeast as an intoxicating beverage will result which is a violation of Federal law."

Good water was the key to good home-brew. Much of the well water was "hard" water and it was essential that cisterns and barrels catch "soft" rainwater. The water situation prompted a humorous saying: "Let's make some home-brew; I can get ten gallons of good creek water."

When the exodus from Thurber and the Junction settled down, there were fewer than one hundred Italian families left in Thurber Junction. While the Italians were the predominant bootleggers, all nationalities were involved so that about one hundred Junction families made and sold beer and whisky during prohibition. For most families this was a necessity, a way of making a living. A few of the more enterprising bootleggers made small fortunes and drove big cars, a far cry from humble origins in Italy. John Bertolli prospered during prohibition. After the repeal of the Volstead Act in 1933 and during the hard times of the Depression and even until WWII, ex-bootleggers were able to live comfortably off their earnings. The suburb of Thurber was first called Coal Mine Junction and then Thurber Junction. During prohibition the name jokingly became "Grappa Junction."

Pete Wasieleski and John Bertolli had several long discussions on the dilemma they faced with the closing of the mines. Pete had a little money saved. He would send his two sons to a mechanic school in Kansas City, which should then qualify them for employment in Argo Corn Products, Argo, Illinois. He did not want to be so far from his sons, but that could not be helped. All Pete's daughters were married. With his twenty acres and nobody dependent on him, he would not need much. Pete's son-in-law, Marche Zimitzski, was building cabins and a restaurant for travelers on the Bankhead Highway in nearby Strawn, and Pete would do the brickwork for these and perhaps some work in Ranger.

John Bertolli's predicament was different. There was a wife and four children, the oldest sixteen, and John's in-laws, the Mazzanos, in their sixties, now lived with the Bertollis. John would have to make and sell grappa and beer, and Pete agreed that John had little choice. John knew it was against the law, but how the law would be enforced or what penalties were involved was unknown. Would bootlegging be embarrassing for Bertolli's family and friends? Perhaps, but not greatly so, because John knew that about a fourth of the Junction's people would be involved. But John had grievous qualms. If prohibition laws were violated, regardless of the circumstances, would this not be a sin? Mortal or venial? This was discussed in the confessional.

Bertolli: "Bless me Father, for I have sinned. Since my last Confession, a week ago, I have sold whisky and beer for money. Is this a mortal sin, Father?"

Father Herkert: "You sold this for money?"

Bertolli: "Yes, Father."

Father: "But is this not against the law?"

Bertolli: "But this is necessary for my family. I am without work. I have no money to move elsewhere. I have a wife, four children and my in-laws with me."

Father: "But you see the church cannot make exceptions to certain laws. It would be the same as if you broke the law by stealing to support your family."

Bertolli: "I understand, Father, but selling whiskey harms no one. Stealing would deprive someone of something they've worked hard for. Selling whiskey hurts no one."

Father: "Perhaps, but the Church teaches obedience. We must obey the laws of the country. Think of this. Pray we can resolve this. For your penance...."

But John could not resolve this to his satisfaction. He would continue to attend Sunday Mass, for he had never missed Sunday Mass at St. Barbara's, but he would have to forsake Confession and Communion. What would it be like without the grace of these sacraments? Then, if his wife and family helped Bertolli make and sell whisky, he would also be responsible for their spiritual deprivation. This wore heavily on John's mind. *"Man does not live by bread alone"*, in the present situation, thought John. *"But neither does man live solely on spiritual graces in our present circumstances."*

Bertolli was not alone in his anguish. Many other devout Catholics no longer took Communion or even attended Mass. But life went on, and bootlegging flourished to become a half-million dollar a year business in the Junction. Thurber Junction became known as the "Bootleg Capitol of Texas." It was three years before enforcement officials were organized to enforce prohibition laws.

First, the Revenue Agents disguised themselves and tried to buy from suspected bootleggers. But the Junction bootleggers stuck together, and when an unknown character was spotted, word quickly got around the small town. Before a bottle was sold to a new customer, a known customer would have to accompany and vouch for the new customer during the initial purchase. If the buyer were a good customer or a friend of the dealer, he was allowed to visit on the back porch or under a secluded shade tree and drink his whisky or beer without having to transport it. Drinking whetted the appetite, and this made the Dutch Lunch very popular around "Grappa Junction." This lunch required no elaborate preparation, no cooking, few dishes and little cleanup in the event of a hasty departure. Slices of homemade salami, Genoa salami, ham, two kinds of cheese, sliced onion, Italian peppers and Italian bread with a bottle of home-brew made a satisfying meal.

The Dry Agents became frustrated with their lack of success and became increasingly ruthless, crude and destructive in their searches. At sunset one summer evening, an agent sped straight to Bertolli's home. There were several cases of freshly brewed beer in the kitchen. As he heard the agent's car drive up, John had no chance to hide the home-brew, so he threw the cases behind an opened door. The agent barged in without knocking. "All right, lawbreaker. Where is it? I got a report you just brewed up a batch. I can smell it."

John Bertolli, nervous and fearful his hasty hiding place would be discovered, asked, "Please, sir. You have a search warrant?"

"Oh, a smart Italian bastard. What if I don't?"

Bertolli politely replied, "Excuse me, sir, but there are ladies in the house. Must you use profanity?"

The cigar-chewing agent loudly proclaimed, "You goddamn right I'll use profanity! It's the only language you wops understand!"

Bertolli stretched his six-foot-two muscular body. "Mr. Agent. This is America. I know a search warrant is required..."

"And I say I don't need one. Now, what the hell do you say to that, smart wop?" And he tromped through the house, looked under beds and in closets before he stomped back to his car without a word. The agent never suspected beer would be hidden in such an unlikely place.

John Bertolli knew the agent's behavior was improper. He drove his new wooden-spoke-wheeled Buick to the Palo Pinto County Courthouse and talked with Judge Ritchie. Judge Ritchie was up for re-election and knew he could not carry south Palo Pinto County without Bertolli's support. Judge Ritchie sent a letter of protest to the Federal Office in Fort Worth. Revenue Agent James Woods never set foot in Thurber Junction again, was reprimanded and transferred.

In 1925 there were 40,000 bootleggers in Texas and only forty Federal Agents to cover all of Texas and Oklahoma. Fortunately for the Junction, local law officers were called upon to assist Federal Agents in raiding. County Sheriff Gib Abernathy and Constable Gabe Mayo of Gordon, Texas, were friendly to the bootleggers, and Gabe Mayo had many friends in the Junction. He liked his drink, and he never had to buy a bottle. On most raids the bootleggers were forewarned by Constable Mayo, and if not forewarned, two houses were all the agents could hit before the alarm was all over town.

The third local lawman, U.S. Assistant Marshal Si Bradford of Strawn, Texas, was a "booger." Si was quick on the trigger, having killed four men in the line of duty. "The law was the law" with Marshal Bradford. On raids he carried a sharp-pointed steel rod with which he tapped and probed for "hollows." Once, when raiding Bertolli, Si struck a hollow sound as he probed freshly dug dirt. "Come on, boys," proclaimed Bradford. "I've found it." The agents dug down to find the stinking, decaying remains of Bertolli's dog which was buried a week previously.

When Si tapped hollow on a false chimney at Lui Broglio's, Lui took off running. Si bellowed, "Stop! Or I'll kill you dead!" Lui stopped because he knew Si would.

In Bertolli's pond Art Rumford kept a minnow bucket at the end of a pole which was suspended out into the deep water. When Si failed to correctly reset the pole, the minnows died, and Si had to pay an irate Rumford for more minnows.

Bertolli made grappa whisky for his own use several years before prohibition. His ingenious, simple still belied evidence of wrongdoing, and it became standard equipment for the local bootleggers. Bertolli used the oval-shaped, copper clothes boiling pot for a still. First, it could be broken down completely with no resemblance to a still. Secondly, all households, bootlegger or not, used a clothes boiling pot. Thirdly, with smoke from the fire under the pot, was someone boiling clothes or making illicit hooch? Agents gleefully destroyed conventional stills on the spot, but they had no right to destroy a woman's clothes boiling pot!

In Bertolli's still, copper tubing ran from the lid of the pot into coils inside a wooden barrel which contained ice or water. The tubing then exited out a cork stopper in the side of the barrel. A jug at the end of the tubing caught the drips of ethyl alcohol. The lid and the tubing hole in the lid were sealed with a paste made of flour and water. A mesquite fire sometimes heated the pot, but a more suitable setup was a double-burner coal oil stove where the heat could be controlled. The distilled whisky came off clear and strong, and sugar browned in a skillet was added to the bottle to give the desired amber color.

One bootlegger stated the advantages of using a copper still: "Nobody in the Junction ever sold any bad whisky. The copper don't mix with the whisky. Hell, I heard of people around Glen Rose poisoned because somebody used a barrel or a tin tub for a still. You don't get a spoiled taste when you use copper."

Most whisky makers used ice for condensing the alcoholic vapors because Thurber ice was inexpensive, and the "Ice drawed the whisky out." For seventy-five cents a 300-pound block, "The Best Ice in the World", made from distilled water, was conveniently available at the Thurber Ice Plant. There was advantage in using distilled water for making ice: there was no residue left in the vats, and the pipes were not clogged with mineral deposits.

The iceman who delivered to the bootlegger was a man who saw nothing and kept his mouth shut. Mr. Lee, a teetotaler Baptist was in charge of the ice plant, and he disliked selling large amounts of ice to icemen he suspected of selling to bootleggers. It was late afternoon and Bertolli had several batches of grappa to run off, but to Mr. Lee, ice this late in the day meant illicit purposes and he refused to sell ice to Bertolli's iceman. Bertolli went to W. K. Gordon and Gordon called Lee. "Mr. Lee, please understand that all ice we make is for sale to anybody, and it's none of our business what it's used for."

With the exception of Bertolli, the big bootleggers had some business as a front. One feed store had three Mexicans working full-time producing grappa. A garage mechanic would back his Model T pickup into the feed store. Bottles of whisky would go on the bottom, sacks of feed on top. This mechanic's services were in great demand, for he got calls at all hours of the night and day to go "fix" broken down cars.

Another trick of the feed store was to put bottles of whisky in sacks of feed. If there were no chickens or cows to feed, the unused feed would be exchanged for another sack of feed, time and again.

The largest dealer was strictly a wholesaler with a dry goods store as a front. He concealed his wealth and activities by banking long distance with a St. Louis bank.

A brakeman on a local train with a daily run between the

Junction and Ranger would buy a gallon of 170-proof grappa from Bertolli and cut it with water to make two gallons, or eight quarts. He stashed the quarts in his working bag and doubled his money daily in the boom town of Ranger.

Under-house basements are not common in Texas, but several bootleggers had basements to conceal their liquor. The trap door was hidden by a rug or a bed or merchandise or flooring nailed back in place.

All foreign-born who remained in the Junction were naturalized citizens. Time and again, during prohibition, the blessings of citizenship in a great democracy were aptly demonstrated. Innocent until proven guilty. Due process. Legal representation. Voting rights. Political influence. *How different from the Old Country,* thought Bertolli. *Although I know I am breaking the law, I still have certain rights and privileges.*

But many native-born Americans still treated foreign-born with disdain and bias. The foreigners were inferior and dumb and practiced a mumbo-jumbo religion, and in the Junction, all native-born Americans lived and owned businesses on the north side of the track, away from the foreigners.

"Judge" Ranspot was a Mineral Wells lawyer who relished a weekly Dutch lunch and home brew. He had no reluctance in representing bootleggers, and to those dispensers of illegal beverages who were unduly harassed by insensitive revenuers, Ranspot offered some advice: call over a non-bootlegging friend or neighbor as witness.

When Bertolli was raided he called for next-door neighbor Engstrom, or sent for Art Rumford who lived a quarter-mile east. Although Rumford was in his late seventies, he was more than a match for the Dry Agents and he still remembered his earlier hassles with the Thurber guards. He was cynical and testy and willing "...to give you bastards a piece of my mind. Even if they was bootlegging, they're not hurting anyone, and doing a hell of a lot more good than you're doing, tearing up innocent people's homes!"

During raids, vegetable and flower gardens would be trampled. Once, an acre of corn was flattened. Gates for livestock and chickens would be left open. Clothes and boxes from closets scattered about. Bricks and rocks from under-house siding were strewn everywhere. The wreckage was left to the family to clean up. A witness discouraged such ruthless activities.

To the people of Thurber Junction, Andrew Marine's warning ride was reminiscent of Paul Revere's ride. The Feds were fed up with the bootleggers being tipped off by local law officers, so one morning at day break; a dozen agents drove into town in two big black cars. Andrew instantly recognized the strangers as agents and rode all over town and back alleys, car horn blaring. With his head out the window, he yelled, "Hide it! Hide it! Law's coming!" Only two bootleggers were caught. A Fort Worth paper's headline the next day reported: PAUL REVERE RIDES JUNCTION'S STREETS TO WARN OF PRO-RAIDERS. The paper could not identify the mystery rider, but the Junctionites knew, and they weren't telling.

One prominent Strawn rancher loved Italian grappa but could not handle it. He would pass out "cold" sometimes during a drinking bout and not remember a thing for a day or two. He had a fear that in such condition he might be mistaken for dead and be buried alive. While he was still living, he had a telephone line strung to the family burial plot in Davidson Cemetery. His Will stipulated that a telephone be placed in his hand, inside his coffin and if he did not call out within three days, he was sure to be dead and not just passed out.

Ma Ferguson, Governor of Texas, issued clemency proclamations right and left, and Ma was easy on bootlegging, a victimless crime. Many times the person seeking clemency was represented by Jim Ferguson, Ma Ferguson's husband, who had previously been impeached as governor. As of August 30, 1926, Ma had issued 2,323 conditional pardons, paroles and furloughs. The reasons for clemency would often be “sickness in family”, “death in family”, “request of Mayor”, “petition of citizens”, or “sole support of family.” Several Junctionites did only short stints in jail, thanks to lawyer Ranspot, but John Bertolli’s friend Sam Hanson received an unfortunate, fatal jail term.

Sam Hanson was sentenced to Huntsville for two years. While drunk and his warning senses lessened, he sold a bottle to an agent. After serving several months, Hanson suddenly died. The body was shipped home to Strawn Merchandise Company Funeral Parlor for burial with closed coffin instructions. The undertaker knew John Bertolli and said, “John, I know you and Sam Hanson were real close. I’m not supposed to do this, but I think you should know there’s something strange about the body. See what you think.” John Bertolli certainly had no compulsion to view a dear friend’s body under “closed coffin” instructions. But he might always wonder, and if anything were remiss, a more suitable explanation than the prison’s “sudden death due to unattributable illness” was due the widow.

The deceased’s face was dark purple. There was an incision from the breastbone to the navel, the internal organs removed and body cavity stuffed with straw. The incision was crudely stitched up with straw sticking out between stitches. Upon query, prison officials would not admit anything. After some difficulty, Hanson’s widow contacted one of Hanson’s cell-mates. He wrote: “I cannot tell you anything, now. In a year’s time, I’ll be out; then I can talk.”

Hanson and two cell-mates were sold some poisonous wood alcohol whisky by a prison guard. Two of the inmates were blinded; Hanson died. All the internal organs were removed to prevent an autopsy and to prevent a prison investigation and scandal. It was a strange twist that after making many gallons of good, pure whisky, Sam Hanson should perish from the bad whisky of a greedy, unethical guard.

Although the coal mines of Thurber closed in 1921, the Thurber Brick Yard and the offices of T P Oil Company, as the company was now called, continued in Thurber until 1933. The several hundred remaining residents danced, drank and were entertained at the Thurber Club, a private club for employees of the oil company. Some Dances were fancy, formal affairs, particularly the New Year's Ball, and prominent citizens of surrounding towns were invited to these dances. The bootleggers of Thurber Junction were happy to provide the booze for members of the Thurber Club. Bars were not legal, even in a private club, but after each dance set, members would beeline to individual lockers for a nip. Lawrence Welk, Jan Garber and Jack Amlunge were some of the big name bands who played at the Thurber Club.

The bootleggers saw nothing morally wrong in an activity which enabled them to provide for their families. Immigrant parents wanted their children to be good Americans; school came first and some children went on to college.

Baseball was an American game. The Thurber immigrants tried the game, but the skills and understanding were not developed; bocce ball was their game. However, sons of immigrants quickly grasped the game with zest and skill because they were exposed to the game from childhood.

Gino Bertolli, John's last born, was a natural baseball player, and John encouraged him by building a backstop in an open field near his house. There would be hours of scrub and practice pitching. In 1924 at the age of sixteen, Gino was invited to play for the Thurber Colts of the Oil Belt League. In Gino's first appearance, he was permitted to pitch the last inning of a game in which the Colts were ahead by six runs. Gino struck out the side with fourteen pitches. He was a sensation in the infield and short relief pitching. He had professional potential, but a torn knee cartilage ended his baseball days.

With money from bootlegging, John Bertolli was able to send his three older offspring to college for degrees. John Bertolli was so proud and grateful, he openly wept at each graduation ceremony. "Just think," John said, "the kids of an immigrant miner with college degrees." Gino, the youngest Bertolli, worked as a mechanic at Bill Peretti's garage in Thurber Junction. In 1932 he married Lena Steppi in St. Barbara's Church.

Mama and Franco Mazzano, the parents of John's wife Giuseppa, died in 1929 within a few months of each other.

In the summer of 1929, Pete Wasieleski, age 61, developed stomach cancer. He had been busy enough since the coal mines closed in 1921. Pete's three married daughters lived nearby with their twelve children and there were births, Baptisms, First Communions and family get-togethers. There were bricklaying jobs, a garden, fruit trees and farm animals to look after. The inactivity induced by the energy-draining cancer galled Pete because he had always been so active and hardworking, but he made no complaints; life had been good to him. He knew he would soon join his beloved Cecelia who had preceded him sixteen years earlier. Pete spent most of his daylight hours on his front porch, thinking or dozing.

John Bertolli found time from his bootlegging activities to visit Pete several times a week. The two old-timers would spend hours recalling the past, or sometimes they silently sat, when nothing had to be said, each reveling in the other's presence. Their friendship went back forty years to 1890, right after the coal mines had opened. They were immigrants from the Old Country who came to America with little but a willingness to work and succeed, and Pete and John had been through it all, from Thurber's prominence to decline. Although John was Italian and Pete was Polish, nationalities were transcended as the two struggled on harsh work and low pay until the Strike of 1903. They were in the thick of the fight for unionization, and both were instrumental in organizing the

Italian Miners Local. During the Strike of 1903 Pete and John left loved ones to travel and to work together in the Illinois coal mines. They both owned homes and land on the Back Road to Thurber. They found stability and happiness in America, raised their children to be good citizens and contributed to the community and to America.

"As my time approaches, John, I think more and more of my childhood in Poland and my parents," Pete quietly stated. "Now I feel bad because I never went back to Poland to see my family or relatives, but I'm sure they understood that with five children it was not possible for us to travel so far. Cecelia and I often talked about going back for a visit, but there never was enough money. Take my advice, John. Your parents are gone too, but take a trip back to Italy, visit your relatives and your hometown before it is too late."

"I know you're right, Pete, and if my luck holds out selling grappa, Giuseppa and I will be able to take a trip back to Italy in a few years. The Federal Agents are raiding more and I have to be especially careful. Why, they're even offering money to my neighbors to report me! Lucky for me, I have good neighbors, but Giuseppa and I help them out, and some beer and a pint of grappa, now and then, helps too."

"John, we had many good times and some sad times."

"Yes, but I think the good times greatly outnumber the sad times."

"Remember the time we stayed too late at Telio's playing bocci ball?" Pete asked, and as he recalled the happening, he smiled, for it now hurt to laugh. "We drank too much. We stumbled home through the darkness and you were showing me a short cut home. 'Just follow me', you said. I did, and we both fell into the Palo Pinto Creek, ten or fifteen feet down, but the water was deep enough to ease our fall or we would have broken our necks. Muddy, clothes torn, bruised and scratched but feeling no pain.

Crazy!"

John laughed as he recalled the incident. "God sure protected his drunkards that time."

"So many of our friends gone from here, and we'll never see them again," Pete ruefully declared. "Hard to believe Thurber was so big at one time. Now, nothing; just a few workers at the brick yard and those who work for the oil company. Where did they all go? Remember that Hungarian fellow who dug his own grave? Never married, no relatives. What's his name - Bascilli? He used to get drunk and walk down the road lighting half-sticks of dynamite."

"Yes. That's Anton. I don't see him much anymore. There will be an iron door just above his casket and another iron door near the top of his grave. Says he wants to be the first out on Resurrection Day."

"Remember that Alfredo Scorzi who used to always bum Miners and Puddlers tobacco off you, and how you broke him from bumming off you?" asked Pete.

"Hell yes! Every time he saw me, he'd ask for tobacco. Said he left his at home, but I wasn't the only one he bummed off. I don't think he ever bought one sack of tobacco. I heard he went somewhere in Illinois."

"I can still remember the look on his face when you told him how you kept your tobacco moist—just three drops of piss a sack! He was still spitting after thirty minutes through that mustache of his." Pete laughed and then grimaced as the laugh brought pain to his stomach.

John Bertolli laughed and said, "Yeah, but he never bummed me for tobacco any more. That broke him of the habit."

When the weather was cloudy or cold, Pete was more depressed, and he sat around the fireplace, recited the rosary and talked with John about the sad events of their life.

"You know, John that was the most horrible thing I've ever seen when the Osborne house burned in the spring of last year and the daughter and father burned to death. I couldn't sleep for a long time after that, and I still have nightmares about it. I was one of the first ones there. I was coming home about midnight from playing pinochle at Punchie's. Through the fire I could see the daddy holding the daughter trying to shield her from the fire. They were trapped inside, and the fire was so hot, we couldn't get closer than twenty yards. There was nothing I could do to save them!"

"Yes, I remember that," John quietly answered. "They're buried in Davidson Cemetery."

Pete was silent for several minutes then resumed his morose memories. "Back in 1916 I was plowing early one morning by Sheffield's when I saw people running towards the coal chute. A man by the name of St. Clair, worked the night shift at the coal chute, and lived a block north of the coal chute. He got off work that morning and went home to find his wife and mother-in-law beaten to death with a crowbar and his daughter near death. They rushed the daughter to the hospital, but she died. They never did find the murderer, but everyone thought it was St. Clair. But for someone to murder a helpless child!"

"Last I heard, he was still living somewhere in south Texas."

"Now remember, John, you get my pallbearers. You, Joe Abraham, John Zinanni, Adam Rogowski, Pete Grabin and Joe Gazzola."

As the cancer progressed and the end neared, Pete talked more often of his beloved Cecelia, something that was hard for him to do before his illness, even though Cecelia had been dead for years. "The only time Cecelia was really mad, very mad at me was when I teased our daughters by showing them a picture of the devil about to stab someone with his pitchfork. She told me I shouldn't scare the kids with that picture. Well, Obsinski came by one evening and we had a few drinks and I thought I'd be cute by showing that picture. Cecelia jerked that book out of my hands, and right in front of Obsinski, she threw that book into the fire. She showed me!"

In February, 1930, Pete was comatose. He suddenly sat up and reached out for something off in the distance and muttered his Polish word of endearment for his Cecelia, "zha voo ha", and he was gone. John Bertolli lost his dearest friend, and Thurber lost another who, by his sweat and sacrifice, helped make Thurber great.

In 1933 the Volstead Act was repealed, one of the first acts of Roosevelt's Democratic administration. The T P Oil Company began moving its offices from Thurber to Fort Worth. The Ranger oil boom had fizzled out. The Great Depression was on. The houses remaining in Thurber were demolished or moved, house by house. Palo Pinto County, a quarter-mile from downtown Thurber, legalized beer and wine, but not whisky. Now, a bootlegger was one who bought distillery whisky bearing a government stamp and sold it in a "dry" area. Eighteen ex-bootleggers opened saloons in Thurber Junction, now that the sale of beer was legal. But not John Bertolli. He had been in the business long enough. With bootlegging out, there was no hope for making money in the Junction, and the population dwindled as people moved elsewhere.

When prohibition ended, John and Giuseppa went immediately to Father Kline for Confession and Communion. It had been thirteen years of anguish and guilt, living without the sacraments, but during this time, the Bertollis had never missed Sunday Mass. When John stepped out of the confessional, tears of joy were dripping down his cheeks. He would no longer sin by violating the nation's laws. America had been kind, and his progeny were established, patriotic Americans. He was moderately wealthy when measured by Depression standards. John and Guiseppa took a trip to Italy. There were joyful, tearful reunions with relatives, and he generously gave money to the needy. It was a touching visit to the seminary where John had first studied Latin and English, and again he gave money to express his gratitude. Italy had not changed much since John left in 1889, for now there was Mussolini. The Bertollis had been born in Italy, but America was their country.

John's return to the sacraments was propitious, for in 1934, shortly after his return from Italy, he was dead of a heart attack. "The Champion of the Italian Miners" died on December 4th, the Feast Day of St. Barbara, patroness saint of the miners.

Life without John in their house was more than Giuseppa could bear, for there had been too many good years together. Giuseppa moved to Fort Worth to be with her daughters and grandchildren. The last remaining Bertollis in Thurber Junction, Gino and Lena, moved to California in 1935 where there was work.

The "Old Bertolli Homestead" on the Back Road to Thurber began a slow deterioration, keeping pace with Thurber Junction; deteriorating towards nothingness, just mesquite and cactus, just as it had been before the railroad built the spur to Thurber mines which gave birth to the Junction.

After the dust of demolition had settled by 1936, the only structures remaining in Thurber were the drugstore, dry goods, smokestack, water filtering plant and two homes: Gordon's and Dr. Binney's.

TWENTY-FOUR

Joe Venutti, in the hectic haste of trying to arrange a Latin Funeral Mass for Gino Bertolli, had completely overlooked the 50th Annual Thurber Reunion which would be held the coming weekend. Over the last few days Venutti had to overcome several sticky problems in making the funeral arrangements: the Bishop's refusal for a Latin Mass, a priest to say the Latin Mass, a place to say the Latin Mass, access to the Thurber Cemetery, lodging and transportation for Bertolli's family who were flying in from California for the funeral.

At Friday evening rosary for Gino Bertolli, Joe Venutti's memory lapse was forcefully jogged into the realities of the upcoming reunion. This year, 1986, would mark the one hundredth anniversary of Johnson's first coal mine, and the reunion would be the biggest ever. Since Joe was kneeling at the front near the casket and leading the rosary, he could not stare around, but he was aware of a large number of people from the chorused response to prayers. The funeral chapel crowd was overflowing, and Joe thought as he prayed: *Sounds like a heck of a lot of people. I didn't expect too many, especially for someone who's been gone from here for so* long...

After Venutti made the Sign of the Cross which marked the end of the rosary, he looked around and was stunned by the large number of people and faces he had not seen in a long time. What was going on, he wondered, as he shook hands with an old friend whose name he couldn't recall at that instant. "Tony Lunardon, from Illinois. We're here for the Thurber Reunion tomorrow. Remember we used to call you 'Vennie'? Do they still call you that?" Of course! The people are here for the Reunion! How stupid I can be; thought Joe. This called for a rethinking of the funeral.

Here it was Friday and people were coming in for the Reunion, and every motel for miles around would be filled: Ranger, Stephenville and Eastland. Many would drive out from Fort Worth or Abilene for one day. Others would crowd Thurber with their motor homes. Some would stay with friends in the Junction, or in Strawn or other towns. Five hundred people were expected. Undoubtedly, many of these people would remember the Bertollis, because Gino's father was so active in the Thurber miners union. With the small chapel overflowing at rosary, tomorrow's Funeral Mass crowd could never be accommodated within the confines of this chapel.

Venutti whispered to the widow, Lena Bertolli, who still knelt in prayer with her family. With Venutti she walked to the back of the chapel, pausing at every step to hug old friends and to accept condolences.

Al Lyons, the Funeral Director, was waiting at the back of the crowd. Venutti quietly made the introductions. "Lena, this is Al Lyons, who's the Funeral Director, and this is Frank Koski, who's president of the Thurber Historical Association. Maybe you remember Frank?"

"I'm sorry, Mr. Koski. I can't think, we've been gone so long."

"Oh, that's all right. I understand," said Frank.

Venutti said, "Lena, I'm sorry, but I completely forgot the Thurber Reunion is tomorrow. There's so many people here tonight for the rosary, you can imagine what a crowd we'll have for the funeral tomorrow; way too many for this chapel."

"Please don't apologize, Joe. You've done so much for us. We put everything on you, and everybody and everything is so nice. But what can we do, Mr. Lyons?" Lena anxiously asked.

"Well, that's just what Joe, Frank and I were discussing. Frank has a good idea; see if it's all right with you. The only way we could handle this big a crowd tomorrow would be to have the Mass in St. Barbara's or St. John's in Strawn..."

"But the Bishop said 'no' to St. Barbara's," Lena interposed."And St. John's would have to be the New Mass—absolutely not!"

"Yes, that's what we thought," said Lyons. "That leaves the American Legion Hall in the Thurber Junction, but if we have to move the funeral, why not move it to Thurber?"

"We can have the funeral where we hold the Reunion, in the old dry goods store," said Frank Koski. "We can easily juggle our schedule an hour or so. This way, people who come to the Reunion in their motor homes wouldn't have to worry about maneuvering their vehicles for parking here at the funeral home. You'd be surprised how many of these people still remember you."

Lena looked at Joe and asked, "What do you think, Joe?"

"I think it's great. There'll be plenty of chairs to seat everybody because there's lots of older folks who can't stand very long. There won't be any problem setting up the altar. We can move in a small organ. We'd be right in the middle of Thurber where most of our folks started out. Thurber's always been like one big family. Everybody always helped everybody. I see no problem with Thurber, Lena, but I do see a problem if we leave it like it is."

Lena nodded her head affirmatively. "I'm sure Gino would approve. The dry goods store is not too far from where St. Barbara's originally stood. To be among old friends, one last time..." And the thought broke her voice and brought tears.

"OK, we'll do it then," said Al Lyons. "I'll stand at the door here and as people leave tonight, I'll tell them of the change in plans and ask them to get on the phone and call everybody who they think will come to the funeral. I'll put a sign outside for people who come here tomorrow. Now, Mrs. Bertolli, you wanted the funeral procession to drive the Back Road to Thurber so we could pause in front of the Old Bertolli Homestead for a minute. We'll have to forego that with our new plans."

Lena agreed. “Gino would understand. It would have been nice, but now we won’t be going by the old place. I know we’re doing the right thing.”

Monsignor Kowalski and Father Brennan arrived at Joe Venutti’s home before eight o’clock on Saturday morning. Monsignor Kowalski made introductions. “Father Brennan from Marble Falls and this is my great-nephew and ace server, Greg Nowak.”

“A pretty drive out here,” commented Father Brennan. “The cedars remind me of the Hill Country. Where we turned off I-20, the tall smokestack, why all the motor homes? I’m fascinated with the history of ghost towns in Texas, but Thurber doesn’t look like a ghost town today.”

Joe smiled. “You’ll be a part of it today, Father, and you’ll learn a lot more about Thurber before you leave here today. That’s where we’re holding the Mass, in the old dry goods store, if you approve, Father.” And Joe continued to explain about the Thurber Reunion and why the change in funeral plans.

“I’m sure it’ll be fine, Joe,” Monsignor Kowalski answered. “I’ll be giving the sermon, so why not let Father Brennan and Greg drive back to Thurber to see if everything’s in place? And you can give me some details for the sermon.”

“Great,” said Venutti. “Joe Grabinski set up the altar, and he’ll be there waiting for you, Father. If you need anything, ask him.” And in an afterthought, “Oh, yes, Father. I might tell you most of us haven’t attended a Latin Mass in a good while, and the people won’t know when to kneel or stand or sit.”

“Don’t worry,” replied Father Brennan. “I’ll help out, and you’re a pallbearer. You’ll be sitting near the front. Put this missal in your pocket. Follow it, and the people will follow you.”

Since this was the hundredth year of the founding of Thurber, the event was newsworthy to Channel 6 of Fort Worth, and a camera and reporter were already in action, much to Joe Venutti’s displeasure; a distraction.

Joe Venutti was right; it was crowded with all the chairs and benches occupied and standees outside. The Mass began.

"In nomine Patris, et Filli, et Spiritus Sancti. Amen. Introibo ad altare Dei."

And the altar boy responded: "Ad Deum laetificat juventutem meam."

Joe Venutti could not concentrate on following the Mass in the missal. Instead, he delighted in just sitting back, listening to the Latin and in following the motions of the priest. The Mass seemed so natural to him, like he had never been away. Monsignor Kowalski's sermon was magnificent.

> How fitting, that everything should come together at this precise time to enable us to celebrate the Traditional Funeral Mass to honor our dear friend, Gino Bertolli.
>
> As many of you know, Gino's father, Giovanni Bertolli, was one of the first Italian miners in Thurber, and one who led the fight for unionization. The bitter fight for a Miners' Union is part of the rich history of this area. Before the Union, working conditions and pay of our forebears were demeaning.
>
> Gino wanted to one day return in retirement next door, in Thurber Junction, his place of birth, a place of memories, a place of good times and hard times, as most of you know. When the mines closed, and the Great Depression lay on this land, the hearts and minds and souls of everyone were squeezed. But Gino did not forget his place of origin. Although he lived his last fifty years in California, he asked that he be buried here, among his friends, in Thurber Cemetery, with his parents, Giovanni and Giuseppa Bertolli.
>
> Nor did Gino forget his religion. Religion back in the old days meant a great deal more than it does today. Many of you are wondering about the Latin Mass and the black vestments. This Traditional Latin Mass was also Gino's request. He was

forever faithful to the religion in which he was baptized. It would perhaps have been more appropriate to hold this service in St. Barbara's Church, which, some of you remember originally stood about a hundred yards north of where we are now gathered. St. Barbara's was the church which the Bertolli family, and perhaps some of your family faithfully attended for fifty years. The church was not available, so it was decided that since many of you would like to pay your respects to our dear friend, it would be fitting to hold the service here.

It is written in Ecclesiastes, Chapter 3: 'All things have their season, and in their times all things pass under Heaven. A time to be born and a time to die. A time to plant, and a time to pluck up that which is planted. A time to weep and a time to laugh. A time to mourn and a time to dance.'

It was Gino's time to be born in neighboring Thurber Junction on December 20, 1908, when Thurber was a promising city, probably the most modern city in Texas at that time. The work then was hard, but there was happiness and more love and concern for one's neighbors than we see today. Gino was the fourth child of Giovanni and Guiseppa Bertolli; two sisters and one brother precede him in death. Now, it is Gino's time for eternal reward.

A time to plant and a time to pluck up that which has been planted. In Gino there was planted a fervent love for God, America and family. This Traditional Mass is a manifestation of his love for God. In today's secular-humanist world, it is so easy to be swept along with the rest of the crowd. Everything is man-centered. Self-gratification comes first. God is not needed. Today, it is not easy to maintain a belief in the Ten Commandments. Getting out of bed for Church, fasting and abstaining, receiving the sacraments and saying prayers. Gino had everlasting faith imbued in him by his family, by Thurber's environment and by the Sisters of the Incarnate Word of Thurber's Hunter Academy.

How well some of remember the proud day for our fathers and grandfathers when they were granted American citizenship. How they dressed in their one good suit, took a day off from work and made the day-long journey to Stephenville or to Palo Pinto to get that prized document of naturalization. The Bertollis were honored to be a part of the New Country. Digging coal six days a week, for sixty dollars a month seems impossibly hard by today's standards. But the Bertollis, like all Thurberites, were grateful for the chance to better them selves. The repressions, hard life and lack of opportunities in the Old Country spurred them to succeed. Gino was thankful to Thurber and America and acknowledged this by proudly, bravely serving his country in World War II. As a staff sergeant combat infantryman, Gino was awarded two Purple Heart medals for wounds received in battles in Europe.

Gino leaves behind his wife, Lena; two children, Maria and Leo; and four grandchildren.

Some of you may remember Gino Bertolli as the youngest player, at age sixteen, on the Thurber Colts baseball team in the 1920s. This was after the mines had closed, but the Brick Plant still operated and the T P Oil Company still had its offices here. Had Gino not hurt his knee, he may have ended up in the major leagues.

Now it is our time to weep and to mourn the passing of a long-time Thurberite and faithful friend.

The Old Bertolli Homestead still stands on the Back Road to Thurber. Gino had plans when he returned to the Junction to restore this old home to its original condition. As Ecclesiastes says: 'A time to mourn and a time to dance.' In spite of the hard times, there were still many times to laugh and to dance in this old house. People say the good old days were not so good when compared to today. But I believe I can safely say that those who experienced life in Thurber back then, would say that while the work was indeed hard, and the pay little, life was uncomplicated, sweeter and more satisfying than today. There was pleasure from the simple things and events in life. All things were relative and everybody was the same. Gino grew up in this environment and nurtured it all his life.

Just as you will share fond memories of Thurber on this, the one hundredth anniversary of Thurber's beginning; please remember Gino Bertolli and his family in your thoughts and prayers.

As Monsignor Kowalski finished, Joe Venutti felt like standing and applauding. It was amazing how Monsignor could take the few facts Joe had given him, and in such a short time, weave them into a masterful eulogy. But Monsignor Kowalski had said many Funeral Masses in his fifty years as a priest, and Kowalski's father was an immigrant tenant farmer in south Texas, so the priest understood perfectly what Thurberites felt.

After the casket was lowered into the grave, those who accompanied the funeral procession to the Thurber Cemetery wandered among the old tombstones and grave markers, and recalled old friends buried there. They were appalled and saddened by the unkempt condition of the cemetery, and they wondered about the surveyor's flags and stakes in the northwest part of the cemetery.

When people gathered in the afternoon to begin the ceremonies for the Reunion, Monsignor Kowalski was asked to give the Invocation. Much of the afternoon's conversation centered on Gino Bertolli, the funeral, the disrepair of the cemetery and the Latin Mass.

On Saturday evening, Bishop Dolezel of the Fort Worth Diocese watched his usual "News with 6 at 6". The TV showed Father Brennan at the altar as the descriptive voice of the reporter narrated:

"The one hundredth anniversary celebration of the founding of Thurber, Texas, began with a funeral and a Traditional Latin Mass. The Latin Mass for Roman Catholics has been banned by Vatican II, but most of the ex-Thurberites, many of Eastern European ancestry, felt the Old Mass very appropriate for the occasion because the Latin Mass was in use when Thurber, a coal mining center, was founded a century ago. The Funeral Mass today, in black vestments, was the last request of Gino Bertolli, son of one of the organizers of the miner's union in Thurber. Bertolli was buried in the almost abandoned Thurber Cemetery..."

And the camera panned the cemetery to show its run-down

condition and conspicuous yellow surveyor's flags.

"This was the fiftieth gathering..."

The Bishop was incensed with what he saw on TV. He would get the name of the priest who dared to say the Latin Mass in his Diocese! He pressed the call button. "Monsignor Flippin, did you see the six o'clock news?"

"Yes, Excellency. Looks as if they got their Mass. I hope they're satisfied."

"Do you know who the priest was?" the Bishop asked.

"No, Excellency. I didn't get a good look at his face. White hair. An older priest. Probably retired."

"You don't suppose it was one of our priests? We couldn't call---What's his name from out there?"

"Venutti. No. He was pretty put out with us, better let him cool off. I'll call the newscaster."

"OK. See what you can find out." Although the Bishop could do little to influence retired priests, the Bishop still wanted to know who the dissidents were and what area of his Diocese required surveillance.

The Channel 6 newscaster told Monsignor Flippin he didn't get the name of the priest; he just assumed it was one of the priests from the Fort Worth Diocese.

Another viewer of the newscast was George Dunlap, President of Peacock Energy and Exploration, who muttered, "Damn! Damn!" as he dialed Joseph Gardner, Peacock's Manager of Mineral Leasing. Dunlap wanted to talk to his subordinate about the surveyor's flags so prominently seen on TV and why they weren't removed when Gardner was at Thurber yesterday. As the phone rang, Peacock's plan for recovering Thurber's coal flashed in review through Dunlap's mind: Enormous profits for many years. Plenty of coal left. Thurber Cemetery never dedicated. We've got plenty of natural gas for making steam and heat. Water. Dam between the two hills. Only forty feet of cemetery land, nobody would ever miss. Move the fence over. Seven unmarked graves. Nobody would ever notice fence was moved, or that graves were outside cemetery fence. If somebody complained about the graves, get a court order to move graves. Damn people in Austin didn't get the bill passed. This gasification would really make me look good throughout the energy industry. Pipe down steam and heat to melt the coal. Suck up the carbon gases and melted coal. The carbon gases injected into our oil and gas wells will increase production. One thing wrong: That stupid damn Gardner dawdled around on moving the fence over and now this damn Bertolli funeral!

Joseph Gardner answered his phone. "Joe, you see the six o'clock news?"

"Yes sir, Mr. Dunlap. I saw the funeral; pretty impressive."

"What did you and the attorney learn when you went out there yesterday?"

"Well, there's no way they can get us on grave desecration. It's obvious somebody did run over the graves, and kind of sunk one in, but the graves are poorly marked and overgrown with weeds. Anyway, it wasn't willful."

"The yellow surveyor's flags sure stuck out on TV. People will wonder what they're for. Did you see Buchannon?"

"No. But somebody put some bricks around some of our flags. I figure it was Buchannon because he's one of the few who knows about the stakes and flags."

"What do you mean?" Dunlap asked as his voice rose to a higher pitch.

"A newly-staked-out burial plot; after our survey. Three layers of freshly-laid brick, cement still not dried. Telling us, 'Don't touch, this is a burial plot.'"

"Yeah. We're starting to get the message loud and clear,"

Dunlap sarcastically replied. "State Representative Goforth will be by Monday to look at our plans for the dam. Implied he'd get a court order if we didn't cooperate, so we'd better kick this thing around first thing Monday morning. This will cost the hell out of us if we have to come up with another plan. The company stands to make millions if we can get this thing going soon. What do you think we ought to do now?"

"Well, it looks like we'll have to show that the cemetery land belongs to Peacock. Then get a court order to move the graves. You know nobody will come forth to say it's their relative's grave because there's absolutely no markers on any of the seven graves."

"Yeah; sounds easy. Just like moving over the fence," Dunlap caustically stated, and for the second time in two days, Joseph Gardner, Manager of Peacock Mineral Leasing, felt rebuke from his boss.

On Sunday Joe Venutti did not attend the New Mass in Strawn. It was the first time in forty years he had missed Sunday Mass. After yesterday's poignant reintroduction to the Latin Mass, he knew he could never again attend the New Mass which was foisted on Catholics by Vatican II. He would talk to Monsignor Kowalski about a weekly Latin Mass in Thurber Junction.

Sunday afternoon, Joe and his wife escorted Lena Bertolli and her family to the conclusion of the Thurber Reunion. There were still many questions and comments about the Latin Mass. Where are Latin Masses held? Weren't these outlawed by Vatican II? Would one be excommunicated for attending a Latin Mass? Where are Father Brennan and Monsignor Kowalski from? Was the Funeral Mass a result of the Pope's Indult? For those with questions Joe couldn't answer, he took their names and promised to reply after he talked with Monsignor Kowalski.

The Thurber Historical Association voted a thousand dollars for restoring Thurber Cemetery, and a committee was appointed to seek a state historical marker for the burial grounds.

Many Reunion attendees were concerned about the surveyor's flags in the cemetery, and Buck Buchannon was asked to tell what he knew of the flags and stakes.

"Right now, I don't know a thing, but I'll durn sure find out. I do know it's Peacock Energy's doing. I expect to have some answers soon because State Representative Goforth of Stephenville is looking into this. I'll give you my telephone number, and you call me then. I'll tell you one thing: I have filed grave desecration charges against Peacock Energy." There was loud cheering and applause.

On Monday morning the DA's office called Buchannon. "Mr. Buchannon, Mike Stone from the District Attorney's office. I've talked with your attorney Don Dowell, and we both agreed it would be tough to make your grave desecration charges stick. We didn't catch them in the act, we don't know if the intent was there, and we'd have a hell of a time proving who ran over the graves. Oh, we could get Peacock to admit the flags and stakes are theirs, but we'd have a time proving they deliberately ran over the graves."

"Well, we could damn well show the lock on the gate was theirs; therefore, they must have been the last ones up there. Obviously no one was up there until we cut the chain for Al Lyons so he could dig Bertolli's grave."

"They might say Al Lyons did it."

"Sure, a funeral director, and the Bertolli grave is fifty yards from Peacock's flags."

"But you know Peacock. They'll fight you all the way to the Supreme Court. They've got the money and the attorneys."

"Yeah; OK. I guess you're right, Mike," Buchannon reluctantly agreed. "If we only knew what Peacock had in mind? Stan Goforth is working on this. There's hell of a lot of history in that cemetery. Of course, Peacock doesn't give a damn, just so they stay number one."

"Well, all right, Buck. If we can help you any other way, call us. Talk to you later."

On Monday morning Peacock's key personnel met in a "Where We Are" session. Now that the Thurber coal gasification was prematurely disclosed, it was agreed that Peacock would go all out on public relations. Call in TV and newspapers. Meet with the locals. Brochures, tours and dinners for local dignitaries. A toll-free hot line for questions. The most irksome problem was still the forty feet of cemetery land required for the dam.

The Peacock attorney had talked with the Erath County DA and there would be no grave desecration charges against Peacock.

The State Water Commission had granted a permit for Peacock to impound 1500 acre feet of water, and the water depth at the dam would be 30 feet.

By proposing electrostatic precipitators to control sulfur and sulfide emissions, Peacock would meet Texas Air Quality Control Board standards.

Peacock's lobbyists reported initial approval from State Highway officials for new access and roads onto I-20, as well as closing a portion of Highway 108 between Thurber and the Junction. State officials were pleased with Peacock's donation of all land for new roads, the proposed two million dollar processing plant on Italian Hill, and a promise of at least sixty new jobs.

An Environmental Impact Statement would be required because of increased traffic and of backup water to I-20, but this would be no problem.

How should Peacock proceed with the acquisition of forty feet of cemetery land required for the dam? How simple everything would have been had the four-strand barbed wire fence been moved over three weeks ago, before the Bertolli funeral forced Peacock into disclosing its plans! Had the same old posts and wire been used, no one would have been aware of the fence-moving or of the seven graves because the graves were remotely located in the northwest corner of the cemetery. Seven unmarked graves, seven unknowns, long neglected or forgotten. Now Peacock would have to appear before Palo Pinto County Court to claim the unused cemetery land was theirs because there was no record of land dedicated as a cemetery. The cemetery, like the Thurber town site and buildings, were included in the 800 acres which Peacock had purchased from Texas Pacific Oil Company.

In conjunction with the court hearing, Peacock would seek permission to move the seven graves to another part of the cemetery. Notice of intent to relocate the graves would be published in the county paper to locate relatives of those buried in the seven graves.

On Monday afternoon State Representative Stan Goforth called Buck Buchannon, "Hey, Buck. I've got the scoop on Peacock's doings. A snotty, sneaky bunch of bastards. I had to threaten them with a court order before they'd let me see the plans. You won't believe what they're doing. They want forty feet of land off the cemetery, where the flags are. They claim the unused land of the cemetery is theirs."

Buck whistled. "Like hell! That cemetery's been there a hundred years bothering nobody, and now Peacock wants some of the land. For what?"

"A dam connecting Graveyard Hill and Italian Hill for a lake. They need lots of water to recover Thurber's coal. A process called gasification where they force the steam down into the coal and take off melted coal and coal vapors. Peacock kept emphasizing to me the people they'll put to work and the recreational benefits of a big lake. It'll be about the size of Thurber's Big Lake."

This didn't sound right to Buck. "What about the buildings and the road?"

"All the buildings go except the smokestack, and they'll build a levee around it because the smokestack already has a state historical marker on it. They propose a new road off I-20, coming off Italian Hill going east, and then turn left for the Junction. A secondary road will cross the dam to the cemetery and then to the smokestack."

"Man, they're crazier than hell!" Buck declared. "There's too much history in those old buildings! Get the State Historical Commission on this..."

"Yeah, but the State Historical Commission doesn't own the buildings or land; Peacock does."

"Hellfire, Stan! They can't cram this down our throats. What about smoke and pollution on my grass? What can we do?"

"Peacock's got some powerful lobbyists down in Austin. Lots of money to throw around. I'll make my colleagues aware of what Peacock's trying to do. You can stir up the locals in the Junction and be prepared to raise hell when they release an Environmental Impact Statement. Of course, Peacock will have a favorable statement. I'll keep you posted, Buck, and I'll talk to some people in Austin, see if they've got any ideas on how we can stop them. I know how badly you want to kick Peacock's ass."

"OK, Stan. Thanks. Stop by sometime. They still have cold beer in the Mingus."

U. S. Senator Phil Burton's office called Buchannon and gave essentially the same information provided Representative Goforth. Evidently, Peacock had its act together.

Buck replied, "Thank you, Miss Godley. Could your office find out for me if Peacock will be required to make an Environmental Impact Statement? An access to a Federal Highway, I-20, will be involved, and I just wonder how Peacock will handle it. Would I have a chance to rebut any statement they make? Call me back when you can."

On Tuesday evening Buck Buchannon addressed the Mingus (formerly Thurber Junction) City Council:

> "Mr. Mayor, members of the City Council, citizens. Most of you know me. I'm Buck Buchannon and I own the Thurber Ranch. I'm here tonight because I want you to be aware of Peacock Energy's latest shenanigan. Without consulting any or us from around here, they plan to block off Highway 108 between Graveyard Hill and Italian Hill and build a dam there. They claim the cemetery is theirs, and they want forty feet of unused cemetery land, and they'll have to move seven graves.
>
> The lake will back water up to I-20 and almost Steam Shovel Mountain. They want to recover the remaining coal by forcing steam down into the coal and capturing the vapors. They chose this site because the coal slopes down toward Number Three Mine, and the coal sludge will ooze that way.
>
> A new access road will have to come off I-20. What will be the pollution from this scheme? Will Gibson Branch be able to handle the dam's overflow? What effect will this have on the Mingus Lake? If the new dam gave way, you people in Mingus are in trouble.
>
> Peacock tried to hide this deal by putting a lock on the cemetery gate to keep us from seeing what they were doing. Had it not been for Gino Bertolli being buried up there, no telling how long it would have taken for us to find out about this..."

There was an hour of questions and answers and discussions.

On Wednesday morning Joe Venutti met with Monsignor Kowalski. "Thank you again for the Latin Mass, Monsignor. Everybody was pleased and surprised. I have a bunch of questions people asked and I'll have to get the answers from you. But my main purpose in meeting with you is to see about a weekly Latin Mass in Thurber Junction. Until the Mass last Saturday at the funeral, I had no idea what I had been missing, and now I'll never go back to the New Mass. As you know, Monsignor, I'm trying to buy St. Barbara's from the Diocese, but until we get the church, we could have Mass in the American Legion Hall. Right now, there's about a dozen who will attend, but when word gets around, I'm sure there'll be people from all around who will come."

"I'd be happy to offer the Latin Mass in Thurber Junction, Joe. Before we get too definite, though, don't you think we'd better have the negotiations for the church sale pretty well sewn up? The Bishop will never sell St. Barbara's if he finds out the Traditional Mass is being said anywhere in Thurber Junction. He'd find out you were behind it. Forgive me, but the Bishop might be obstinate in selling the church now, because you went ahead with the Latin Mass for Bertolli's funeral."

"He might be mad and stubborn with me, Monsignor, but I've got the hammer in the form of my Will. Right now, the Fort Worth Diocese is the beneficiary and I'm leaving everything to them, but I'm planning to change my Will. I'll use my Will to pry the church loose, and when this is in my hands, I'll change my Will. I know that sounds terrible, Monsignor, but it's not nearly as bad as what Vatican II did to us."

"What you do and how you handle it is none of my business, Joe, and I can't be involved with any of that," the Monsignor cautioned.

"Yes, I understand, Monsignor. I'll ask my attorney to get right on with buying the church. You're right, maybe we better hold off on the Mass a couple of weeks. Buying the church shouldn't take too long, and I'll get back with you as soon as I have something definite."

Peacock's Community Relations of the Thurber Gasification Plant was given special treatment and was covered by all TV stations and newspapers. There were briefings and luncheons at the Thurber Lake clubroom, and tours of the site were available for reporters, newscasters and politicians. Favorable comments which emanated from the governor, union officials and the State Industrial Board were splashed across the papers and TV, but only suspicion and doubt came from Junctionites and ex-Thurberites.

Peacock made a presentation to a Thurber Junction town meeting and State Representative Stan Goforth attended, along with Mayors, council members and citizens from surrounding towns. Brochures were handed to each attendee, and wall maps, a scale model and screen projections covered all aspects of Peacock's plan, but the accent was on jobs and recreation. The gasification plant would be the biggest happening in the region since Comanche Peak Nuclear Power Plant.

Sam Hartsell, Peacock's Community Relations man, was articulate and adroit. His briefing at the Mingus/Thurber Junction meeting was first rate, but he felt oddly out of place. He was one of the few men in suit and tie. His long hair, carefully shaped over his ears and the collar of his coat, was fine for the city folk he normally worked with, but the Mingus/Thurber Junction citizens were mostly older, conservative, short-haired and simple-living folks. *"The 'M & M' crowd, Menopause and Medicare"*, thought Hartsell. His manicured nails and artificially cultured voice branded him a "city slicker" in the minds of the local folks.

Sam Hartsell was well prepared with all his charts and briefing aids, but he could not get a feel for people who were so plain-spoken, so set in their living ways and who still bitterly remembered the hard times of their parents after the mines closed in Thurber.

Buck Buchannon asked the first two questions: "What was Peacock trying to hide when they put the lock on the Thurber Cemetery?"

“Sir, I can assure we weren’t trying to hide anything. The surveyors, just as a matter of routine, put a lock on the gate, not thinking folks were being denied cemetery access.”

“Then what were you going to do with the seven graves which are on the forty feet of cemetery land you want?”

“There would have been an attempt to locate relatives, and then work with the legal authorities to relocate the graves, but this might have been difficult because the graves are unmarked.”

A retired school teacher asked the next question: “What happens to us if you have a ground leak and all the fumes escape into the air?”

“Well, ma’am, we can immediately shut off the pressurized steam we’re feeding underground. Then we’ll drill down into the rupture, set a pipe, and then cement much like you do in oil drilling.”

The questions continued. “There’s coal all over this area; why did Peacock select this particular location? Can’t you put this some other place? Why mess up Thurber and Thurber Cemetery and put in an earthen dam which threatens all of us in Mingus? I remember back in 1919 when the Big Lake dam busted.”

“A very good question, sir. Number one: While Peacock owns mineral rights to 30,000 local acres, we own only 800 acres of surface area, right here,” Hartsell pointed to his map. “Number two: Water is critical for an operation of this kind. We can’t take water from the Thurber Big Lake because the city of Gordon depends on this water, and there’s no other location suitable for a good-size lake. A dam between Cemetery Hill and Italian Hill is the only possible solution. If you analyze all aspects of it very carefully, as we have, this location is the only logical choice.” Hartsell paused to think through the next part of the question. “Three: The coal at Number 3 Mine is deeper than anywhere else, which means the sludge and coal tar will flow toward this point where we can extract it. Four: Peacock wants to help this area prosper. We can help this area by providing a number of jobs and a recreational area. The monthly payroll will be over $100,000. We're certainly aware of the history of this place, and we intend to preserve its past. I..."

In the beginning Hartsell's responses to questions were polite, concise and confident, but as the questions became more caustic, Hartsell's suit and a non-air-conditioned building made him sweat. After an hour of biting, intensive questioning; negative, derogatory thoughts intruded Hartsell's mind.

"Baloney! Preserve the past by putting the remaining buildings under water? They may not mean a durn thing to you or Peacock, but to us, there's a lot of history, meaning and symbolism in those old buildings. Sounds to me like you're going to drown our history, not preserve it!" By now, Hartsell had removed his coat and was wiping the sweat off his face, and he did not like his credibility questioned. He thought: W*hy you toothless bastard, I just work for the company.* But he gave a fake smile and said, "The smokestack will still be available, but the other buildings are beyond repair."

"Bull! I've been in both the dry goods building and the drugstore, and they're still structurally sound and in fair shape. Peacock just doesn't want to spend the money to repair them, and they stand in the way of the almighty dollar Peacock will make from this dam and plant!" And Hartsell bristled again and thought another mean thought: *Dumb ass. You're so old and senile, you won't be here when we get this thing going,* but Hartsell again put on his good community relations demeanor and replied, "But sir, this will mean dollars for everyone and a growth in Mingus/Thurber Junction."

"A hell of a lot of good that will do me at my age. Why didn't you think of this thirty years ago, or when the Depression was on?"

"They kicked our parents and grandparents out of Thurber years ago; now they want to kick somebody out of their final resting place and us out of our homes if the dam breaks." This was followed by another malevolent Hartsell thought: *Why you dried up old fart, drowning would be too easy a death for you,* but Hartsell forced a smile and gave a vague answer. "Our engineers assure us Gibson Branch will handle all emergencies."

"While your lake is filling, it'll shut off all water to Mingus Lake, and all the fish will die." A final intrusive, summarizing thought crossed Hartsell's mind, a thought which also reflected his company's attitude: *You ignorant hick SOB's! You can bitch and moan all night, but in the end, Peacock will do what it damn well wants to do,* and Hartsell again forced a gracious reply.

The citizens wanted no part of Peacock's dam, and they remained threatened, suspicious and hostile, but that was too bad, because what Peacock wanted, Peacock got. The energy giant did not become a dominating power by being timid. Hartsell knew Peacock could steam-roller opposition, and the one little thorn on the gasification plant, forty feet of cemetery land, was nothing more than a minor irritation to Peacock.

Led by Rancher Buck Buchannon, residents organized and hired an attorney to represent their case at Peacock's hearing before District Judge Sam Cleever in Palo Pinto County Court at Law.

TV and newspapers ran stories on Thurber and on Peacock's attempt to claim cemetery land and to relocate seven graves. Lone Star Monthly magazine had a feature with colored photos of Thurber and the cemetery. There were letters to editors, to the Thurber Historical Association and to the Mayor of Mingus, all expressing ill will toward Peacock Energy. While there was no record on file with the County Clerk in either Palo Pinto County or Erath County which described such land for interment purposes, and while the grounds were not cared for, tombstones and the fenced enclosure were sufficient to show the cemetery had not been abandoned. The recent burial of Gino Bertolli confirmed the purpose of the land.

True to form and expectations, Peacock was not through; they immediately announced they would go to Appeals Court to escape the parochial emotions. Peacock's lawyers insisted that a semi-abandoned, ten-acre cemetery with more surplus land than would ever be used should not constitute a valid objection to Peacock's need for a mere forty feet of unused cemetery land.

For the hundredth time, Peacock President Dunlap cursed the stupidity of his subordinate, Joe Gardner. If Gardner had just gotten off his ass and had that fence moved, all this crap we're going through could have been avoided! Now, we're really into it; all this unfavorable publicity. If Appeals Court turns us down, we'll have to go to the State Supreme Court.

TWENTY-FIVE

Joe Venutti's attorney Don Dowell met with Monsignor Flippin of the Fort Worth Diocese concerning Venutti's offer to buy St. Barbara's church.

After the handshake, Monsignor surprised Dowell with the blunt comment, "I didn't know St. Barbara's was on the market."

Although taken aback by this strange introductory comment, Dowell imperturbably replied, "It might not be, Monsignor, but can we not explore the possibility?" Could the Monsignor be perturbed because Venutti had a Latin Mass against the Bishop's wishes?

With his offhanded comment, the Monsignor was sparring with Dowell, but when Dowell showed no reaction, the Monsignor said, "I was making light conversation, Mr. Dowell. As I recall, the only previous mention of selling was made by Mr. Venutti, who offered $2000 to buy the church for the State Historical Society. But the Bishop wanted to help out by letting the Historical Society use the church, put an historical marker on it and maintain it while the church would remain under the control of the Diocese. Mr. Venutti has been an important benefactor, so the Bishop wanted to reciprocate."

"Well, that sounds all right, Monsignor, except for one point: If the Historical Society is to maintain it, they would not want any encumbrances placed on the church by the Diocese so they'd have to come to you every time they needed to make a minor repair. The church is in need of repairs right now. Have you seen the church lately, Monsignor?"

"Well, no. I rely on Father Hooper for information; the church is in his parish. By the way, did you see the news last Saturday evening? They showed a Mass in Thurber, but it wasn't in this church, and it wasn't one of our priests. I wonder who the priest was."

Dowell recognized the asinine attempt for information, and thought he should do a little jousting, too. "Sorry, but I did not attend the Latin Mass, and I don't know who the priest was, but I heard it was a very moving experience. I do know Joe Venutti went through a great deal of trouble to arrange the Latin Mass, and he was a little put out."

Monsignor perked up at this hint of a rebuke. "Well, yes, I can understand. We tried to help him, but he decided his was the only way."

Don Dowell continued to press Monsignor Flippin. "Joe Venutti is normally a very mild, kind man, but I wouldn't want him mad at me, like last week when he was trying to arrange Bertolli's funeral. But that's neither here nor there. Have you spoken with the Bishop about Venutti buying the church for the Historical Society?"

"Yes, but in the context that the Diocese would maintain control so than any religious activity would be harmonious with current practices throughout the Diocese because the church would still be in the geographical confines of the Diocese."

Dowell stifled his irritation and said, "As I mentioned, Monsignor, the historical people would want complete control of any property they maintain. There's no church services held in the church now, and I don't think the Historical Society is into religion."

"Yes, Mr. Dowell, but what if somewhere down the line somebody decides to have services, or wants to use the church as a meeting place..."

"Well, let them," Dowell cut in. "That's what the Ecumenical Catholic Church is all about, isn't it? Besides, that would be up to the Historical Society if they had the church, and it would be out of your hands."

“It’s still the Roman Catholic Church, not the Ecumenical Church, Mr. Dowell,” the Monsignor tersely corrected. “People would still regard it as the Catholic Church. Why, they might even decide to have a Latin Mass.”

“Might as well,” Dowell testily replied. “Today’s Ecumenical Church; excuse me, Roman Catholic Church, allows every other kind of religious service in the church. Just recently the Pope invited the Moslems, Hindus, atheists and even the peyote believers into the Church at Assisi in Rome. But I didn’t come here to argue religion, Monsignor; that’s not my expertise. My client Mr. Venutti has given me a $2000 check with instructions to purchase this church. That’s all, pure and simple. Either you want to sell a church which is no longer in use, or you don’t.”

“I’m not sure the Bishop would want to turn loose of this church for $2000. The church is in good shape. It has a great deal of history...,” the Monsignor procrastinated.

“Monsignor, you’re not reading my subliminal message. Do you know my client’s worth?”

“I understand it’s substantial.”

“Yes. Here is a deed for the church, made up for the Bishop’s signature. I also have a copy of a Will which I made out several years ago. It says the Diocese is the beneficiary. Now, do you get the message, Monsignor?” And he handed over the deed.

“Yes, I see,” the Monsignor replied, lips tight. He went into the Bishop’s office and after several minutes, he returned with the Bishop’s signature.

Dowell handed over the $2000 check and took the deed from Monsignor Flippin. Dowell, with sardonic amusement, commented, “My client grows impatient, Monsignor.”

Before the church was turned over to the Historical Society, Monsignor Kowalski celebrated the first Mass in St. Barbara’s since 1962. The walls of the church echoed the Latin prayers which were first said on her altar in 1892. Her bell, shipped over from Italy years ago, a gift of the Italian miners, again gave off its dull, monotonic "thuong", and the Mingus residents began listening on Sunday for the distinctive sound. St. Barbara, patroness saint of miners. But there were no miners left whom she could watch over, only the descendants of miners.

Eleven people attended the first Mass. Twenty-seven the second Sunday. After several Sundays, attendance averaged seventy. Attendance fell sharply at St. John's in Strawn and St. Rita's in Ranger. People who had not been to church in years came to St. Barbara's, many out of curiosity.

Bishop Dolezel was alarmed and infuriated. He countered by using the Pope's Indult to authorize a Traditional Latin Mass at St. John's in the neighboring parish of Strawn. But Father Hooper was not trained in Latin, and the Bishop's proposal alienated those who had grown accustomed to the New Mass. The Bishop next issued a letter which was read by all his priests from the pulpit. The letter was an implied threat of excommunication for Latin Mass adherents. When told of the Bishop's letter, the Latin Mass worshippers scoffed, for excommunication could only come from the Vatican. After the recent controversy over Gino Bertolli's burial, media hopped on this latest flare-up which increased the pressure on the Bishop for Traditional Latin Masses throughout the Diocese.

When Joe Venutti heard of Bishop Solezel's threats, he saw a prime moment to negate his Will, and he fired off an angry letter which was laced with religious history gleaned from Monsignor Kowalski.

Your Excellency:

I am appalled at your recent threat of excommunication for those of us who have the privilege of worshipping as our ancestors did.

At the Council of Trent in July, 1570, Pope St. Pius V defined for all time the ritual for saying the Roman Catholic Mass. His Papal Bull QUO PRIMUM decreed his order "is to last in perpetuity", and no Pope ever destroyed or discarded any previous Papal Bull until Paul VI threw out the Tridentine Roman Catholic Mass.

As regards excommunication, let me cite part of the CORONATION OATH OF THE POPE: "I vow:

To change nothing of the received tradition...or to permit any innovation therein...to guard the holy canons and decrees of all Popes.

Accordingly, without exclusion, we subject to severest excommunication anyone---be it our self or be it another---who would dare to undertake anything new in contradiction...or would concur with those who undertake such blasphemous venture."

Now, I ask you, Bishop Dolezel, who are the excommunicated, those who have denied the Roman Catholic faith and changed the Church, or those of us who have never separated themselves from anything which Christ instituted?

Accordingly, I have excommunicated you and your Diocese from my WILL, effective this date. My estate will be used to foster the true Faith and to train priests in the Tridentine Latin Rite.

Yours in Christ, Joe Venutti

St. Barbara's was completely restored and repainted. Joe Venutti felt continuous pleasure and peace which he had never before experienced, and he discussed this with Monsignor Kowalski.

"The Hand of God has touched your soul, Joe. When one gives freely of himself, and truly sacrifices for the good of others, this is his reward."

"Whatever it is, it's a good feeling, and I hope it continues."

Monsignor said, "Joe, what you have accomplished is amazing. This church is already self-sustaining. Notice the fervor of the parishioners. The people have been starved for the Mass. They're very generous, and the Sunday collection is averaging about $500. I'm happy to be a part of it, and I, too, feel some of that rapture you speak of."

"No, Monsignor. I haven't done anything. It's you who has his neck stuck out and the courage to openly say the Latin Mass. At this rate, you'll soon need an assistant, but where can you find young priests who can say the Latin Mass?"

"Well, I have some ideas, Joe. See what you think."

"I'm listening, because as I mentioned some time back, I've voided my Will benefiting the Diocese, and I'll now use my resources to help train priests in the Latin Rite so that the Traditional Latin Mass will continue in perpetuity, as it was intended to."

"Word sure gets around, Joe. In the few months we've been saying the Mass, I've received letters from three retired priests wanting to help us, including Father Brennan, who said the Funeral Mass for us. This is great for now, but what about after we're gone?"

"Like I said, Monsignor, I'll provide the financial support and you take care of the spiritual end; whatever you decide."

"Let me digress a bit, here. There was an eighty-five year old Vietnamese Archbishop, Ngo-Dinh-Thuc, now deceased, whose family was of Vietnamese royalty and this family, sacrificed themselves in fighting Communism. Bishop Thuc's brother, Diem, was president of Vietnam from 1954 to 1963, if you remember. Bishop Thuc feared he would not be allowed back into Vietnam if he left for Vatican II, but upon command of the Vatican he went to Rome. When he saw the Church's bending on Communism, he refused to participate in Vatican II and was forced into retirement. As a retiree, he grieved for his Roman Catholic Church and concluded that with the Vatican II changes, the Church no longer had possession of the Sacrament of Holy Orders. Under the new ordination rites, there would soon be no valid priesthood and the Apostolic Succession forever would be broken. The venerable Archbishop could not go to his grave knowing that as a Roman Catholic Bishop he held the only power on Earth which could ensure the continuance of the Roman Catholic priesthood and Apostolic Succession. He therefore consecrated two Mexican priests, Carmona and Zamora, in 1981, who in turn consecrated two American priests, Martin and Baker, and regardless of what the Vatican says, these consecrations are probably theologically valid."

The Monsignor continued his discourse. "Now, the very foundation of Catholicism is the idea of a leader, a Bishop. The Pope, for example, is the Bishop of Rome. Bishops Martin and Baker have split the United States into the Eastern and Western Dioceses, and Bishop Martin has asked if we would like to come under the umbrella of his Diocese. There's no way we can operate on a permanent basis without a Bishop, because there's Confirmation and Holy Orders and hundreds of other religious questions which come up."

Venutti asked, "What about Bishop LeFebvre and his Pius X Society?"

"Well, right now I think we'll need somebody in the United States who is convenient. LeFebvre's getting on in age, and I'm sure he'll have to consecrate some Bishops if the Pius X Society is to continue. Do you have any concerns with what I've talked about, Joe?"

"Gosh no, Monsignor. That's so tragic about Bishop Thuc. I'd never heard of this before, but then there's so much that has gone on with Vatican II, and the average person will never know just what has happened."

"That's true, but it'll all work out some way; it always has for the Church. I believe the Vatican will eventually have to appoint a Patriarch or an overseer for the Latin Rite, because there are millions of people world-wide who feel like we do, but they don't have the opportunity to attend the Latin Mass. One day the Church will be united again; maybe not in our lifetime, but it's coming."

"Lots of good things happening, Monsignor."

"Speaking of good things, Joe, did you know that several parishioners have already asked me about Christmas Midnight Mass? Isn't that exciting?"

TWENTY-SIX

State Representative Stan Goforth did not approve of Peacock's methods in forcing through the dam and gasification plant at Thurber. Peacock Energy was impervious to criticism, and their attempt to hide the moving of the cemetery fence, their disregard for Thurber's history and their indifference to the concerns of the citizens were all vexing to Goforth. District Court had ruled against Peacock using some of the cemetery land for the dam. In a few months there would be another hearing at the State Appeals level. If the Appeals Court ruling were negative, Peacock would go to the Texas Supreme Court. There was no end to Peacock's persistence; they'd keep hammering away, and eventually they'd get their way. Peacock's lobbyists in Austin had approached Goforth about a special bill which would permit Peacock to use the cemetery land. If the legal maneuvering failed, Goforth knew Peacock would "buy" enough legislators to get the bill passed.

Goforth's interest in Thurber was more than just votes and looking after his constituency. Goforth's father had worked in the Thurber Brick Plant until 1933, and Stan had often heard his father talk about the brick yard: 80,000 bricks a day from eighteen kilns, and thirty-five different kinds of Thurber brick. But paving brick was the specialty, and Thurber brick paved many streets and miles of highways throughout Texas before giving way to asphalt and concrete. The fastest man in laying paving brick was Tom Kitchens who could put down over a hundred bricks a minute. That was almost two bricks a second, which seemed incredible, but Stan's father averred that Kitchens had been timed on several different occasions.

The Goforth family had moved to Stephenville, thirty miles south of Thurber, in 1933 when Stan was ten years old. Stan was educated at Stephenville's John Tarleton College and Texas A and M with a degree in Civil Engineering. After WWII service, Stan worked several years for an engineering firm in Fort Worth before setting up his own surveying firm in Stephenville. He was in his mid-sixties and had served four terms as State Representative. Having grown up during the Depression, he knew hard times and had never lost the common touch which set well with the ranchers and dairy farmers of his district.

Goforth was nicknamed "High Pockets" to fit his tall, lanky stature. The voice was country, and this masked a sharp mind. A close-cropped haircut crowned facial features befitting the cigarette advertisements, even down to blue jeans, Stetson and boots. His land surveying firm was now run by his son while Stan looked after his Charolais cattle and golf.

Like his close friend Buck Buchannon, who owned Thurber Ranch, Stan Goforth knew how Peacock operated because ranchers often came to Goforth with complaints about how Peacock was tearing up their land when drilling or laying pipe lines. Peacock had approached Stan Goforth several times about doing survey work for them, but Goforth declined because he did not want his friends to think he was in any way responsible for Peacock's rough-handed methods.

What could Goforth do to stop Peacock from building the dam and destroying the remaining structures in Thurber and obliterating the colorful past? Peacock owned all the buildings and 800 acres surrounding Thurber. They claimed ownership of the cemetery, but that was for the courts to decide. The cemetery was the key to stopping Peacock, but Goforth knew Peacock would prevail in the end. Peacock was so powerful and ruthless they would find a way to get the cemetery land, and Thurber would be submerged forever under twenty feet of water. For the hundredth time Goforth thought: W*hat a waste. We've got to stop them, but how*?

Stan Goforth drove to Buck Buchannon's home to talk over the Peacock dilemma. After a long sip of beer from a frosted mug, Stan smacked his lips and declared, "Man! That tastes good. Makes a man want to forget about his troubles, and we do have big troubles with Peacock. They're going to steam roller us, Buck, and I don't see how we can stop them."

"Yep. I've thought and thought about it, but it doesn't come to me," Buck ruefully replied. "Like you say, we'll contest them at the Appeals Court, but they'll just go to the legislature with the special bill. You can raise hell on the floor about the bill, but we know they'll buy off enough lawmakers. A bunch of crooked bastards down there at Austin, and they'll justify their actions by stating that with the oil patch bust, Texas needs ventures like Peacock's to bolster the economy. What a crock!"

After three beers, the two were no closer to a solution. "Well hell, Buck. Why don't we just go talk eyeball to eyeball with them? Ask them why they can't pipe water in from Lake Palo Pinto, or drill down and use salt water. Looks like they could find a way to take the salt out. They'll heat the water to make steam, and the salt will be left behind and ..."

"Yeah, but what do you do with the salt residue that's left?"

"Hell, I'm sure they've already thought about saltwater," Goforth dejectedly sighed.

"And you don't want me with you when you talk to Peacock," Buck advised. "I've raised so much hell with them the last several years, when they see me; it's like waving a red flag at a bull."

"Speaking of the bull, I'd better go check on my cows," said Goforth as he looked at his watch. "OK. I'll go to Dallas Monday to see the bastards. Just go over the whole damn thing, see if there's something we've overlooked. The Appeals Court doesn't come up until next month, so we've a little time. If you come up with anything, call me. But damn! Looks like they'll break it off in our back. Thanks for the beer. See you later, Buck."

George Dunlap, President of Peacock Energy, effusively

greeted Goforth. "Well, well! So good to see you again, so soon, Representative Goforth! Looking forward to your next session down in Austin? Remember what Sam Rayburn said about the Texas Legislature? 'Nobody is safe as long as the Legislature is in session.'" Dunlap loudly laughed at his own humor.

Goforth didn't think the quote worthy of such a brash laugh, but he politely emitted a few laugh sounds.

"I hope you can stay for lunch at the Petroleum Club, Mr. Goforth."

"Well, that depends on you giving me some good answers," chided Goforth.

"Oh hell! You're after something. Still on Thurber, right?"

"Yes, sir. But I'll be up front with you, George. We know you'll finally kick our butts on this, because you and I know, 'What Peacock wants, Peacock gets'. But if I may, I'd like to hash over some ideas. I want to be able to look my constituents in the eye and truthfully say, 'I tried.'"

"Well, you make Peacock as a mean bastard. Nah, we're not that bad, just trying to do our job. The directors make the policy, and we carry it out," Dunlap summarized.

Dunlap was almost sixty. His deep-set, penetrating eyes could bore right through you, subordinates said. His bushy eyebrows sharply contrasted with a fringed but bald top. A large, stout build made a domineering presence which lent authority to Dunlap's philosophy of "Results, not excuses." Peacock Energy had done well under Dunlap's leadership, but his heavy-handed tactics had made many enemies within and outside the industry. Land and royalty owners and small businesses could not stand up to the powerful Peacock who sneered at any who dared challenge Peacock's questionable practices. "Results, not excuses" had give Peacock a dominant position in the energy industry.

Dunlap continued, "I think your friends around Thurber will

reap enormous benefits from our plant and lake, if they'll just sit back and analyze this. We'll spend over a million just to get started out there."

"Yes, and you'll make more than that in one year, and with 127,000,000 tons of coal remaining, right smart profits for years to come," Goforth wryly observed.

"Well, yes. That's the name of the game, isn't it?"

"George, surely you must have considered other ideas about this before you settled on the dam between Graveyard Hill and Italian Hill. We admire your initiative in undertaking this project, and yes, it will put a lot of people to work, and we don't begrudge you making profits. But this dam and taking over the cemetery is what's bad about this. I'd like to review some of your other ideas on this; maybe I could use what little influence I have to help with an alternate plan. I hate to see such an important historical site like Thurber wasted."

Leaning back in his chair, hands clasped over his slight paunch, Dunlap listened, then replied, "Oh, yes, we looked at this from all aspects, but there were only two major considerations: water and the slope of the coal. We can't do anything about the slope; it all slopes toward Number Three Mine, and that's the extraction point. Look at the water sources around Number Three. Thurber Big Lake, Little Lake and Mingus Lake, but the Big Lake is the only one with capacity, and with the city of Gordon drawing its water from there, it's out."

"What about piping water in from Lake Palo Pinto?" Goforth asked.

"You name it, we've looked at it. Do you know what it'll cost for a ten-mile, six-inch water line and right of way from Lake Palo Pinto? Close to $4 million. So from cost standpoint, that's out. I'll tell you one thing; people don't realize this gasification will be the first venture of its kind in the United State. Russia's way ahead of us on this. Right now, Peacock is an eminent energy company, but with this project we'll be pre-eminent, worldwide," Dunlap boasted.

Goforth recoiled at the conceit and use of self-esteeming words such as "eminent" and "pre-eminent", but that was the nature of the man and the company. Still, something about the choice of those words rankled Goforth, but he checked his anger and asked, "Could you drill down and use the salt water? Plenty of that."

"No way. Too corrosive and clogging. No, we made the only choice there was. If you look at a topographical map you can see that on our 800 acres, or for several miles around us, there's no other place we could build a dam."

"Eminent" and "pre-eminent" thought Goforth. Eminent in bullying and pre-eminent in cramming it down our throats. "Are you aware of Thurber's rich, colorful past?" Goforth queried.

"Hell, yes! It's all in the company history, and there's several books and magazine stories about Thurber."

"But doesn't Peacock understand it's more than just words written down, George? It's a feeling, a reverence of a past way of life, and those buildings are symbolic, something Thurber folks can hang onto."

Dunlap defensively replied, "Hell, the buildings are in terrible shape; in a few years they'll all cave in. You people should have thought about those buildings years ago, before we went for gasification. You know we're saving the smokestack by building a costly protective levee around it."

"Those buildings have stood there for eighty years and nobody in his wildest dreams could see them submerged under water."

"Well, we sought bids to salvage the bricks, but nobody would touch it. We thought about demolishing the buildings and using the rubble in the dam, but the engineers said that wouldn't be good." There was a slight pause before Dunlap added, "I don't understand it. You people out Thurber way have given us more trouble than any other venture we've ever undertaken, and Peacock's domain stretches from Texas to Alaska."

The word "domain" triggered another bristly reaction in Goforth, and he thought: *there he goes again, the ego centrically bastard. Now, he speaks of a domain, like he was master of all!* And again, Goforth had to force himself to curb his anger. "But George, the sneaky way Peacock first tried to take over the cemetery was what made us folks out there mad. And when you speak of Peacock's vast domain, it looks like Thurber's the crapping place for Peacock." And the word "domain", like "eminent" and "pre-eminent", annoyed Stan and stuck in his mind for some reason.

"Ha! Cute metaphor, Stan," Dunlap cynically replied.

"Speaking of your domain, George, Peacock's into everything, mostly oil and gas, but there's lignite and other coal deposits. Why didn't you try gasification in some of your other coal fields?" The three words, *"domain", "eminent" and "pre-eminent"* continued to subliminally play in Goforth's mind.

"Well, our other coal deposits are from four to six feet thick, and it's profitable to mine this coal, but with Thurber's thirty-inch seam, gasification is about the only way we can recover Thurber's coal."

"I guess the thing that really bugs me is that the buildings will be destroyed, regardless of how Peacock goes about it. Can you imagine being in a boat and looking down into the water and saying, 'There's the old Dry Goods Store where I bought my first pair of shoes?' Or, 'There's the Drug Store; my grandmother used to tell about the delicious sundaes she got there when her family went to the Sunday band concerts.'" *Why do the three words keep buzzing around in my mind,* thought Goforth. Is there some connection?

"You sound like it's a foregone conclusion we'll win in Appeals Court, Stan."

"Hell, George, you and I both know Appeals Court won't make a damn bit of difference. A couple of weeks ago one of your Austin people offered me a good chunk of money to vote for a special bill entitled 'Use of Exempt and Unused Public Land for Industrial Development.' I told him it'd take a hundred times what he offered me. So if you lose in court, you'll get a special bill passed. A little delay, but business as usual, huh George?"

Dunlap, red-faced, gave Goforth a steady, penetrating glare which was characteristic of Dunlap when he was perturbed. "Let me say this, Goforth," Dunlap loudly enunciated each word. "We'll do what we have to do, and it's nobody's damn business but ours."

"Oh, but it is my business, George, because it's in my district," Goforth evenly replied. Dammit! What was it about the words *"domain", "eminent" and "pre-eminent"* that kept pestering Goforth's mind, as if the words were trying to impart a meaning, an understanding, or a revelation? *Domain, domain. Eminent, eminent.* Then it hit Goforth, like an exploding light bulb! Of course! EMINENT DOMAIN! It was so obvious in retrospect, why hadn't he thought of it before? There might be a way to stop Peacock after all!

Dunlap was puzzled by the deep smile of relief that lit up Goforth's face, and he became more puzzled when Goforth abruptly stuck out his hand, and as he vigorously pumped Dunlap's hand, he said, "Thanks for your time, George. I've got to run. You've answered all my questions. I've got all I need to know." And as an afterthought, to throw off his adversary, Goforth said, "I know when I'm licked. Good luck on your gasification." Goforth seemed to float out of Dunlap's office and into the first pay phone booth.

"Hey, Buck! I think I found a way to kick Peacock's ass.

Eminent Domain! Too much to talk about over the phone! It'll take some money and a little finagling, but I bet we can do it! Can we meet at your place in a couple of hours? You, me, Joe Venutti and your lawyer Dowell. Ask Dowell to counsel us on Eminent Domain, and if he can't make it, ask him to look it up and we'll talk with him by phone. I'm so excited I'm about to pee in my pants! I don't know why I didn't think of this before; it might have saved us a lot of trouble. See you in a little while."

Attorney Don Dowell explained Eminent Domain, the right of a governing body to condemn land for public use as long as a fair price was paid the owner.

Stan Goforth's plan was to make a State Historical Park at Thurber by getting the State to use Eminent Domain procedure to acquire the Thurber townsite. Attorney Dowell assured the three men a State Historical Park certainly was for public use; therefore, Eminent Domain was applicable.

Goforth looked at Buck and said, "Buck, you remember Willie Hicks during our college days at Tarleton? We called him 'Gaspergou Willie' because his word for a drum fish was 'gaspergou'. Came with us several times to Mingus to drink beer at Ma Tibbs'. Remember we took off from school to go fishing at Possum Kingdom? He studied Wildlife Management in school. Guess what? He's now executive director of State Parks and Wildlife. The top dog. You and I need to pay 'Gaspergou Willie' a visit."

"Hell, yes, I remember him. He was always smiling, laughing. I'd like to see him again. Man, that's great!"

"Now money… The Parks people love it when somebody donates property for parks. In our case it will be even more important because we're asking them to implement Eminent Domain. Approval for Thurber State Park would be more likely if we could say, 'Hey, here's a perfect spot for an historical park.

Use Eminent Domain and here's the money to buy the Thurber site.'" Between Joe Venutti and Buck Buchannon, a half-million was pledged and the two promised to seek out other individuals, corporations and foundations who might contribute additional funds.

"OK. Let me tell you how the rest of this should work—if we're lucky. If we can sell 'Gaspergou Willie' Hicks on this, and if we can get on the agenda for the next Parks Board meeting and if we can get to five or six of the Parks Commissioners, we can swing this. If, if, if; but this is our only shot."

A brief meeting with 'Gaspergou Willie' Hicks, Executive Director of Texas State Parks and Wildlife, turned into an hour-long meeting. However, the talk was more of old college days than of a state park because Buck and Goforth quickly convinced their old school buddy of the feasibility of the Thurber site as a state park.

"I've been in Austin four terms now," Goforth said. "Funny I haven't run into you before, Willie. They still call you 'Gaspergou?'"

"Nah. A few of the old Tarleton bunch, now and then."

"Been doing any fishing?" Buck asked.

"No, because I don't seem to have time for fishing now, but I'm fixing to retire in a year or two, and I'll make up for lost time."

"Well, when you're ready, I've sure got a good fishing lake," Buck said. "Mother's Lake. Way back in the sticks and stocked with Florida bass. I only let very special people fish there, and I guarantee you won't find any gaspergous in there."

Before they left, Hicks gave Goforth a list of the nine Parks Commissioners with addresses and telephone numbers, and then mentioned friends and legislators known to be close to certain commissioners. The next Parks meeting would be in five weeks and Goforth would be on the agenda to speak for the Thurber State

Park.

Representative Goforth called on several legislators and friends of Parks Commissioners and asked them to personally urge the commissioners to support a Thurber State Park.

Joe Venutti and Buck Buchannon obtained pledges from corporations for another half-million dollars which made a total of one million dollars for a state park. Venutti, Buchannon and a dozen others from the Thurber Historical Association made the trip to Austin when Stan Goforth made his presentation to the State Parks Board.

> "Members of the Parks Board:
>
> I'm Stan Goforth of Stephenville. I represent the 14th District, which includes the ghost town of Thurber, Texas, and Thurber is what I want to discuss with you this afternoon..."
>
> Goforth outlined the major historical aspects of Thurber: its coal and brick industries, its contribution to the labor movement in the southwest, its ethnic diversity and its role in the Ranger Oil Boom.
>
> Goforth then presented Thurber's optimal features for an historical park: the location, the unique history, the picturesque beauty of the site, the fervent attachment to Thurber by ex-residents, the lack of restrictions on construction, the original buildings, and the self-supporting ability through concessions and private donations of one million dollars for development.
>
> "We ask the Parks Board to institute Eminent Domain immediately, or else the rich history of Thurber will be annihilated forever, for at this time one of the large energy corporations of America is ready to build a dam and flood the site. If we don't act now, Thurber is doomed."

There were twenty minutes of friendly questions from Parks Commissioners, and Goforth could tell from the nature of the questions and from the comments that the Parks Commissioners were convinced.

When the Parks Chairman asked for additional comments, a man who introduced himself as "Roy Shelton, a member of the legal staff of Peacock Energy and Exploration Corporation," adjusted the microphone at the podium. *The bastards*! thought Goforth. *They never give up! Now how in the hell do they propose to fight the state on Eminent Domain? And how did they know we were going this route with the Texas Parks? But Peacock had its own inimitable methods.*

Attorney Shelton began by accusing Stan Goforth of misrepresenting the facts. "The land which Representative Goforth refers to is owned by Peacock Energy of Dallas. It is not for sale, nor will it be for sale, and Eminent Domain is not in order because we are in the process of building a dam and a gasification plant at Thurber to recover the remaining coal there. My company will stand irreparable damages which will be considerably more than the sale of the land by Eminent Domain. I remind the Parks Board that after all these years nothing historically has been done with Thurber, but now when we propose an industrial development, Representative Goforth comes up with a plan for a Historical park. What we're weighing here is whether the state derives considerable income from our industrial installation, or whether the state spends tax dollars for an untried, unproven tourist park. And I might add we're putting over $1 million dollars into this plan, and there will be a monthly payroll of $100,000."

The Parks Board Chairman dryly replied, "Mr. Shelton, let me note that tourism also brings in considerable revenue for the state." Then turning to Goforth, "Representative, are you aware Peacock Energy is building this dam and gasification plant?"

"Sir, Peacock has plans, but they are not building at this time. Whether they build depends on how the Appeals Court rules, or if there might be special legislation passed for Peacock's project." Goforth then explained how Peacock needed forty feet of cemetery land and relocation of seven graves before they could proceed, but Goforth did not elaborate on Peacock's shoddy attempt at taking over the cemetery land. "As for irreparable damages, there can be no damages if something doesn't exist to be damaged. There may be alternate plans, other than drowning Thurber. If the Appeals Court decides Peacock can take forty feet of cemetery land and relocate the graves, then Peacock might have grounds for damages. But at the present time, Mr. Shelton, your company can show no damages."

The Parks Board Chairman concluded by stating, "We'll send a Parks Feasibility Team to Thurber in the next few weeks to determine whether this is tourist attractive and if it's up to standards. Frankly, I have no problem with the state using Eminent Domain, as long as it's for good public use and is not an undue burden upon the state. After we hear from the Feasibility Team and the Appeals Court, Representative Goforth, the Parks Board will decide whether we should proceed with Eminent Domain. It's much easier when there's a willing seller and willing buyer, but I think Mr. Shelton has made it clear his company is not willing to sell. If we decide Thurber is indeed, of great historical interest, we should not hesitate to use Eminent Domain. We know that in the past, historical sites have taken a beating, and that's why we take a strong stand for history now. We address this issue in no uncertain terms in our Parks Manual, General Statement of Texas Parks Concerning Historic Sites; let me read the second paragraph."

> "The Commission recognizes that historic sites and structures are being irretrievably lost through neglect, ill-advised restoration and nearsighted economic considerations; and with the disappearance of these sites are lost valuable reminders of the rich and varied heritage of Texas and the nation."

"So you see, we are charged with the responsibility of ensuring that historical sites are preserved. Thank you, Mr. Shelton, for giving us your company's position."

A State Parks Feasibility Team of five members spent a day in Thurber and was impressed with the history, location, museum plans and the cooperation of the locals. The Team was taken to Graveyard Hill to view Peacock's scheme for the dam and takeover of the cemetery land.

Based on the Feasibility Team's report, the Park's Staff recommended that the Parks Board approve Thurber State Park and Museum.

The Appeals Court concurred with the District Court on rejecting Peacock's claim to the cemetery land: "Regardless of the condition, or whether it was a dormant cemetery, the purpose of the land was clearly for interment and not for industrial development, as witness the many burials."

With this decision and the Feasibility Team's recommendation, the Parks Board instructed Executive Director Hicks to proceed with the acquisition of the Thurber land and to use Eminent Domain if required.

It was a conniption fit at Peacock Energy when George Dunlap, Peacock President, learned Texas Parks would use Eminent Domain to acquire the Thurber site. "That sneaky bastard Goforth!" muttered Dunlap, as it all came back to him: the meeting with Goforth, Dunlap's reference to Peacock's domain and being eminent, and Goforth's referring to Thurber as the "crapping place of Peacock." And now the Appeals Court denied Peacock! Here was the biggest coup of George Dunlap's career, Thurber gasification, about to go under because that stupid bastard, Joseph Gardner, Peacock's Manager of Leases, did not get off his ass and move the cemetery fence before the Gino Bertolli funeral! Gardner was made the scapegoat, and Dunlap shipped him off to a branch office in Abilene.

There was still one shot, however: the legislative bill which would allow Peacock to use the cemetery land; but the bill would have to be passed before the Parks people began Eminent Domain. Since the legislature was not in session, Dunlap would have to persuade the governor to call a special legislative session.

Dunlap phoned the governor and reminded him of Peacock's generous financial help in his race for the governorship, but the governor had no pressing issues to call a quick special session, and openly, Peacock's bill would be political anathema.

For one of the first times in his career, Dunlap was totally defeated, and this time he was not able to extricate himself. When Peacock's Board of Directors met, Dunlap's cold, clandestine plot for taking over the cemetery land was thoroughly discussed, and all the attendant fall out of bad publicity was aired. Peacock's feathers were in disarray. The necessity of Dunlap's callous leadership was questioned, and Dunlap was forced into early retirement.

The first priority for the new Peacock president was to restore Peacock's tattered image. Accordingly, Peacock donated the Thurber site for a State Park, and the state did not have to exercise Eminent Domain. However, the gasification method for recovery of Thurber's coal did not die with a change in Peacock's leadership; instead, it was resurrected in a new form. The lake at old Number 10 Mine, two miles northwest of Thurber, was drained, dredged and the dam built up. This would triple the lake's capacity, and water would be piped from this lake to the plant on Italian Hill. The revised plan would be more costly and would delay gasification six months, and since the improved Number 10 Lake was on Buck Buchannon's land, Peacock would pay Buck a "Water Rights Fee." There was little objection from locals on the revised plan.

EPILOGUE

Thurber State Park was opened two years later. The old Dry Goods Building contained dioramas, Thurberabilia, minor research facilities and a small theater. Number 4 Mine was reopened with tours to show how coal was dug back in Thurber's days. The Drug Store Building was restored to an old time drug store and soda fountain. Joe Venutti moved St. Barbara's Church back to its original site at the foot of Graveyard hill. In the summer, in a reconstructed Opera House, drama and music students from area universities would present a musical depicting Thurber's history.

At the Park's dedication, and on opening night at the Opera House, Representative Goforth, retired Parks Executive Director 'Gaspergou Willie' Hicks, Buck Buchannon, Joe Venutti and Lena Bertolli were honored and recognized. Why Lena Bertolli, some people wondered. It was soon evident that one of the characters in the musical was an immigrant Italian miner; and even though the name was not Bertolli, the characterization was clearly that of Giovanni Bertolli.

On Graveyard Hill, a few hundred yards from the Opera House, exciting musical sounds of Thurber's past wafted over the graves of Giovanni, Giuseppa and Gino Bertolli and Pete and Cecelia Wasieleski. And on Sundays, St. Barbara's bell tolled a solacing knell.

End

Thurber, TX November 1888. In the midst of a Knights of Labor miners strike against the Johnson Brothers Coal Co., Robert D. Hunter's Texas and Pacific Coal Company bought the Johnson's coal interests. The angry miners contended they were still on strike when Hunter took control. But Hunter thought otherwise. "How can you strike against my company?" Hunter smirked. "You've never worked for me, nor received pay from me. Right now you are trespassing. I'm paying a dollar-fifteen a ton and no more Union business!"

As the sounds of protest echoed around him, Hunter slammed his fist down against the desk top. "Dammit to hell!" he bellowed, "I'll make a dollar look as big as a wagon wheel before I'm through with you! Go back to looking at a mule's rear end! See how much you make then! Just get off my damn land and take your shanties with you."

Hunter abruptly sat down at his desk, facing sidewise to the strikers. He reached way back in the middle drawer, his fingers searching. The men quieted down as they contemplated the intimidating movements of Hunter. Then the ominous "click" of a trigger cocking and sounding as loud as the voice of God in the breathless room. Hunter's actions gave the message that he meant business.

Hatred mingled with fear as the miners scrambled through the doorway. "We ain't through with you yet!" one of the braver miners yelled once outside Hunter's office. "You're a lily livered SOB and you're gonna' pay!"

LEO S. BIELINSKI

THE

BACK ROAD

TO

THURBER

2009

Thurber Historical Association

Box 192

Gordon, Texas 76453